Rhetorical Analyses of Literary Works

RHETORICAL ANALYSES OF LITERARY WORKS

Edward P. J. Corbett
OHIO STATE UNIVERSITY

New York
OXFORD UNIVERSITY PRESS
London 1969 Toronto

Library of Congress Catalogue Card No. 68-56180

Printed in the United States of America

For Charlie, with gratitude and admiration

Preface

THIS BOOK presents a collection of rhetorical analyses of literary works, exercises in a mode of criticism I have defined in the Introduction. In preparing it I found my chief problem to be one of selection, for I could have assembled critiques of works from a single period, such as the Renaissance; or critiques of a single author, like John Donne; or critiques of a single genre, the Lyric, for instance, or the Essay. Ample material was available, and any one of those principles of selection would have given the collection unity, but I decided instead to gather rhetorical analyses of works in various genres, by a wide range of authors, English and American, from the sixteenth to the twentieth century. I have given precedence to variety over unity mainly because I want to illustrate for teachers and students the amazing versatility of rhetorical criticism. It seems to me no other method of practical criticism has been applied to such a diversity of texts with such illuminating results.

I have further decided to concentrate attention on those authors and works commonly studied in the college classroom. This rule has required me to exclude many exemplary critiques, but I hope that what is printed here compensates for what is missing. The full bibliography will direct readers to the large body of rhetorical criticism that is available, and I trust it will fill in many of the gaps left by the necessarily limited offerings of such a collection as the present one.

My diverse, wide-ranging selections also posed a problem of organization. Originally, I thought of arranging the critiques chronologically, according to the publication date of the literary work being analyzed, but it soon seemed to me that such an arrangement could be justified only if it served to reveal an evolving method of rhetorical criticism or a changing rhetorical rationale in the construction of literary works. Neither revelation seemed likely, so I have grouped the essays under heads which reflect some of the traditional concerns of rhetoricians: Argument, Arrangement, Audience, and Style. If I have printed a critique under one heading,—under Arrangement, for instance—I do not mean to suggest that the critic concentrates on the structure of the work to the exclusion of all other rhetorical concerns; I am suggesting only a strong emphasis on that particular aspect.

The headnote for each individual selection is intended to orient the reader, so let me say here only that he will find analyses of many kinds of poetry and of prose (dramatic monologues, lyrics, and narrative, didactic, and satiric poems; drama, satire, polemics, autobiography, history, and the novel). The texts of most of the poems and a few of the prose works being analyzed are reproduced in the critique. The texts of all other literary works, with the exception of the novel *Emma,* Newman's *Apologia,* and possibly the prose passages from Shaw, are readily available in almost any anthology of English and American literature. I regret that I have no rhetorical analysis of a short story; I simply could not find one. I wish that I could have offered more rhetorical analyses of twentieth-century and American literary works. Some were available, but either I found them not to be consistently rhetorical, or I judged them not to be as good as the other pieces I had selected.

This collection will have served a useful purpose if it encourages students of literature to try their hand at rhetorical analyses of modern literary texts. Contemporary writers are not less rhetorical than earlier writers in the composition of their works, but because of the disappearance of rhetorical training from the schools, modern critics have not been aware of how valuable rhetoric can be as a means of explication. There has been a revival of interest in rhetoric, but in this revival rhetoric has for the most part been regarded as useful only in the synthetic process of composing a prose discourse. I hope the performances of the critics in this volume will make other critics realize that rhetoric can also be useful in the analytic process of breaking down a literary artifact to see what makes it work.

For the production of this book I owe many debts. To rhetoricians like Aristotle and Longinus and Hugh Blair, whose works first taught me what rhetoric is. To those authors of works on the history, theory, and practice of rhetoric who broadened and deepened my knowledge. To the many critics listed in the bibliography who showed me how rhetoric might be applied to the reading of literary texts. To the authors and publishers who granted me permission to reprint the essays in this book. To Dudley Bailey of the University of Nebraska; James J. Murphy of the University of California, Davis; and Wayne C. Booth of the University of Chicago, who saw the manuscript in various stages and guided me with their judicious comments and suggestions. To George R. Allen of the Oxford University Press whose critical sense frequently brought my own judgment back into focus. To my many students over the years who endured my fervent homilies about the value of rhetoric as a critical tool. And to my wife, who only stood and waited.

E. P. J. C.

Columbus, Ohio
June 1968

Contents

STYLE

Introduction

THE EDITOR of a collection of "rhetorical analyses of literary works" is obliged to make clear what a rhetorical analysis is and how this mode of analysis differs from other critical methods of examining literature. The obligation, however, is much easier to acknowledge than to fulfill. Since the term *rhetorical analysis* would seem to derive from the term *rhetoric,* one's concept of what constitutes a rhetorical analysis depends on one's concept of what rhetoric is. Yet despite the recent revival of interest in rhetoric, a certain haziness about it persists, even—I was tempted to say *especially*—among teachers of English. A series of conferences on Rhetoric and Literature at Modern Language Association conventions from 1964 to 1967 pointed up dramatically the diversity of notions about rhetoric and the consequent disagreements among teachers about the relevance and value of rhetoric for literary study.[1]

As the editor of this volume, I will not presume to dogmatize about the meaning of the term *rhetorical analysis.* I will set forth my definition of the term and hope that my exposition is clear enough and persuasive enough to elicit at least provisional acceptance from my readers. And if I do not win even that provisional acceptance, such a stipulative definition can at least serve to give this collection some unity and coherence.

Perhaps I should begin by exposing what I mean by the term *rhetoric.* This exposition inevitably involves me in a history of the discipline for which the term is a label. One of the denotations that *rhetoric* has for me is "the art of persuasive oratory"—a discipline that had its origins in fifth-century Athens and that was codified by, among others, Aristotle. Aristotle classified rhetoric, along with politics and ethics, as one of the practical arts, distinct from speculative arts like metaphysics and mathematics and from productive arts like poetics and carpentry. As a practical art, rhetoric was concerned more with process than with product, with an optimum way of acting or doing rather than with the artifact that resulted from the activity. Rhetoric texts presented a set of principles or prudential techniques, arrived at inductively from the practice of skillful speakers and writers, governing that activity in which men sought to persuade their fellowmen, through the use of the spoken or written word, to adopt a certain

[1] For a summary of the discussion at the first two conferences, see James J. Murphy, "The Four Faces of Rhetoric: A Progress Report," *College Composition and Communication,* XVII (May 1966), 55–59.

point of view and perhaps to act or to make judgments in accord with that induced point of view. Aristotle defined rhetoric as the "faculty or power [*dynamis*] of discovering all the available means of persuasion in any given case" (*Rhetoric*, Bk. I, chap. 2).

On the foundations that Aristotle established in his *Rhetoric*, successive generations of rhetoricians—often referred to as "classical rhetoricians"—erected an elaborate superstructure. Although, as Professor Duhamel has pointed out,[2] classical rhetoric was not as monolithic in its rationale as some histories have led us to believe, the system of rhetoric that prevailed in the schools for the next 2000 years was remarkably uniform in its main orientation and in a good many of its accidental features. Since the terminology inherited from classical rhetoric will appear in some of the rhetorical analyses in this volume, it might be well to deal briefly with a few of the key terms of this system.

Classical rhetoricians divided the study of rhetoric into five parts: *invention*, which was concerned with the discovery of arguments or proofs; *arrangement*, which dealt with the organization or disposition of the matter made available by invention; *style*, which dealt with the expression or verbalization of the discourse, treating such things as choice of diction, syntactical patterns, rhythm, and figures of speech; *memory*, which recommended techniques for memorizing a set speech; and *delivery*, which dealt with the oral presentation of the composed speech. These pedagogical divisions of the rhetorical art were all brought to bear in the composition of the three categories of persuasive discourse (although, obviously, memory and delivery had no bearing on written discourse): (1) *political* or *deliberative* discourse—that type of discourse, dealing primarily with the future, which sought to win assent or dissent from an audience, usually about some matter of public policy, and/or to influence action in accord with that assent or dissent; (2) *forensic* or *judicial* discourse—originally the persuasive discourse of the courtroom but ultimately any discourse whose objective was the indictment or defense of past actions; (3) *epideictic* or *ceremonial* discourse—discourse of "display," whose temporal province was primarily the present and whose objective was praise or blame of persons or groups or institutions. In all three of these genres, persuasion was effected by one or a combination of three modes of appeal: (1) the *appeal to reason*, including—whenever available—those demonstrative devices from logic or dialectics, such as induction, analogy, and the syllogism, and the rhetorical equivalents of these de-

[2] P. Albert Duhamel, "The Function of Rhetoric as Effective Expression," *Journal of the History of Ideas*, X (June 1949), 344–56.

vices, the example and the enthymeme; (2) the *appeal to the emotions* of the audience; and (3) the *appeal of the ethos* of the speaker or writer—the appeal exerted by the confidence and admiration that the speaker or writer inspired in his audience by his display of good sense, goodwill, and moral integrity.

These three modes of appeal tie in quite neatly with the three elements that figure in any rhetorical situation—the speaker, the speech, and the audience or, to put it in pronominal terms, the *I*, the *it*, and the *you*. The appeal to reason was concerned primarily with the discourse itself; the ethical appeal, with the speaker or writer; the emotional appeal, with the audience. It is this concern with the interlocking relationships among the speaker, the speech, and the audience which helps to differentiate Aristotle's treatment of persuasive discourse in the *Rhetoric* from his treatment of mimetic discourse in the *Poetics*. In the *Poetics*, Aristotle, once he gets past his historical account of the evolution of the various poetic species and concentrates on just two types of mimetic discourse, tragedy and epic, remains *inside* the work itself. There is no discussion of the author as a causal element in the *making* of the work, and the only nod he gives in the direction of the other external factor, the audience, occurs when he mentions, ever so briefly, the effect of tragedy as being the catharsis of pity and fear. As the opening paragraph of the *Poetics* makes clear, Aristotle is mainly concerned in this treatise with determining the essence, the various species, and the several functions of poetry, with the ways of constructing plots, and with the number and nature of the constituent parts of poetic works. He uses the *means*, the *objects*, and the *manner* as the criteria for discriminating the various species of imitative works, and when he comes to treat of the six constituent parts of tragedy, he links these parts with the three criteria—Diction and Music being associated with the *means* of imitation; Plot, Character, and Thought with the *objects* imitated; and Spectacle with the *manner* of imitation.

This brief look at some of the key terminology of classical rhetoric and at the difference between Aristotle's treatment of rhetorical composition in the *Rhetoric* and his treatment of poetical composition in the *Poetics* will eventually lead us to the definition of rhetorical analysis and to the differentiation between this mode of criticism and other modes. But perhaps I should first try to account for the confluence of rhetoric and poetics that later developed, with the result that either the two arts became almost indistinguishable or one of them tended to absorb the other.

As Richard McKeon has pointed out, "What later writers learned from Aristotle applicable to literature, they derived from the *Rhetoric* rather than from the *Poetics*."[3] Aristotle did acknowledge that two of the six parts of tragedy, Diction (*lexis*) and Thought (*dianoia*), were common to both poetics and rhetoric and that one of these, Thought, more properly fell within the province of rhetoric. But it is clear that for Aristotle, as for Plato, rhetoric and poetics were distinct disciplines. Partly because of the pre-eminence of rhetoric in the classical schools, however, the concept of *mimesis* as the distinguishing mark of poetic discourse became less and less influential, and the notion of discourse as communication gained ascendancy. This shift had firmly established itself by the time that Horace published his *Ars Poetica*. "It is not enough," Horace said, "that poems be beautiful; they must also please and lead the minds of the listeners whither they will" (ll. 99–100). The classic statement of Horace's view of the function of poetry is contained in the lines, "Poets strive either to improve [*prodesse*] or to please [*delectare*], or to unite the agreeable with the profitable. . . . Make it a point to unite the pleasant [*dulce*] and the useful [*utile*] for the advice and the delight of readers" (ll. 333–34, 343–44). The aesthetic function of poetry is still recognized by Horace, but it now shares, if it is not dominated by, a didactic function.

According to Bernard Weinberg,[4] it was Francesco Robortello, with the publication in 1548 of the first full-scale exegesis of Aristotle's *Poetics*, who was mainly responsible for the acceptance by Renaissance critics of the Horatian notion of the function of poetry. In Robortello's commentary, the union between rhetoric and poetics had become almost complete; the only real difference that he saw was that poetry used meter and rhetoric used prose. Professor Weinberg sees Robortello's basic departure from the Aristotelian notion of poetry as being the view that "the effect produced is no longer one of artistic pleasure resulting from the formal qualities of the work, but one of moral persuasion to action or inaction, in which the pleasure involved is merely an accompaniment or an instrument; and the audience is composed of men capable of yielding to this persuasion rather than of men capable of enjoying this pleasure."[5]

This notion of the utilitarian, communicative function of poetry was picked up and circulated by all the later Renaissance commentators on the *Poetics* and was adopted by most of the Renaissance critics. For all of its Aristotelian air, even Sir Philip Sidney's famous

[3] "The Concept of Imitation in Antiquity," *Critics and Criticism*, ed. R. S. Crane (Chicago, 1952), p. 171.

[4] "Robortello on the *Poetics*," *Critics and Criticism*, pp. 319–48.

[5] Ibid. pp. 346–47.

definition of poetry in his *Defence of Poesie* (1595) is essentially Horatian: "Poesie therefore is an art of imitation, for so Aristotle terms it in the word *mimesis,* that is to say, a representing, counterfeiting, or figuring forth—to speak metaphorically, a speaking picture: with this end, to teach and delight." The final cause in this formulation is a combination of *utile* and *dulce.* That this notion persisted with some English critics well into the eighteenth century is evident from Dr. Johnson's pronouncement in his *Preface to Shakespeare* (1765): "The end of writing is to instruct; the end of poetry is to instruct by pleasing."

"Measured either by its duration or the number of its adherents," says M. H. Abrams, "the pragmatic view has been the principal aesthetic attitude of the Western world." [6] But inherent in the rhetorical tradition of the ethos of the speaker or writer, Abrams goes on to point out, were the elements that contributed to the decline of this rhetorical disposition in criticism. Under the influence of the psychological contributions from men like Hobbes and Locke, Abrams says, "the stress was shifted more and more to the poet's natural genius, creative imagination, and emotional spontaneity, at the expense of the opposing attributes of judgment, learning, and artful restraints. As a result, the audience gradually receded into the background, giving place to the poet himself, and his own mental powers and emotional needs, as the predominant cause and even the end and test of art." [7]

The diagram that Abrams sets up in the first chapter of his *The Mirror and the Lamp* provides a convenient schema for classifying the four main varieties of literary criticism that have prevailed in the Western tradition. In Abrams's scheme, the Work itself is set up in relationship to three external elements—the Universe, the Author, and the Audience. If a critic confines his attention to the work itself, concerned only with the formal integrity and structure of the work, he is engaged in what Abrams calls Objective Criticism. This is the kind of criticism in which, for instance, the New Critics and the Chicago School of neo-Aristotelians were engaged. In this mode of criticism, the literary work is analyzed as an autonomous whole, irrespective of the author that produced it and the audience that hears or reads it. The literary artifact is regarded as an object for contemplation, as an object to be experienced and enjoyed, and the critic is interested in the constituent elements of matter and form which make it an aesthetic whole.

[6] *The Mirror and the Lamp,* Norton Library Edition (New York, 1958), p. 21.

[7] Ibid.

Then there is that school of criticism which studies the work in relation to the "universe" outside of it—the world or the reality that the work attempts to represent. This is Mimetic Criticism, the fountainheads of which are Plato and Aristotle (although, it should be pointed out, Aristotle becomes an Objective Critic when he settles down in the *Poetics* to an analysis of tragic drama and the epic). Here the critic is interested in the truth, the verisimilitude, the plausibility, of the representation or *mimesis* embodied in the literary work. The standard of judgment is not, as in Objective Criticism, the internal coherence of the parts, but the fidelity of the work to the universe of reality.

Expressive Criticism, as Abrams labels it, is that mode of criticism which regards the work in relationship to its author. This is the kind of criticism that is interested primarily in the psychology of the creative act. So the Expressive Critic "reads back" from the work to its efficient cause. We see this mode of criticism exemplified in the critical treatises of Romantics like Wordsworth and Coleridge, who deal in such terms, many of them appropriated from faculty psychology, as *genius, imagination, fancy, will, judgment, taste, understanding, emotions*. Such a critic focuses his attention on, and derives his criteria from, the author as generator of the artistic product.

The fourth relationship—that between the Work and the Audience—constitutes the main orientation for what Abrams call Pragmatic Criticism and what I call Rhetorical Criticism. As Abrams puts it, Pragmatic Criticism "looks at the work of art chiefly as a means to an end, an instrument for getting something done, and tends to judge its value according to its success in achieving that aim." [8] The literary work is viewed as a vehicle of communication, as a means of interaction between the author and the audience. For the Pragmatic Critic, the poet is not Shelley's nightingale, "who sits in darkness and sings to cheer its own solitude with sweet sounds." The poet's song is not simply something *expressed* and maybe *overheard;* it is an *utterance* that seeks its terminus in the response of an audience, an utterance that, in a sense, is not completed *until* it finds an audience.

Clearly, this view of the function of literary works is not the view of Aristotle, the man who wrote both a *Rhetoric* and a *Poetics* because he saw two distinct modes of discourse. One might be inclined to believe that pragmatic or rhetorical criticism was the legacy of another great Greek rhetorician and critic, Longinus. In his *On the Sublime,* Longinus did indeed pay attention to the triadic relationship of author, work, and audience. He starts out with a consideration of

[8] Ibid. p. 15.

the effect (transport, "ecstasy") in the audience; works back from that effect to the quality (sublimity) in the work which produced that effect; and then works back from that quality in the work to the author who created that quality. Adopting for literary works the triadic framework that Aristotle saw as characteristic of rhetorical discourse, Longinus does seem to be a prototype of the rhetorical critic of poetic discourse. But Longinus quite clearly distinguished the art of the sublime from the art of rhetoric. For one thing, the effect of rhetorical discourse is persuasion, whereas the effect of "sublime" discourse is transport. For another thing, the effect of rhetorical discourse is exerted by the successfully integrated whole, whereas the effect of the sublime can strike instantaneously ("like a flash of lightning") from the brilliance of a single part.

On a closer look, Longinus is really a prototype of the Expressive Critic—a fact borne out by his great popularity and influence among the Romantic critics. Although three of the five sources of the sublime —those that can be acquired by art (diction, figures of speech, composition)—are stylistic skills traditionally studied in rhetoric, Longinus' primary concern is with the author. It is significant, as Elder Olson has remarked,[9] that all the sources of the sublime are stated as predicables of a human subject—"having power of expression," "capable of great conceptions," "inspired by vehement passion," etc. In other words, the sources of the sublime reside not in "weighty conceptions," "intense passion," "noble diction" but rather in the ability of the author to conceive of and to articulate these. As Longinus says in the first sentence of Chapter VIII, where he first names the sources of the sublime, the common denominator of the five sources is "a natural faculty of expression" (*legein dynameōs*). And of course there is that most famous line in the treatise—"Sublimity is the echo of a noble mind."

Although rhetorical criticism of literary works then is essentially neither Aristotelian nor Longinian but stems rather from the Horatian cast that Renaissance critics gave to poetics, it is nevertheless a distinctive, respectable, and viable mode of criticism. And having set it in a context with other modes of criticism, I can now go on to sharpen the picture of its *modus operandi.*

It can be said, first of all, that rhetorical criticism is a mode of analysis that focuses on the text itself. In that respect it is like the practical criticism that the New Critics and the Chicago School indulge in. It is unlike these modes of criticism in that it does not remain *inside* the literary work but works *outward* from the text to consider-

[9] "The Argument of Longinus' *On the Sublime,*" *Critics and Criticism,* p. 243.

ations of the author and the audience; because of its concern with the interrelationships among the author, the work, and the audience, it cannot remain closed up inside the work.

But if rhetorical criticism goes outside the work to consider the author and the audience, how does it differ from such other modes of criticism as biographical criticism, historico-sociological criticism, and psychological criticism? And how does it avoid falling into what W. K. Wimsatt calls the Intentional Fallacy and the Affective Fallacy? These are pressing questions, which need a firm answer if rhetorical criticism is to be clearly distinguished from other modes of criticism.

One of the benefits of the New Criticism, which became so popular in the schools after World War II, was that it brought students back to a close reading of the text itself. New Criticism effectively counteracted the practice that had prevailed for a long time in the schools of exploring the biography and the philosophical-aesthetic underpinnings of the author and of establishing the historical context of the work. Students were expected to read literary works outside the classroom, but classroom time was spent largely in reviewing the life and times of the author or exploring the history of ideas. Admittedly, this picture of the situation is an extreme one; anyone might be hard-pressed to adduce a single example of a classroom in which attention was never paid to the literary text itself. But anyone who had taken literature courses before the 1940's can attest that the emphasis in many of these courses was predominantly on the life of the author and the historical background of the work. One of the objections later leveled against the New Critics was that by concentrating on the work in isolation from external considerations, they had swung the pendulum to the opposite extreme. Nevertheless, there has been general agreement that by putting the emphasis where it belonged—namely, on the work itself—the New Critics had effected a salutary redress of the imbalance.

Rhetorical criticism too gets the student back to the text, but it also allows him to consider the author who wrote the work and the audience who receives the work. What differentiates rhetorical criticism from other modes of criticism that consider external factors is that rhetorical criticism uses the text for its "readings" about the author and the audience. In talking about the ethical appeal in his *Rhetoric,* Aristotle made the point that although a speaker may come before an audience with a certain antecedent reputation, his ethical appeal is exerted primarily by what he says in that particular speech before that particular audience. Likewise, in rhetorical criticism, we gain our impression of the author from what we can glean from the text itself—from looking at such things as his ideas and attitudes, his stance, his tone, his style. This reading back to the author is not the same sort of thing as the attempt to reconstruct the biography of a writer from his literary work.[10] Rhetorical criticism seeks simply to ascertain the particular posture or image that the author is establishing in this particular work in order to produce a particular effect on a particular audience.

So too with respect to the audience—the rhetorical critic uses the text as the basis for his speculations about the disposition of the audience and the probable effects of the work on the audience. The rhetorical critic would not disdain to use any biographical or historical information he had gained from other sources to help him assess the author or the audience or the occasion, but the literary work itself is the primary document for his "readings" about the author and the audience.

Does not this type of criticism run the risk of falling into the Intentional Fallacy and the Affective Fallacy? A closer look at what W. K. Wimsatt had to say about these pitfalls for criticism reveals that he is not referring at all to the kind of interest that the rhetorical critic has in the author and the audience. Wimsatt summarizes the character of these two aberrancies in this fashion:

> The Intentional Fallacy is a confusion between the poem and its origins, a special case of what is known to philosophers as the Genetic Fallacy. It begins by trying to derive the standard of criticism from the psychological causes of the poem and ends in biography and relativism. The Affective Fallacy is a confusion between the poem and its results (what it *is* and what it *does*), a special case of epistemological skepticism, . . . It begins by trying to derive the standards of criticism from the psychological effects of the poem and ends in impressionism and relativism. The outcome of either Fallacy, the Intentional or the Affective, is that the poem itself, as an object of specifically critical judgment, tends to disappear.[11]

That Wimsatt does not see rhetorical criticism as necessarily liable to these fallacies is evident from his own indulgence in rhetorical criticism in articles like "Rhetoric and Poems: The Example of Pope," where he defined rhetoric as "the theory of poems with emphasis on their verbal aspects."[12] And in his essay "The Affective Fallacy" (p. 34) he shows us what saves rhetorical criticism from falling into this fallacy:

> The more specific the account of the emotion induced by a poem, the more nearly it will be an account of *the reasons for emotion, the poem*

[10] For the inception, in the first third of the nineteenth century, of the attempt to reconstruct the life of a writer from his literary works, see Richard D. Altick, *Lives and Letters* (New York, 1966), pp. 93–103.

[11] "The Affective Fallacy," *The Verbal Icon* (Noonday Press, 1960), p. 21.

[12] *English Institute Essays, 1948* (New York, 1949), pp. 153–78.

> *itself*, and the more reliable it will be as an account of what the poem is likely to induce in other—sufficiently informed—readers. It will in fact supply the kind of information which will enable readers to respond to the poem. (italics added)

As was once said of Wimsatt's mode of criticism, "He would rather have us, on the whole, in discussing poetry, use the technical language of rhetoric than of psychology." [13]

Some students of rhetoric are wary of any rhetorical criticism that studies the literary work in relation to the external author and audience. Robert M. Browne, who is represented in this collection, prefers a rhetorical criticism that remains inside the work for its study of these interrelationships. He puts it this way:

> The rhetoric which derives from the poet's extrapoetic intention [somewhat the same thing that Wimsatt means by "intentional fallacy"] may be called *external* rhetoric, external because both poet and readers are outside the poem. But rhetoric enters the poem in a third and more intrinsic way: inside the poem there are speakers and hearers and processes of persuasion. We sometimes use the term *rhetoric* to apply to this *internal* rhetoric of the poem, and consider its speakers as rhetoricians.[14]

One can gain some valuable insights into the workings of a literary piece by concentrating on the rhetorical strategies operating within the work—and some of the critiques in this collection do just that—but those critics, like Kenneth Burke and Wayne Booth, who have examined what Browne calls the "external rhetoric" of a literary work, obviously do not feel that they are engaging in a bastardized form of rhetorical criticism. The production of any literary work is a public act, a "transaction" between an author and an audience, whether that audience is made up of the author's contemporaries or of readers many centuries later. We have long since been disabused of the idea that the spokesman or narrator or "I" or persona in a literary work necessarily represents the point of view of the author. But even where we recognize that a persona, like Swift's Gulliver, does not speak for the author, we are conscious still of an author behind the scenes manipulating various elements in order to influence our reactions to events, emotions, thoughts, and characters in the work. Gulliver, for instance, is manipulating his audience within the work, but Swift too is manipulating the readers of *Gulliver's Travels*. And that authorial manipulation is as much a part of the rhetoric of the piece

[13] "Cognitive Criticism," *The Times Literary Supplement*, February 20, 1959, p. 97.

[14] "Rhetorical Analysis and Poetic Structure," *Rhetoric: Theories for Application*, ed. Robert M. Gorrell (Champaign, Illinois, 1967), p. 91.

as is the manipulation going on inside the work. Thomas O. Sloan puts the case this way:

> Our response to the character of the author—whether it is called ethos, or "implied author," or style, or even tone—is part of our experience of his work, an experience of the voice within the masks, personae, of the work. . . . Rhetorical criticism intensifies our sense of the dynamic relationships between the author as a real person and the more or less fictive person implied by the work.[15]

Wayne Booth has put the case in even stronger terms:

> In short, all of the clichés about the natural object being self-sufficient are at best half-truths. Though some characters and events may speak by themselves their artistic message to the reader, and thus carry in a weak form their own rhetoric, none will do so with proper clarity and force until the author brings all his powers to bear on the problem of making the reader see what they really are. The author cannot choose whether to use rhetorical heightening. His only choice is of the kind of rhetoric he will use.[16]

The study of the audience's response to a literary work, perhaps the principal concern of rhetorical criticism, is liable to another set of pitfalls. If the critic uses his own reactions to the work as a gauge of other readers' responses to the work, the result could very well be the kind of impressionistic comment we get in critics like George Saintsbury. On the other hand, the attempt to measure the actual response of a particular audience to a literary work runs the risk of falling into a rather tenuous kind of subjectivism. Despite all our advances in technology and psychology, we have not yet devised any adequate tools to measure accurately and objectively the responses of an audience to a literary work. About the best we have been able to do is to cite a number of published reactions to the work.

The rhetorical critic can best protect himself against impressionism and subjectivism by confining his analysis as much as possible to those elements in the work which are capable of producing an effect of a certain kind on an audience. As O. G. Brockett puts it, "While the impressionistic critic tends to assume that his response somehow contains the work, the internal critic tends to see the response as contained in the work." The response, he says, "is deduced from an analysis of the structure, the relationship of characters, the implied and expressed meanings, the mood, and similar factors."[17] By con-

[15] "Restoration of Rhetoric to Literary Study," *The Speech Teacher*, XVI (March 1967), 95–96.

[16] *The Rhetoric of Fiction* (Chicago, 1961), p. 116.

[17] "Poetry as Instrument," *Rhetoric and Poetic*, ed. Donald C. Bryant (Iowa City, 1965), p. 24.

centrating on the response as it is potentially contained in the work, the critic can render his analysis of effect as objective as such an analysis can be. As Bernard Weinberg says, "Our analysis reveals, simultaneously, an 'effect' built into the poem and an 'effect' that will occur in an audience because of what is in the poem. Moreover—and here the situation is the direct opposite of what we find in rhetoric [i.e. in didactive or persuasive discourse]—what happens in the audience happens because of what the poem is, not because of what the audience is."[18]

It should begin to be clear from the foregoing that rhetorical criticism is that mode of internal criticism which considers the interactions between the work, the author, and the audience. As such, it is interested in the *product,* the *process,* and the *effect* of linguistic activity, whether of the imaginative kind or the utilitarian kind. When rhetorical criticism is applied to imaginative literature, it regards the work not so much as an object of aesthetic contemplation but as an artistically structured instrument for communication. It is more interested in a literary work for what it *does* than for what it *is.*

Because rhetorical criticism is more interested in a literary work as *utterance* than as *artifact,* as *impression* than as *expression,* it works best with—or at least is applied most often to—those forms of literature which, as I like to put it, "have designs on an audience." Satire, didactic essays and poems, problem dramas, propaganda novels, parables, exempla, are some of these forms—where the author is more interested in teaching than in delighting, or at least in teaching *through* delighting. So we often find rhetorical criticism applied to those pieces which have been called "occasional literature"—literary works which were prompted by contemporary events or concerns of some political or social import.

Satire is the most obviously rhetorical of all literary works. It is always prompted by some contemporary situation or tendency, and the author is always intent on effecting a change of attitudes or on moving people to take some course of action. On this score, satire is very much akin to that persuasive oratory with which the art of rhetoric began. Like the deliberative or forensic or epideictic orator, the satirist tries, as James Sutherland puts it, "to persuade men to admire or despise . . . to see, or think, or believe whatever seems good to the writer."[19]

It may be this affinity of rhetoric for certain types of literature

[18] "Formal Analysis in Poetry and Rhetoric," *Rhetoric and Poetic,* p. 40.
[19] *English Satire* (Cambridge, 1958), p. 5.

that prompted Northrup Frye to view rhetorical criticism as a basis for a theory of genres. "The basis of generic distinctions in literature," Frye says, "appears to be the radical of presentation. Words may be acted in front of a spectator; they may be spoken in front of a listener; or they may be written for a reader. . . . The basis of generic criticism in any case is rhetorical, in the sense that the genre is determined by the conditions established between the poet and his public." [20] Using the "radical of presentation" as a criterion, Frye distinguishes four genres: drama, where words are acted out for spectators; *epos,* where words are recited for a listening audience; lyric, where words are recited but not in front of a listener (the lyric is *overheard,* if it is heard at all, because the audience is concealed from the author); "fiction," where words are printed or written for a reading audience.[21]

Frye makes valuable distinctions among a direct or actual address, a *mimesis* of direct address, and a *mimesis* of assertion—distinctions we would do well to keep in mind when dealing with discourse as it appears in imaginative literature and as it appears in utilitarian prose:

> In *epos,* where the poet faces his audience, we have a *mimesis* of direct address. . . . As we progress historically through the five modes, fiction increasingly overshadows *epos,* and as it does, the *mimesis* of direct address changes to a *mimesis* of assertive writing. This in its turn, with the extremes of documentary or didactic prose, becomes actual assertion, and so passes out of literature.[22]

The discrimination between direct address and an imitation of direct address or of assertion will be easy enough to make in extreme instances. No one, for instance, will have trouble discriminating the mimetic address of Absalom in Dryden's poem from the real address of something like Lincoln's Second Inaugural. But how do we classify Pope's *An Essay on Criticism* and Arnold's *The Function of Criticism at the Present Time?* Are they both instances of mimetic assertion? Or is one a *mimesis,* and the other the real thing? If so, which is which? And where is the line of demarcation between the two? It is to the question of why some occasional essays pass over into the realm of art or literature that George Levine directs his attention in his article "Nonfiction as Art." [23] But let us not be lured into pursuing that question here.

[20] *Anatomy of Criticism* (Princeton, 1957), pp. 246–47.

[21] It should be remarked that Frye's distinction between "fiction" and the other genres blurs when he admits that these other genres can also appear in a printed or written medium.

[22] *Anatomy of Criticism,* p. 250.

[23] *Victorian Newsletter,* No. 3 (Fall 1966), 1–6.

It is a fact of literary history, in any case, that for a long stretch, from about 1540 to at least 1800, English creative writers looked as much to rhetoric as to any system of poetics for a rationale governing the construction of literary works. It would be hard to find a major English writer, from Chaucer on, who had not had rhetorical training in the grammar schools and universities or at least had not been influenced by the rhetorical bias of his age. When these writers sat down to compose a poem or a play or a novel or a prose essay, they quite naturally harked back to the lessons that their rhetoric books had taught them about the construction of a real address or assertion. Accordingly, when a critic turns his attention to a literary work produced during the long period when rhetoric was a reigning discipline in the schools, he finds ample and unmistakable evidence in the text itself, aside from any documentary evidence he may have, that the principles of rhetoric had helped to inform the work.

When I was searching for instances of rhetorical criticism for this collection, I had my choice of dozens of analyses of works produced during the sixteenth, seventeenth, and eighteenth centuries, but I found few instances of rhetorical analyses of works produced in the nineteenth and twentieth centuries, those periods when the influence of rhetoric had waned. There are two explanations for the dearth of rhetorical analyses of modern literature. For one thing, because many modern critics have had no formal training in rhetoric and may not even be aware of the long tradition of rhetoric, they have not recognized rhetoric as a means of unfolding a literary work. For another thing, since most modern writers have had no formal training in rhetoric, they do not consciously make use of rhetorical principles in composing their works—even though a rhetorical critic might be able to demonstrate that rhetorical principles help to account for the particular form that the works have assumed.

When rhetoric has played a prominent part in the synthetic process of composition, it is easy for a critic to make use of rhetoric in the analytical process of examining the constituent parts of the composition. Perhaps the commonest form of rhetorical criticism is the one that applies the principles and the terminology from classical rhetoric to an examination of a literary work. When Sir Philip Sidney felt the need to rise to the defense of poetry against those of his contemporaries who were impugning its worth, he readily recognized, because of his rhetorical training in the schools, that one of the ways in which he could enhance the efficacy of his defense was to structure his written discourse as a forensic oration. So when Kenneth Myrick analyzed the *Defence of Poesie* in his *Sir Philip Sidney as a Literary*

Craftsman (Cambridge, Mass., 1935), it was easy enough for him to demonstrate that the *Defence* does indeed have the seven-part structure of a classical oration—exordium, narration, proposition, partition, confirmation, refutation, and peroration. Other critics might outline the organization of the essay in a different fashion—topically, for instance. But it is hard to see how those other views of the organization could be as illuminating about the form of the essay as the designation of the organizational principle that the author himself had deliberately adopted. They might be able to show that the author did not successfully execute the form or to argue that he had chosen the wrong form for his subject-matter or audience or purpose, but they could not make even those judgments until they had determined, from an examination of the text or from external testimony, what structure the author had chosen to impose on his work.

Rhetorical criticism that derives from the canons of ancient rhetoric may manifest itself also in an analysis of the strategies of argument in a poem, a play, a story, or a prose work. Such an investigation will be brought to bear when the work as a whole or parts of it are viewed as an attempt to persuade an audience of something—that audience being either the hearers within the work or the readers outside of it. Such a critic will be variously concerned with the kinds, the sources, the cogency, and the validity of the arguments. If he is concerned simply with the kinds and sources of the argument, he may use as his exploratory tool the "topics" or "places of argument" that figured so prominently in the techniques of invention proposed by the classical rhetorics. So he may see the "lines of argument" as having been yielded by such topics as "definition," "similarities," "differences," "cause and effect," "antecedent and consequence." For his evaluations of the cogency and validity of the arguments he will use as criteria not only the truth and logical consistency of the propositions but also considerations of audience, subject-matter, occasion, and purpose. He may go beyond this assessment of the logical appeal to a consideration of those other two strategies of rhetorical proof, the emotional appeal and the ethical appeal—an examination that will invariably involve him in considerations of the author and the audience. Whatever facets of the argument the critic chooses to analyze, he will be dealing in one way or the other with Thought (*dianoia*), that constituent part of an imitative work which, as Aristotle admitted in the *Poetics,* belongs more properly to rhetoric.

The kind of criticism that strikes students of literature as being most characteristically "rhetorical" is that which concerns itself with style. In fact, some of the pejorative connotations that cluster about the word *rhetoric* stem from its association in many people's minds with stylistic artifice—with all those notions of style as "ornament," as "purple patches," as "verbal smoke-screen," as "sound and fury signifying nothing." The association of style with rhetoric is historically warranted, for not only was style the main preoccupation of some of the Greek and Roman sophists and all of the seventeenth-century disciples of Peter Ramus, but style (*elocutio*) was originally and persistently regarded as one of the five parts of rhetorical studies. It is significant that when the New Critics emerged into prominence after World War II, they were often referred to as "rhetorical critics" because of their concentration on the verbal strategies of a literary text. It is notable too that three of the most famous practitioners of New Criticism—Allen Tate, Robert Penn Warren, and John Crowe Ransom—were products of Vanderbilt University, where Donald Davidson has done much to preserve the tradition of rhetoric. In recent years, the most impressive and most advanced development in the so-called "new rhetoric" has occurred in the area of style or, as it has come to be called, stylistics.

In the study of the style of a literary work, rhetorical critics turn their attention to such things as diction, imagery, sentence structure, sentence rhythm, tropes and schemes, and the typology of styles ("low, medium, and high"; "tough, sweet, and stuffy").[24] Not all critics, however, who comment on the style of a literary work can be called "rhetorical critics." What makes attention to style peculiarly rhetorical is some attempt to relate the stylistic features not only to other formal and material elements in the work itself but also to the ethos of the author and to the effects the author is seeking to produce in an audience. For the rhetorical critic, style represents the choices that an author has made from the available lexical and syntactical resources of a language. A critic becomes "rhetorical" when he tries to show that the choices from among the available options were made in reference to subject-matter or genre or occasion or purpose or author or audience—or some combination of these.

That last sentence epitomizes the rationale of rhetorical criticism. The term *choices* gets us to the heart of rhetoric in general and of rhetorical criticism in particular. If rhetoric is the art of making judicious choices from among available resources, there must be some norms or reference points to guide decisions about the best choices. Those reference points in rhetorical criticism are those named above

[24] For a commentary on the subjectivism of some methods of stylistic analysis, see Louis T. Milic, "Metaphysics in the Criticism of Style," *College Composition and Communication*, XVII (October 1966), 124–29.

—subject-matter, genre, occasion, purpose, author, audience. When a critic asks why an author did *this*, in *this* order, and in *these* words, and answers his question in relation to one or more of these reference points, he is probably operating as a rhetorical critic. If there is a hierarchy among these reference points, *audience* would have to be put at the head of the list. Aristotle and all the other major rhetoricians considered the audience to be the chief determinant of the means adopted to achieve an end. And this notion of the primacy of audience is implicit in Gene Montague's definition of rhetorical criticism:

> When I speak of a rhetorical critical method, I mean the investigation of the use of traditional devices to produce an effect on an audience, of the presence of materials in a poem, novel, or short story which can best be accounted for by a pragmatic rationale—in other words, the presence in a work of elements that are there for one chief specific purpose: to manipulate an audience.[25]

As I have been pointing out, a good deal of the rhetorical criticism of literary works that has been done by modern critics is conducted according to the rationale and in the terminology of classical rhetoric. But an exercise in practical criticism does not have to be rendered in terms of the ancient system in order to qualify as being distinctly rhetorical. Some modern critics, even when they are well versed in the tradition of rhetoric, have produced rhetorical critiques which have not used a single term from the classical or Renaissance rhetoric books—and there are several examples of that kind in this collection. And I have read a few critiques in which the author presented no evidence, either explicit or implicit, that he had any knowledge or even awareness of the rhetorical tradition. The point is that one does not have to be committed to any particular rhetorical school in order to operate as a rhetorical critic. And I suspect that some teachers and critics would be surprised—maybe even shocked—to learn that they have all along been engaged in rhetorical criticism of literature. Indeed it would be a great gain for criticism if we could invent a new vocabulary in which to conduct rhetorical analyses. As a matter of fact, though, some of the common terms in modern criticism are nothing more than new words for old rhetorical concepts—terms like *stance, voice, tone, textures, attitude, ambiguity, tension.*

In presenting this collection of rhetorical analyses, I make no claim that this method of explication is *the* method to adopt in explor-

[25] "Rhetoric in Literary Criticism," *College Composition and Communication,* XIV (October 1963), 168.

ing a literary text. I am merely proposing that for those who prefer to concentrate on the literary work itself this is another and a fruitful method of internal criticism. Because it permits us to ask questions about a literary text that are not part of the exploratory technique of other systems of internal criticism, it can return us answers that are not yielded by other systems. If I were to make a special plea for this system of practical criticism over others, I would say that it is not liable to the charge of "critical monism" that R. S. Crane once leveled against such critics as Cleanth Brooks, Allen Tate, John Crowe Ransom, Robert Penn Warren, and I. A. Richards.[26] Allowing the critic to move back and forth between the work and the author and the audience, with glances, if need be, at external documents for supplementary or confirmatory evidence, rhetorical criticism enables him to discover a variety of the causes and conditions for a literary work being what it is. Most teachers have now come around to the view that they must be in command of a number of critical approaches to a literary work. "Pluralism of critical method" was Professor Crane's plea in his polemical Introduction to *Critics and Criticism* back in 1952. It will be enough if the rhetorical method can provide critics and teachers with another tool for their diagnostic kit.

[26] "The Critical Monism of Cleanth Brooks," *Critics and Criticism*, pp. 83–107.

ARGUMENT

A Rhetorical Analysis of John Donne's "The Prohibition"

THOMAS O. SLOAN

[On the basis simply of the number of rhetorical analyses that have been done on John Donne's prose and poetry, one would be inclined to pronounce that he was the most rhetorical of all English literary artists. Whether he deserves the title of "most rhetorical" is perhaps debatable, but there is no question that he had absorbed his rhetoric lessons very well and that he consciously put them to work when he came to write his prose and poetry.

Thomas O. Sloan shows how rhetorical even a lyric poem can be. Viewing "The Prohibition" as a persuasion-situation, in which the "I" of the poem addresses a "you," Sloan analyzes the strategies of persuasion according to the Ramist system of logic and rhetoric which was very much in vogue in England at the time that Donne wrote the poem. One of the things revealed by this analysis is that dichotomy is the basic principle of organization in the poem. The argument for the basic dichotomy of structure is further supported by Professor Sloan's investigation of Donne's diction, imagery, irony, syntax, and grammar. Throughout the analysis Sloan is intent on exploring the connection between form and meaning. "Form," he concludes, "communicates poetic meaning, but does not contain it."

Like the New Critics, Sloan does spend a good deal of time "inside" the poem, but unlike the New Critics, he does not hesitate to range "outside" the poem also for his explanations of the strategies that Donne adopted. As he says at the end of his article, a rhetorical analysis can at least reveal those constituents of poetic meaning that the New Critics call "structure" and "texture" and that the Ramist rhetoricians called "*dispositio*" and "*elocutio*."]

From *Quarterly Journal of Speech,* XLVIII (February 1962), 38–45. Reprinted by permission of the Speech Association of America and Thomas O. Sloan.

Take heed of loving mee,
At least remember, I forbade it thee;
Not that I shall repaire my'unthrifty wast
Of Breath and Blood, upon thy sighes, and teares,
By being to thee then what to me thou wast;
But, so great Joy, our life at once outweares,
Then, least thy love, by my death, frustrate bee,
If thou love mee, take heed of loving mee.

Take heed of hating mee,
Or too much triumph in the Victorie.
Not that I shall be mine owne officer,
And hate with hate againe retaliate;
But thou wilt lose the stile of conquerour,
If I, thy conquest, perish by thy hate.
Then, least my being nothing lessen thee,
If thou hate mee, take heed of hating mee.

Yet, love and hate mee too,
So, these extreames shall neithers office doe;
Love mee, that I may die the gentler way;
Hate mee, because thy love is too great for mee;
Or let these two, themselves, not me decay;
So shall I, live, thy Stage, not triumph bee;
Lest thou thy love and hate and mee undoe
To let mee live, O love and hate mee too.

THOUGH READERS have been intrigued by the poetry of John Donne for over three hundred years, critical interest in his poetry has reached its highest peak in our time. Since the turn of the century few poets have been the subject of such wide and varied critical attention—particularly during the last three decades, when the viability of a critical method appeared to depend upon its usefulness in analyzing a poem by Donne. However, regardless of their type of analysis, modern critics frequently indicate that the uniqueness of Donne's poetry lies in its modes of persuasion. "Disputatious," "argumentative," "having the look of logic"—these are typical of the terms critics use to characterize the special qualities of Donne's poetry. Perhaps it was inevitable, then, that our time should see the publication of a major scholarly work devoted in part to exploring certain possible connections between

Donne's poetry and Renaissance rhetoric.[1] And, considering the nature of modern criticism, perhaps it was also inevitable that a major modern critic should respond by warning readers against viewing Donne's complex, many-sided poetry through the unavoidable narrowness of rhetoric.[2] Yet in the midst of these positions a basic question remains to be answered: of what value, if any, is a specific Renaissance rhetorical theory in examining a specific poem by Donne? Though the question is limited, its answer should have relevance for larger theoretical questions concerning the use of rhetorical theory in exploring the province of poetry.

For a rhetorical analysis of Donne's poetry the Ramist system of "logic" and "rhetoric" is most serviceable, not only because Ramism has received extensive treatment in recent scholarship but also because it is representative of intellectual developments of Donne's day. Recent scholarship in the history of Renaissance rhetoric [3] and in the relation of rhetoric to Renaissance poetry [4] has underscored the importance of Ramism and increased modern understanding of Ramist theories. One of the most striking aspects of these theories is that they were in many ways a natural outgrowth of the Renaissance intellectual heritage. For example, at the time that Peter Ramus began his educational reforms in France in the middle of the sixteenth century, the precepts of *inventio* and *iudicium* in "logic" (actually, dialectic) virtually duplicated the precepts of *inventio* and *dispositio* in rhetoric. As part of his reform, Ramus resolved the confusion by depriving rhetoric of its first two processes and telling poets and orators that henceforth they were to seek invention and disposition in logic and only *elocutio* (style), plus *pronuntiatio* (delivery) for orators, in "rhetoric." When Ramus's treatise on logic is coupled with the rhetoric written by his disciple Omar Talon, the two works

[1] Rosemond Tuve, *Elizabethan and Metaphysical Imagery* (Chicago, 1947). See esp. ch. xii.

[2] William Empson, "Donne and the Rhetorical Tradition," *Kenyon Review*, XI (1949), 571–587.

[3] For example, Wilbur Samuel Howell, *Logic and Rhetoric in England, 1500–1700* (Princeton, 1956); and Walter J. Ong, S.J., *Ramus, Method, and the Decay of Dialogue* (Cambridge, Mass., 1958).

[4] For example, Tuve; and Sister Miriam Joseph, *Shakespeare's Use of the Arts of Language* (New York, 1947).

can be seen as clever reorganizations of four of the traditional five parts of rhetoric. Ramus's Protestantism and his "martyrdom" in the St. Bartholomew's Day Massacre (1572—the year in which, according to many scholars, Donne was born) served to increase the popularity of his theories in England. By the time Donne entered Cambridge, Ramism had already become a strong influence at that university, and Ramist logic and rhetoric remained the single most important rhetorical system throughout Donne's lifetime.[5]

But analyzing Donne's poetry by means of Ramist invention, disposition, and elocution need not necessarily assign Ramism any singularly influential role in the creation of that poetry. In the first place, Ramism certainly mirrored its own time, but in the complexities and turbulence of that time there were countless aspects which could have conspired to produce the special qualities of Donne's poetry. For that matter, in those few characteristics which distinguish Ramism from other rhetorical systems of its time, Donne is distinctly non-Ramist: e.g., his involute, paradoxical, ambiguous statements are unlike the "plain style" the Ramists favored. Secondly, like most rhetorical systems in the Renaissance, Ramism emphasized the similarities between oratory and poetry, but it was peculiarly indifferent to the unique powers of poetry. So far as the Ramists were concerned, the characteristic which distinguished poetry from the rest of rhetoric was merely rhythm.[6] Thus, any attempt to characterize Ramism as a complete theory of poetry is useless. However, once these facts are recognized, Ramist theory remains the most useable one for a *rhetorical* analysis of Donne's poetry.

"The Prohibition" is a good example of Donne's poetic manner. It was probably written during Donne's prodigal youth, and perhaps belongs to that group of poems Ben Jonson had in mind when he remarked to Drummond that Donne had written his best poetry before the age of twenty-five. All of these early poems employ the conventions of a persuasion-situation in which Donne speaks in monologue to convince another person or in soliloquy to convince himself. Also, "The Prohibition" contains

[5] All of the Ramist textbooks examined for this discussion, and cited in the footnotes, were published during Donne's youth.

[6] Ong, pp. 281–283.

Donne's characteristic, striking images. Finally, the arrangement of material in "The Prohibition" is conspicuous, as it is in many of Donne's poems.

Except for the obvious fact that the poem is a monologue addressed to a loved one, the full persuasion-situation of the poem is only implied. In realizing these implications, certain assumptions can be made on the basis of the careful wording Donne employs, and these assumptions in turn are strengthened by correspondences and contrasts in form. In a general way all three stanzas correspond: each has eight lines; each has the same rhyme scheme; and each has the same statement-proof-conclusion movement with the statement and conclusion expressed in couplets and the proof in the enclosed four lines. But certain differences serve to segregate the third stanza from the other two, differences more subtle than the variation in the couplet rhymes. Ramist disposition provides terminology that indicates these subtle differences, and Ramist invention gives their rationale. But, having named the tools, we are still left with the problem of meaning, and to complete our search we have no recourse but verbal analysis. To anticipate this discussion somewhat, the rest of the persuasion-situation appears to be this: first, though now the woman addressed appears indifferent toward him, he loves her so intensely that she cannot remain indifferent (how like Donne to confront this indifference with "Take heed of loving mee"); second, her present attitude toward him is so vague that she may yet choose to love him or to hate him, or both to love and to hate him, while he has no choice but to love her; third, her capacity for emotion is less than his.

He begins the statement of his argument in the first stanza by warning her not to love him, but in order to exonerate himself of the consequences should her emotions turn to love for him, he begs her to "remember" that he has warned her. The proof (lines 3–6) contains an interesting quality comparison which sharply indicates the difference in their capacities for emotion. Sighs and tears, as Elizabethan psychology believed, were "the two most immediate and natural ways" whereby the heart found relief from the dangers of excessive passion.[7] But so far greater is Donne's passion that he could find relief only through the expenditure of

[7] J. B. Bamborough, *The Little World of Man* (London, 1952), p. 128.

breath and blood, which being made of the same elements as "sighes" (air) and "teares" (water) heighten the directness of the quality comparison. This was an "unthrifty wast" on his part, for the returns of his investment were less than profitable, so much so that the loss could be repaired only by causing a like waste on her part. But if she loves him, or when she loves him, he could repair this waste not upon her breath and blood, but merely upon her sighs and tears—her capacity for emotion is that much less than his. The proof is expressed in the "not this, but that" form which the Ramists call the discretive axiom.[8] Donne tells her to beware of loving him, not because he plans to repair his loss by showing her that indifference which she has shown him, but because great passion—both of them in love—can cause death. Probably not her death, however. The concluding couplet indicates that it is he, with his always greater intensity of passion, whose life would be suddenly, "at once," outworn by an excess of Joy. He concludes persuasively, his concern apparently only for her, that her love could be frustrated by his death. The conclusion is expressed conditionally: *if* you love me (and I don't really know that you do), beware.

It is the denial of this condition which leads Donne to the point of his second stanza, if you do *not* love me. . . . Perhaps because of his own intensely emotional state, he cannot conceive a passionate alternative any less extreme than the direct opposite of love. Another reason why hate is the subject of the second stanza (and why the negation of both love and hate naturally follows in the third) lies in a rhetorical principle of arrangement. For this principle we must turn not to disposition but to the one place in invention that is most important to questions of arrangement, *distribution,* "when the whole is distributed into his partes." According to Fraunce, "the more that the partes doo disagree among themselues, the better is the diuision. By which it appeereth that the best diuision must be of partes that be most

[8] See Abraham Fraunce, *The Lawiers Logike* (London, 1588), fol. 96v; Dudley Fenner, *The Artes of Logike and Rhethorike* (Middelburg, 1584), sig. Cir; and Roland MacIlmaine, *The Logike of the Most Excellent Philosopher P. Ramus Martyr* (London, 1581), p. 79. Although all three writers exemplify this axiom with an "although . . . yet" construction, Fenner and Fraunce state that the axiom is fittest to dispose arguments from the place *divers,* and all three state that among the signs of the *divers* argument are the "not this, but that" constructions.

repugnant, which can bee but two, therefore *Dichotomia* is most excellent, a diuision consisting onely of two partes." [9] Though the Ramists cannot claim to be the sole exponents or defenders of the persuasive force of argument by dichotomy, the dichotomizing arrangement was associated with the Ramist movement,[10] which could have brought fresh attention to this ancient device. In any case, the dichotomy is the basic principle of arrangement in this poem. Donne moves from one extreme in the first stanza to its opposite in the second; these two extremes in turn become half of a dichotomy which is completed in the third stanza. As noted below, this dichotomizing arrangement both accounts for and is enhanced by subtle structural characteristics.

Donne warns her not to hate him, but the hate of which he speaks is the hate that would arise from her exulting in the fact that she has brought him to his knees. He is completely at her mercy, and once she takes "too much triumph in the Victorie," her emotion becomes hatred. Again, the proof (11–14) of the statement is expressed in a discretive axiom. But while in the first stanza he employed images from commerce and psychology, in this stanza (both statement and proof) he speaks in terms of organized hate, war. The imagery of these two stanzas aids their contrast, and their structure aids their correspondence. Particularly in his psychological concepts in the first stanza, Donne gives the signs and terms of passionate intensity ("Breath," "Blood," "sighes," "teares," "outweares," "frustrate"), but the imagery of war produces the opposite effect; it makes the hate formal and cold. He tells her that he would not return her hate (he gives himself no alternative to his present state), but her day as conqueror would be shortened by the death of her conquest. The conclusion, too, is expressed in exactly the same syntactical form as that used for the conclusion of the first stanza, conditionally; *if* you hate me (and I don't really know that you do), beware, for my death, caused by your hate, would make you less than that conqueror you had become.

[9] Fraunce, fol. 57r.

[10] According to Howell, Ramus's "followers tended to construe the natural method and the law of justice to mean the severest kind of dichotomizing, as if any given idea had only two members, one completely insulated from the other" (p. 163); see also p. 186.

The function of "Yet," which begins the third stanza, is best described with the Ramist phrase "segregative conjunction," for this stanza completes the argument of the entire poem by forming the argument into a dichotomy. As in the first two stanzas, the proof is expressed in a sentence of two parts (19–22); but whereas in the first two stanzas these two parts began with "Not that" and "But" to form discretive axioms, in this stanza the two parts are segregated by "Or" to form a disjunctive axiom—the best form for disposing a distribution of two opposites, a form which accords with the increasingly strict dichotomizing movement of the poem. Moreover, since the discretive and the disjunctive are the two types of segregative axioms,[11] there are both correspondence and contrast between the proof in the third stanza and that in the other two stanzas. In proving his opening statement, Donne asks her to love him that he "may die the gentler way"; the comparison is between his actual death, which would be caused by the absence of her love, and the "gentler" death of sexual intercourse (the last three words in the line cause "die" to lose some of its dimension as an Elizabethan trope and to become more of a literal statement than a pun). And he asks her at the same time to hate him because her love alone could cause his (literal) death. Or, as he explains, there is the other sense in which "these extreames shall neithers office doe." Having first considered the effect of her love-and-hate emotions on himself, each serving to counteract the effects of the other, he now considers a possible effect within her. The two emotions may destroy themselves, so that she may become incapable of feeling either emotion toward him; he may therefore be saved, beyond the dangers of death, to serve as a live demonstration of her powers and not as a dead "triumph," as temporary as a funeral procession. The conclusion of the stanza accords with the conclusions of the first two stanzas; it begins with a "lest" clause and ends with a command. In the "lest" clause, he is logically the last member of the list, for throughout the poem he has maintained a position secondary to her, to her love, and to her hate, and in every instance he has heightened the persuasiveness of his appeals by showing that the worst effect of his destruction is that it would undo her love and her hate. "To let me live," which begins the

[11] See Fraunce, fol. 95v; Fenner, *loc. cit.;* MacIlmaine, *loc. cit.*

final line of the stanza, is a dramatic change from the conditional clauses that began the last lines of the first two stanzas; furthermore, having mentioned himself last in the preceding line, he comes first in this, thereby achieving added emphasis.

The whole poem eventually creates one dichotomy: she may (1) either love or hate him, or (2) both love and hate him. It is proper that the two parts of the first alternative be disposed in stanzas which closely correspond in structure, because such an arrangement helps the reader to see that these two parts form the first alternative of a dichotomy, and because such an arrangement enhances the argument that although the nature of love may differ from the nature of hate, the two as causes produce the same fatal effect. It is precisely because these two produce the same effect—his death and the consequent frustration of her love or lessening of her victory—that the first alternative is ruled out. The second alternative would not undo her love, her hate, and him, and the contrasting structure of the third stanza enhances the difference. But the third stanza also needs *some* correspondence to the others, not only because of the prosodic requirements of songs and sonnets, but also because of the unvarying grammatical-logical-rhetorical insistence on parallelism in the construction of alternatives in a proposition. Therefore, the proof in the first two stanzas is disposed in discretive axioms and the proof in the third stanza is disposed in a disjunctive axiom, but both types belong to the category of segregative axioms. Furthermore, although there is a correspondence in the couplet form of the statement and conclusion of each stanza, the couplets of the last stanza employ rhymes which differ from those of the couplets in the first two stanzas. Or we may note this last correspondence and contrast in another way: each stanza is a kind of figure the Ramists call *epanalepsis* "when the same sound is iterated in the beginning and ending." [12] The epanalepses of the first two

[12] Abraham Fraunce, *The Arcadian Rhetorike* (London, 1588); reprint ed. Ethel Seaton (Oxford, 1950), p. 45. Unlike Henry Peacham (*The Garden of Eloquence* [London, 1593]), who in discussing the figures of repetition makes neat distinctions between "members," "clauses," and "sentences," both Fenner and Fraunce use the word "sentence" loosely. Fraunce's examples indicate that repetitions may be made at the beginning, middle, or end of some unit that may properly be thought to have a beginning, middle, or end—be that unit a phrase, a clause, a sentence, or a line, or even a stanza of poetry.

stanzas ("Take heed of loving mee . . . take heed of loving mee," "Take heed of hating mee . . . take heed of hating mee") correspond to each other but contrast with the epanalepsis of the last stanza ("love and hate mee too . . . love and hate mee too").

Finally, no Ramist analysis—not even a partial one such as this—would be typical without the use of a bracketed, dichotomized diagram to represent arrangement.[13] Whereas the Ramists would cast a paraphrase of the entire poem in diagrammatic form, the following diagram is a simplification. The statement and development (proof and conclusion) of each stanza is represented; the brackets indicate the dichotomized arrangement of the poem.

Yet
- "Take heed of loving mee"
  - discretive axiom
  - "Then, least . . . take heed of loving mee"
- "Take heed of hating mee"
  - discretive axiom
  - "Then, least . . . take heed of hating mee"
- "love and hate mee too"
  - disjunctive axiom
  - "Lest . . . love and hate mee too"

It would appear that a rhetorical analysis of this poem is useful in exploring the connection between structure and meaning. This analysis of arrangement and the observations concerning style encompass a large part of what is meant by *form*, which in poetry helps to communicate meaning. Although this analysis

[13] An excellent example of the use of the dichotomized diagram in literary analysis is given by Fraunce, *The Lawiers Logike*, foll. 120r–124r.

may not suggest that the form is extraneous or obtrusive or even absurd (qualities of form often denoted by our modern pejorative *rhetorical*), this analysis does suggest that the form is isolable, that it somehow has its own purposes to serve, or that it can even be enjoyed for itself without a full realization of meaning. The proportions of arrangement and the contrasts of imagery satisfy, perhaps even cloy, the mind's desire for order; at the same time these qualities help the reader to a partial understanding. For example, the conditional conclusions of the first two stanzas indicate the vagueness of her present attitude, and the correspondence in stanzaic structures helps indicate the formation of dichotomies. Form communicates poetic meaning, but does not contain it. Although a fuller realization of meaning than that so far arrived at will be indicated in terms of a trope, the whole poem, with all its variations, shades, and ambiguities, will not stop at the boundaries of rhetoric.

What does the poem finally come to? Donne is deeply vexed by the fact that the woman he is passionately in love with is treating him with indifference. He shows first that neither love nor hate is preferable to this indifference. Then he shows in the last stanza that the best, the safest, attitude for her to take toward him is compounded of love and hate, in which the two emotions cancel one another—leaving her with an attitude of indifference! With no choice but to love her, he actually protests her indifference (which in the past has caused his waste of breath and blood) by begging for her indifference so that he may serve as a living pageant of the extreme devotion she can inspire in one man. What the poem finally comes to is best characterized by that overused term of modern Donne criticism, a term well known to the Ramists: *irony*. The poem is a carefully stated plea for her love. Perhaps she loves him now. If she does, the intensity of her love is so much less than his that it is difficult for him to tell whether she loves him or not. In fact, she may even hate him. In either case, however, his death is certain. Her emotions, vague though they may be, are too great for him! Therefore, it is best that her emotions be compounded of love and hate—so that he may know the joys of love with the opposite emotion as a safeguard against its fatal effects, or so that she becomes totally indifferent toward him and he lives on as her conquest, not dies as her captive. It is not a large logical jump, and no emotional jump at all, to see that Donne is begging for the return of his love, in kind. Nor must one make a much larger jump to state that in light of the quality comparisons of her capacities for emotion and his, Donne is virtually defying her to return his love.

Irony is a term not confined merely to formal considerations, such as the development of the argument from protesting indifference to begging for indifference. It could also describe the voice of the speaker, as Fraunce realized when he stated that irony is "perceiued by the contrarietie of the matter it selfe, or by the manner of vtterance quite differing from the sense of the wordes, for then it is apparent that wee speake but iestinglie, and not as wee thinke." [14] However, there is more to the quality of Donne's voice than ironic jesting, just as there is more to the poem than ironic pleading for her love. Donne presents his indifferent loved one with a brilliantly conceived and cogent argument for continuing her indifference, and at the same time he interfuses the argument with his desire for her love; for example, the drama enacted on this "Stage" could only be an "unthrifty wast" of his "Breath and Blood."

In short, the poem has both cogent argument and irony. Because it is a poem, we are not forced to choose between the two. We can have the poem both ways: in terms of its organization (*dispositio*) and in terms of its tone (*elocutio*). Or these two ways can be regrouped by employing a strategy honored by at least two decades of New Criticism, to speak of a poem as possessing both "structure" and "texture." The "structure" is the formal means of establishing the argument; essentially it involves the procedures of reasoning in a poem. In this analysis, "structure" would be virtually synonymous with *dispositio*. By making us aware of the dichotomy convention, the "structure" of this poem shows us the validity of Donne's plea for her indifference as the safest course for her emotions to take. Although the poem has the look of reason, it has the manner of irony. "Texture" involves everything not included under "structure": situation, meter, rhyme, imagery. In this analysis it would be virtually synonymous with *elocutio*. It is the "texture" which gives the poem its

[14] *The Arcadian Rhetorike*, p. 10.

irony—for example, the force given the quality comparison in the first stanza by "Breath," "Blood," "sighes," and "teares," or that in the last stanza by "Stage" and "triumph," or the persuasion-situation in which a man in love protests his loved one's indifference. "Structure" and "texture" are two not necessarily discrete views of the same phenomenon; after all, both "structure" and "texture" are *in* the poem; the voice that presents the poem is not just ironic, it is also pleading a rigorously established case. At the very least, a rhetorical analysis provides local habitations and names for these constituents of poetic meaning.

The Voices of Seduction in "To His Coy Mistress": A Rhetorical Analysis[1]

JOSEPH J. MOLDENHAUER

[JOSEPH J. MOLDENHAUER views Andrew Marvell's *carpe diem* lyric "To His Coy Mistress" as an instance of persuasive discourse—not as an actual persuasive discourse but as a *mimesis* of persuasion. In examining the interrelations of speaker, speech, and audience he remains inside the poem, concerned not with the poet who wrote this work but with the *persona* in the poem who seeks to seduce his mistress, and not with the readers of the poem but with the *addressee* in the poem, the coy mistress. What we have then, as Professor Moldenhauer puts it in a paraphrase of John Stuart Mill, is "rhetoric overheard."

Professor Moldenhauer touches on several aspects of the rhetoric of this seduction: the syllogistic structure of the argument in this three-part poem; grammar (the mood and tense of verbs, pronoun shifts, etc.); diction, both for its denotations and connotations; subtle shifts of rhythm; imagery, symbols, and figures of speech. Many critics have commented on this fascinating poem (see footnote 3), but Professor Moldenhauer, by examining the poem as an exercise in persuasive rhetoric, has added another dimension to our understanding and appreciation of it. By the time we get to the end of his thorough analysis, we are ready to agree with him that by "persuasive no less than by poetic criteria, 'To His Coy Mistress' stands the unchallenged masterpiece among lyrics of seduction." His critique provides further confirmation of the claim that any exegesis of a literary work is itself an exercise in persuasion. The critic must sell his interpretation to his readers in much the same sense that the persona in Marvell's poem must sell his "line" to his reluctant mistress.]

From *Texas Studies in Literature and Language,* X (Summer 1968), 189–206. Reprinted by permission of the University of Texas Press and Joseph J. Moldenhauer.

[1] This essay, in a somewhat different form, was one of a series of lectures on "Poetry and the Varieties of Love," presented by members of the English Department of The University of Texas during the 1965–1966 academic year.

OBEDIENT TO the neoclassical aesthetic which ruled his age, Andrew Marvell strove for excellence within established forms rather than trying to devise unique forms of his own. Like Herrick, Ben Jonson, and Campion, like Milton and the Shakespeare of the sonnets, Marvell was derivative. He held imitation to be no vice; he chose a proven type and exploited it with a professionalism rarely surpassed even in a century and a land as amply provided with verse craftsmen as his. Under a discipline so willingly assumed, Marvell's imagination flourished, producing superb and enduring examples of the verse types he attempted: of the emblem poem in "On a Drop of Dew"; of the allegorical debate in "A Dialogue between the Resolved Soul and Created Pleasure"; of the devotional meditation in "The Coronet"; of the philosophical elegy in "The Nymph Complaining for the Death of Her Fawn"; of the metaphysical lyric, following Donne, in "The Definition of Love" and "The Garden"; of the pastoral love lament in the four "Mower" poems; of the commendatory verse portrait in "The Picture of Little T. C."; and of the ode in "An Horatian Ode upon Cromwell's Return from Ireland." Like Jonson's and Herrick's best poems, these by Marvell are conspicuous for their grace, their poise and balance, their architectural firmness of structure, their precision of language, and their sure command of tone.

When he undertook to write a *carpe diem* lyric in "To His Coy Mistress," Marvell was working once more within a stylized form, one of the favorite types in the Renaissance lyric catalogue. Again he endowed the familiar model with his own special sensibility, composing what for many readers is the most vital English instance of the *carpe diem* poem. We can return to it often, with undiminished enthusiasm—drawn not by symbolic intricacy, though it contains two or three extraordinary conceits, nor by philosophical depth, though it lends an unusual seriousness to its theme—but drawn rather by its immediacy and concreteness, its sheer dynamism of statement within a controlled structure.

The *carpe diem* poem, whose label comes from a line of Horace and whose archetype for Renaissance poets was a lyric by Catullus, addresses the conflict of beauty and sensual desire on the one hand and the destructive force of time on the other.[2] Its

[2] Horace, *Odes*, I, xi:

. . . . . Dum loquimur, fugerit invida

theme is the fleeting nature of life's joys; its counsel, overt or implied, is Horace's "seize the present," or, in the language of Herrick's "To the Virgins,"

> Gather ye Rose-buds while ye may,
> Old Time is still a flying.

It takes rise from that most pervasive and aesthetically viable of all Renaissance preoccupations, man's thralldom to time, the limitations of mortality upon his senses, his pleasures, his aspirations, his intellectual and creative capacities. Over the exuberance of Elizabethan and seventeenth-century poetry the pall of death continually hovers, and the lyrics of the age would supply a handbook of strategies for the circumvention of decay. The birth of an heir, the preservative balm of memory, the refuge of Christian resignation or Platonic ecstasy—these are some solutions which the poets offer. Another is the artist's ability to immortalize this world's values by means of his verse. Shakespeare's 19th and 55th sonnets, for example, employ this stratagem for the frustration of "Devouring Time," as does Michael Drayton's "How Many Paltry, Foolish, Painted Things." In such poems the speaker's praise of the merits of the beloved is coupled with a celebration of his own poetic gift, through which he can eternize those merits as a "pattern" for future men and women.

The *carpe diem* lyric proposes a more direct and immediate, if also more temporary, solution to the overwhelming problem. Whether subdued or gamesome in tone, it appeals to the young and beautiful to make time their own for a while, to indulge in the "harmless folly" of sensual enjoyment. Ordinarily, as in "To

> aetas: carpe diem, quam minimum credula postero.

Catullus, *Poems,* V:

> Vivamus, mea Lesbia, atque amemus,
> . . . .
> soles occidere et redire possunt:
> nobis cum semel occidit brevis lux,
> nox est perpetua una dormienda.
> . . . .

Famous translations and adaptations of the latter poem include Campion's "My Sweetest Lesbia," Jonson's "Come, My Celia," and the concluding stanza of Herrick's "Corinna's Going A-Maying."

His Coy Mistress" and Herrick's "Corinna's Going A-Maying," the poem imitates an express invitation to love, a suitor's immodest proposal to his lady. Such works are both sharply dramatic and vitally rhetorical; to analyze their style and structure is, in effect, to analyze a persuasive appeal.[3]

Before turning to the text of "To His Coy Mistress," I would declare certain of my critical presuppositions, even at the risk of rehearsing commonplaces. If "rhetoric" is taken to mean "verbal embellishment" or "decorative writing," all literature is necessarily rhetorical. But the narrower and commoner definition, "persuasive discourse," is also applicable. When we speak of the rhetoric of a poem in this sense, we do not imply that its author steps forth and confronts us, man to man, to engage in instruction or special pleading. Rather, we refer to a persuasive effort within the poem's hypothetical situation, and we attribute this effort not to the author as a biographer would regard him, but to the *persona,* the personality he has devised as the speaker of his work. The persona is technically distinguishable from the author (the human agent, "doing and suffering") even in didactic poetry. And when an author creates two or more speakers for a dialogue poem

[3] The standard readings of "To His Coy Mistress" are those by Herbert J. C. Grierson, Introduction to *Metaphysical Lyrics & Poems of the Seventeenth Century* (Oxford, 1921), xxxvii–xxxviii; T. S. Eliot, *Selected Essays* (New York, 1950), pp. 253–256; M. C. Bradbrook and M. G. Lloyd Thomas, *Andrew Marvell* (Cambridge, 1940), pp. 42–44; Douglas Bush, *English Literature in the Earlier Seventeenth Century* (Oxford, 1945), pp. 163–164; Ruth Wallerstein, *Studies in Seventeenth-Century Poetic* (Madison, Wis., 1950), pp. 161, 336–337, 339; and Joan Bennett, *Five Metaphysical Poets* (Cambridge, 1964), pp. 125–126. Each has in some manner and measure influenced my treatment of the poem. Also relevant, though they did not come to my attention until after the preparation of this paper, are J. V. Cunningham, "Logic and Lyric," *MP*, LI (1953), 33–41; Harold E. Toliver, *Marvell's Ironic Vision* (New Haven, 1965), pp. 154–161; and J. B. Leishman, *The Art of Marvell's Poetry* (London, 1966), pp. 70–79. With these three discussions the present essay shares elements of interpretation. See also George Williamson, *The Donne Tradition* (Cambridge, Mass., 1930), pp. 154–156; John Wheatcroft, "Andrew Marvell and the Winged Chariot," *Bucknell Rev.*, VI, no. 3 (December 1956), 22–53; Anthony E. Farnham, "Saint Teresa and the Coy Mistress," *Boston Univ. Studies in English,* II (1956), 226–239; Lawrence W. Hyman, "Marvell's 'Coy Mistress' and Desperate Lover," *MLN*, LXXV (1960), 8–10; and Hyman, *Andrew Marvell* (New York, 1964), pp. 59–63. Problems in the third strophe are examined by Frederick L. Gwynn, *Explicator*, XI, no. 7 (1953), item 49; Lawrence A. Sasek, *Explicator*, XIV, no. 7 (1956), item 47; Walter Sedelow, "Marvell's *To His Coy Mistress,*" *MLN*, LXXI (1956), 6–8; and John J. Carroll, "The Sun and the Lovers in 'To His Coy Mistress,'" *MLN*, LXXIV (1959), 4–7.

or a play, none of the voices of the work will be his own, however much one of them may serve as spokesman for his values.

Confining the discussion to univocal poems, we understand, moreover, that the speaker's rhetoric is directed toward another literary personage. Though silent, the *addressee* of the poetic situation is more or less definable. Between him and the audience proper there exists an imaginative distance similar in kind to that which separates the author from the speaker. To be sure, many poems address a "generalized audience." It would seem that epics, for instance, speak to us directly. Yet in reading such works, are we not invited or required to put on a "generalized" identity distinct from our particular selves? The univocal poem appeals at the very least to some *abstraction* of ourselves. Insofar as we obey this summons we are made over into that sort of addressee which the poet has designed.[4] The addressee is more objectively realized as a "character" in dramatic monologues, verse prayers, and love poems. Here the poet's authority in creating the addressee is obvious; in the former case it is less conspicuous but equally significant. Like the reader of a devotional lyric or a love poem, the reader of the epic enjoys a measure of detachment. This distance between the actual audience and the addressee of a poem was of sufficient importance to John Stuart Mill that he made it central to his conception of poetry. Defining literary discourse by contrast to overt persuasion, Mill wrote, "eloquence is *heard;* poetry is *over*heard." [5]

Implied throughout these reflections is an analogy between poems—however lyrical or "personal"—and dramas. This relationship has been examined by John Crowe Ransom, who observes that while the two are not generically identical, poetry "maintains faithfully certain dramatic features. The poet does not speak in his own but in an assumed character, and not in the actual but in an assumed situation." Poems are "little dramas, exhibiting actions in complete settings." [6] Tension is the grand

[4] This notion has been advanced by Walker Gibson, "Authors, Speakers, Readers, and Mock Readers," *College English,* XI (1950), 265–269. For another, opposing view, see Walter J. Ong, S.J., "Voice as Summons for Belief," in *Literature and Belief: English Institute Essays, 1957,* ed. M. H. Abrams (New York, 1958), pp. 80–105, esp. p. 101.

[5] *Dissertations and Discussions* (New York, 1882), I, 97.

[6] *The World's Body* (New York, 1938), pp. 254, 249.

prerequisite of drama, and in stage plays (as in dialogue poems) the conflicting interests are assigned to separate personae. Only slightly less dramatic are those numerous poems (including "To His Coy Mistress") in which the presence of a particular addressee, with particular interests and motives, is assumed in the very mode of address. The dramatic view may be extended even to the meditative poem. Though the speaker here muses in solitude, addressing himself alone, the tensions among the themes, images, and structural units of the lyric comprise the dramatic agon of the work. Standing for various motives or attitudes in the speaker, they serve as so many "voices," so many "characters," in the poem.[7]

Analysis of "To His Coy Mistress" need not begin with this refinement of the dramatistic approach, however useful it may prove at last, for the poem presents a distinct dramatic and rhetorical situation. Its central agon pits the speaker's desire for erotic fulfillment against the hesitancy of his lady. Within its dramatic confines the language of the poem is a mimesis of persuasion, or (in a variation upon Mill's aphorism) "rhetoric overheard":

Had we but World enough, and Time,
This coyness Lady were no crime.
We would sit down, and think which way
To walk, and pass our long Loves Day.
Thou by the *Indian Ganges* side 5
Should'st Rubies find: I by the Tide
Of *Humber* would complain. I would
Love you ten years before the Flood:
And you should if you please refuse
Till the Conversion of the *Jews*. 10
My vegetable Love should grow
Vaster then Empires, and more slow.
An hundred years should go to praise
Thine Eyes, and on thy Forehead Gaze.
Two hundred to adore each Breast: 15

[7] The theorizing and practical criticism of Kenneth Burke often suggest, and sometimes make explicit, such a "dramatic" and "attitudinal" concept of the language of lyric. See, for example, Burke's *Attitudes Toward History* (Boston, 1961), pp. 242–243, 312, and *A Grammar of Motives* (New York, 1945), pp. 243–244, 403.

But thirty thousand to the rest.
An Age at least to every part,
And the last Age should show your Heart.
For Lady you deserve this State;
Nor would I love at lower rate. 20
But at my back I alwaies hear
Times winged Charriot hurrying near:
And yonder all before us lye
Desarts of vast Eternity.
Thy Beauty shall no more be found; 25
Nor, in thy marble Vault, shall sound
My ecchoing Song: then Worms shall try
That long preserv'd Virginity:
And your quaint Honour turn to dust;
And into ashes all my Lust. 30
The Grave's a fine and private place,
But none I think do there embrace.
Now therefore, while the youthful hew
Sits on thy skin like morning dew,
And while thy willing Soul transpires 35
At every pore with instant Fires,
Now let us sport us while we may;
And now, like am'rous birds of prey,
Rather at once our Time devour,
Than languish in his slow-chapt pow'r. 40
Let us roll all our Strength, and all
Our sweetness, up into one Ball:
And tear our Pleasures with rough strife,
Thorough the Iron gates of Life.
Thus, though we cannot make our Sun 45
Stand still, yet we will make him run.[8]

Rhetorical analysis of the poem requires first an adequate conception of the persona, his lady, and the circumstances which evoke his argument or appeal. The speaker's urbanity is at once apparent. No newcomer to love, no apprentice to the craft of wooing, he exhibits a sophistication born of long experience. He

[8] Text: *The Poems & Letters of Andrew Marvell,* ed. H. M. Margoliouth (Oxford, 1927), I, 26–27, deriving from *Miscellaneous Poems by Andrew Marvell* (London, 1681). The last word of line 34 is printed "glew" in the 1681 edition, but is usually emended to "dew" or "lew" (warmth, heat). Margoliouth adopts the latter.

must therefore be envisaged, I think, as a man of mature years—neither youthfully sentimental and self-indulgent about love, nor so exhausted by age that he can summon no energy for the present endeavor. His eloquence, his wit, and his concern for the logic of his argument place him among the educated, while his self-assurance and poise are the attributes of a courtier. A virile, attractive figure, he seems quite as impatient of delay as that persona of Suckling's, who exclaims,

> Out upon it! I have loved
> Three whole days together.

Marvell's speaker, however, enjoys a finer gift of self-control and a more flexible wit.

Though the lady of the poem is given no active verbal role, we derive an image of her through her suitor's statements and implications. She is by no means his concubine: to take "Mistress" in its derogatory modern sense would be to reduce the poem to nonsense. We learn, of course, that she has preserved her virginity; but even if this information were not given, the speaker's rhetoric would lack an intelligible motivation were the lady his accomplished lover. "Mistress" here carries its older meaning of sweetheart or beloved—the woman who commands one's affections. Like her distant literary grandame, the Laura of Petrarch's sonnets, and like the numberless ladies of the courtly love tradition since Petrarch, the mistress in Marvell's poem is both fair and cruel. Proud of her beauty, she not only relishes but *expects* her lover's praise. Her coyness, her reluctance to yield to his advances, has about it an air of deliberate display which again recalls the disdainful women of earlier lyrics, who demand that their suitors prove their worthiness by interminable gestures of adoration and patient fidelity. Her social position is no lower than the speaker's; if she were, say, the innkeeper's daughter, his eloquence would be gratuitous. She is probably younger than he, and somewhat less sophisticated—though worldly enough, it would appear, to appreciate his wit.[9]

[9] The setting of "To His Coy Mistress" is nowhere announced; but, given the characteristics of the speaker and his lady, we cannot think of the appeal as occurring on the moors, in the hayloft, or even in the bedroom. A suitable setting, should we care to visualize one, would be a drawing room or a formal garden. This last possibility might find some justification in the poem's garden imagery.

Like Donne's "The Canonization," "To His Coy Mistress" implies a remark by the addressee, before the poem proper, to which the speaker's language constitutes a response. In the former lyric the addressee is a practical man who has advised the persona that love is wasting his time and substance. In "To His Coy Mistress" the lady's assumed remark is something on this order: "Not yet; we have time. Court me further, and keep saying beautiful things." Her suitor's response, accordingly, discusses their courtship and love under the categories of those "Iron gates" of life—the mortal limitations, specified in the opening line, of space and time. The structure of his statement is neatly tripartite, each strophe or verse paragraph possessing its own distinctive grammar, imagery, and tone or quality of voice and each serving a precise logical function in the *carpe diem* argument. Structurally, the poem resembles a syllogism of which the first section is a suppositional premise and the second a premise of refutation. The concluding third part, in the light of these premises, has all the authority of a necessary deduction.[10]

In the opening section, the speaker presents the vision of a courtship wholly free from the restraints of space and time—a condition in which the lady's reluctance, far from being objectionable, takes on positive value, since it provides the continual occasion for praise. All history becomes the lovers' own: they "*have*" time in their power as their wooing extends backward into the remote past—ten years before the Flood—and forward into the unimaginable future—till the conversion of the Jews. It is an idyllic, almost a paradisic, vision: like the unfallen first parents, the lovers enjoy eternal life, and the world is their moist and pleasant garden. Images of water and of leisurely growth are conspicuous in this section, as the lady is imagined in a setting appropriate to her beauty and social rank—the exotic banks of the Ganges—while the speaker, with stylized, painless melancholy, laments her coyness by the shores of the chilly Humber. The grandeur and power of the antique world are further evoked by the image of the speaker's love growing "Vaster then Empires, and more slow." With the magnanimity of an ancient monarch, he pours forth his treasures and bestows them on his queen. As well as gathering rubies in their realms, she receives from him the

[10] See especially Eliot and Cunningham.

richer gift, the higher "state" or ceremonial tribute, of a flattery protracted through centuries, millennia, ages. Within the terms of this vision, then, the opening section is a stupendous act of homage to the lady's charms.

But the vision is at all times undercut by reminders of its unreality. First and most importantly, the grammar of the section is subjunctive, and every verb conforms to the mood of the opening condition: "*Had we but* World enough, and Time." Behind any optative or conditional statement lurks the rejoinder that what it expresses might not, or cannot, be true to fact. Each image of delight and each gesture of flattery in the first paragraph contains its own refutation, as the persona makes the subjunctive mood his grammatical instrument of irony. The development of the section, furthermore, can be described as a progressive joke or a *reductio ad absurdum* of the notion that there is "World enough, and Time." Each of the pleasant situations the speaker envisages is more unlikely than its predecessor. The first, "We would sit down, and think which way / To walk, and pass our long Loves Day," seems plausible; and "long . . . Day," as the first elaboration upon "enough," does not arouse disbelief. But that the speaker and his lady should be found, in the next three lines, at opposite ends of the earth is distinctly improbable. The two ensuing couplets propose an impossibility, taking the condition beyond the realm of fact, and taking the vision of extended courtship far beyond all human reality. From this point onward the ludicrous dominates—both in the image of the suitor's "vegetable Love" (of which more will be said presently) and in the hyperbolic sequence of time units from "An hundred years" through "An Age at least." These lines, 13 through 18, may remind us of Bergson's definition of the comic predicament: "something mechanical encrusted on the living." [11] Devoid of spontaneity, devoid almost of will, the machine-like speaker will turn out huge quantities of praise.

Behind the ironic mask his point is, of course, that time and space do not suffice for the kind of wooing which the lady expects and which the courtly love conventions prescribe. The opening section parodies several of these formulas: the inventory of the

[11] *Laughter: An Essay on the Meaning of the Comic,* trans. C. Brereton and F. Rothwell (New York, 1921), p. 37.

lady's matchless features, the requirement upon her suitor to offer her an almost religious admiration, and the indefinite suspension of the physical act. I would by no means suggest that Marvell was the first or only writer to ridicule courtly conventions. The stereotypes and the whole system of love-Platonism which underlay them had been fair game for ironic poets throughout the high Renaissance. Shakespeare's 130th sonnet—to glance at but one English instance—mocks the standard similes for women's charms:

> My mistress' eyes are nothing like the sun;
> Coral is far more red than her lips' red;
> If snow be white, why then her breasts are dun;
> If hairs be wires, black wires grow on her head.
> I have seen roses damask'd, red and white,
> But no such roses see I in her cheeks;
> And in some perfumes is there more delight
> Than in the breath that from my mistress reeks.
> I love to hear her speak, yet well I know
> That music hath a far more pleasing sound;
> I grant I never saw a goddess go;
> My mistress, when she walks, treads on the ground:
> And yet, by heaven, I think my love as rare
> As any she beli'd with false compare.

Like Shakespeare's speaker, the suitor of "To His Coy Mistress" exposes the inadequacy and insincerity of the conventional modes of praise. His emphasis upon the mechanical character of his flatteries demonstrates to his mistress that such gestures are at best a hollow and passionless routine.

These major ironies are supported by a number of lesser ones in the imagery of Section I. "Ten years before the Flood" and "Till the Conversion of the *Jews*" serve most directly to describe an enormous tract of time for the pleasures of wooing; but both of these termini suggest the death of the world. If the waters of the Ganges are timeless, mystical, and romantic, those of Noah's flood imply human fallibility and catastrophic punishment. As for the conversion of the Jews, it was supposed that this would take place just before the final destruction of earth. Equivocal implications are likewise to be found in the phrase, "My vegetable Love." According to an Aristotelian distinction, popular in Renaissance science, man's nature was compounded of three elements or "spirits," which linked him—for he was a microcosm or little world—with the macrocosm or universe. He shared the highest of these elements, the *rational* with God and the angels. The intermediate element, called the *sensitive* spirit, he held in common with the beasts: it provided him with sensation, mobility, and will. The last of the three was the *vegetative* spirit, the principle of simple life and growth, which he shared with the plants. A "vegetable Love" is not, then, merely a love which grows slowly: it is a *rudimentary* love, something less than human and even less than bestial. Inevitably, too, the phrase "My vegetable Love" evokes a visual image, the absurd picture of a gigantic plant—a squash vine, say—spreading itself over the earth in green imitation of Alexander's conquests. The final irony of Section I lies in its last word, "rate," by which the persona calls attention once more to the mechanical, statistical nature of the praise he would bestow upon his mistress. In addition, the commercial meaning of the term dehumanizes the lady, transforming her organic features into things—rare commodities on the market—which command, it seems, an excessive price.

Low over this strophe hangs an air of artifice and unreality which cannot be attributed entirely to the supposition contrary to fact. Everything in these lines seems remote, dreamlike, somehow drugged. The cadences are slow and regular; the images lethargic or static. The timeless world of the vision is motionless as well: the lovers do not walk but "think which way / To walk" as they *sit down* to plan their leisurely courtship, and they simply *appear* by the Ganges and the Humber. The speaker's vegetable love grows imperceptibly. In the itemized flattery of lines 13–18, the rate of progression slows down to less than a snail's pace. Thus, while the main rhetorical function of Section I is to refute its own vision, to show that the lovers are *not* free in space and time, the speaker also reveals that even in imagination, immunity from human restraints would be intolerable.

If in the opening verse paragraph the speaker's voice is jocular or teasingly ironic, with an undertone of pessimism, in the second it is essentially somber, though tempered by macabre humor. The transitional term "but" signals a shift in logic and rhetoric, and the suitor's argument turns from hypothesis to fact, from a wish-fulfillment dream of freedom to an authentic nightmare of mortal constraint. The dominant verbal mood is now indicative rather than subjunctive, and the tense is future rather than indefinite. The prospect the speaker offers in this strophe *will* come to pass if the lady persists in her coyness.

The world he projects in this portion of the argument is at once the antithesis and the echo of the idyllic suppositional vision. There he examined time as a function and servitor of love; here he considers love *sub specie temporis,* love as a function of time and of time's instrument, death. Both worlds, it should be noted, are equally static and enervated; but the immobility which reigns in the second vision differs significantly from the suspended animation in the first. The stillness now results from time's authority over the lovers, rather than the reverse. Pleasure and perpetual life are superseded by pain and a quite different version of timelessness, the "vast Eternity" of oblivion in death. No longer does the speaker pretend that he and his mistress "have" time; he now acknowledges how fatally time possesses *them:*

> But at my back I alwaies hear
> Times winged Charriot hurrying near:
> And yonder all before us lye
> Desarts of vast Eternity.

"Times winged Charriot" most immediately designates the mythological car of Apollo, the sun god, which measures off the passage of the days; but in this context it suggests, further, the armored vehicle of some ancient lord of war. The imagery of imperial conquest, associated earlier with the speaker himself, is now attached to time—the speaker becoming, by contrast, a helpless and hunted wretch. Time, in this metaphysical symbol, looms as a pursuer so terrible and merciless that his victim dares not turn to face him. Barbaric time behind them and emptiness ahead, the lovers can flee in no direction. Though eternity is "vast," vaster yet than the empire of love, their lot will be enforced confinement as time and tomb alike close in. There will indeed be endless space and time, the speaker suggests, but not for *them* to rule over, to enjoy in courtship, or even to understand.

Unlike the hospitable and watery vistas of Section I, the landscape of the future is parched, sterile, and desolate. The faculties of sensual delight are reduced to "dust" and "ashes"; and in the "Desarts of vast Eternity" no refuge can be seen. The rich rubies of the earlier vision are succeeded by pale memorial marble; and the languid image of a vegetable love gives way not only to the sterility of the inorganic desert and dust, but also to the animal rapacity of the charioteer and the hungry grave-worms. The rhythms of the antistrophe, ponderous as a knell, are even slower than those in Section I. "Desarts of vast Eternity," its most important line with respect to cadence, begins with a solemn trochaic thud, proceeds, in seventeenth-century pronunciation, through the threefold repetition of the long *a* sound on alternating syllables,[12] and comes at last to the full stop of a period.

Both visions presuppose that the mistress will continue to withhold her favors; and in the second, the suitor declares outright that no courtship can take place in the grave. In developing this theme, however, he portrays a ghastly *equivalent* of love in death—a version of Eros so shocking as to constitute the most powerful of arguments against coyness and "quaint Honour." We might summarize the major irony of Section I as the denial, through conditional grammar, hyperbolic progression, equivocal allusion, and comic imagery, of the timeless condition and the lavish praise to which that strophe is devoted. In Section II, on the contrary, the speaker's irony resides in his *affirmation*, through metaphor, of a morbid species of love, at the same time as he declares love impossible in that none-too-distant future. Even as he asserts that his "ecchoing Song" will not be heard in the lady's tomb, he creates the very image he excludes. Together with the lady, we hear a futile lyric resounding from the pallid walls. Death becomes, in the images of the antistrophe, a seducer who will not be refused, taking the place of the unsuccessful speaker; and death as a lover is to the last degree unflattering and crude. In that "fine and private place," the grave as love-nest, death clasps the now wholly defenseless and unresisting mistress: "Worms shall try / That long preserv'd Virginity." The grim image of deflowerment is echoed in the next line, "And your quaint Honour turn to dust," where the persona puns on "quaint."

12 Margoliouth, *The Poems . . . of Andrew Marvell*, I, 222 (notes).

"Honour," in seventeenth-century diction as today, refers to woman's chastity and good reputation for the same virtue. "Quaint" has more numerous meanings in this context: "peculiar," "prim," "fastidious," "ingenious," and "artful" or "cunningly designed." Most interestingly, "quaint" is an old vulgarism denoting, in the Elizabethan John Florio's definition, "a woman's privities." To paraphrase, then: long preserved or defended in life, and however well preserved or embalmed in the tomb, the mistress's celebrated maidenhead is not proof against worms. The curious and pretentious honor associated with her "quaint," and the "quaint" itself, will yet be reduced to insubstantial dust.

The pun on "quaint" amplifies a bawdy overtone in "Vault." Trained Latinist that he was, Marvell would have been at least as sensitive to the word's possibilities as was Shakespeare, who wrote in *Henry the Fifth* of "caves and womby vaultages of France" (II, iv, 124). The anatomical meaning of "vault," "one or another of certain concave structures or surfaces normally facing downward," was used as early as 1549, while the denotation of drain or sewer (and thus, by extension, privy) is even older. "Vault" as a verb had been first applied to sexual congress well before Marvell's day: the *OED* illustration, "Whiles he is vaulting variable ramps (prostitutes)," is taken from *Cymbeline,* I, vi, 134. "Vaulting-house" was a common seventeenth-century synonym for "brothel." The connection between the architectural reference and the anatomical and erotic senses goes beyond parallels of shape and motion: the Latin word for arch or vaulted chamber was *fornix,* from which "fornicate" derives. In a transferred sense *fornix* also designated a brothel, while the English adjectives "fornicate" and "fornicated" have been employed since the sixteenth century for vault-shaped structures. Milton exploited this association in *The Reason of Church-Government,* where he punned, "[she] gives up her body to a mercenary whordom under those fornicated arches which she cals Gods house" (Columbia ed., III, 268). Although "vault" refers to the womb or vagina in none of the instances recorded in the *OED,* it would appear that Marvell has concealed such a reference, either metaphorical or punning, in "To His Coy Mistress": he could draw upon both the current vulgar meanings of "vaulting" and the subtle etymological and semantic links between "vault," *fornix,* "fornication," "brothel," "sewer," and "privy" (cf. "private place," line 31). The context of the term permits the interpretation of an "ecchoing Song" in the "marble Vault" as another obscene parody, in death, of the sexual consummation which the lady presently denies her suitor.[13]

Sexual innuendo had played a minor role in the opening vision, as the speaker pledged himself to devote "thirty thousand" years to adoring the "rest" of his mistress's charms—gazing, that is, upon what lies below eyes, forehead, and breasts. In the second section, erotic *double-entendre* and the incongruous prospect of death as seduction are the major resources of irony. And common to the innuendo in both sections is the idea of abnormal love: in the first, voyeurism, or the substitution of visual for all other forms of gratification; in the second, necrophilism, or the substitution of a dead for a living partner. More specifically yet, these implied perversions are both, like the ruling atmosphere of parts I and II of the argument, characterized by an unwholesome passivity.

It has been objected on historical and philosophical grounds that Hegel's dialectic formula of thesis-antithesis-synthesis does not accurately label the structure of "To His Coy Mistress."[14] Perhaps the special kind of syllogism Marvell's persona employs is named in scholastic philosophy; but the critics have not, to my knowledge, discovered its proper descriptive label. I see no hazard in using the term "dialectic" for the relationship of the three parts of this poem, particularly of the first with the second, or in describing the third as a "synthesis" of the oppositions which precede. In so doing I assign no particular philosophical meanings to the words, but construe them in a logical and rhetorical sense only.[15]

The opening word of Section III, "Now," establishes the

[13] I am indebted to Professor Robert L. Montgomery, Jr., of The University of California, Irvine, for setting me on the trail of an ambiguity in "vault."

[14] Wallerstein, pp. 153–154. Miss Wallerstein debates a remark on the structure of "To His Coy Mistress" and "An Horatian Ode" in Bradbrook and Thomas, p. 73.

[15] See again Burke, *Grammar of Motives,* p. 403: "Other definitions of dialectic are . . . any development (in organisms, works of art, stages of history) got by the interplay of various factors that mutually modify one another, and may be thought of as voices in a dialogue or roles in a play, with each voice or role in its partiality contributing to the development of the whole; or the placement of one thought or thing in terms of its opposite; or the progressive or successive development and reconciliation of opposites . . . ."

present as the speaker's temporal reference, and the next word, "therefore," signals a necessary synthesis or resolution of conflict. We note at once the shift of verbs into the present tense, and the change of mood into the imperative, the true modality of *carpe diem*. This grammatical transformation has a clear psychological purpose in the suitor's argument, insofar as the present tense affords release from the dreamlike conditional of the first strophe and the terrifying future of the second. Two trances are broken, two unhealthy visions of inactivity are dispelled, as the speaker adopts the imperative mood for his statements. The imperative present verbs at last depict the lovers as *agents* in the realm of possibility. Having advised his mistress of what they *would do* under wildly impossible conditions, and what *will be done to them* in the future, he now tells her what they *can do* in a realistic present—or, to be more precise, he exhorts that they do these things. Any imperative implies that what it enjoins can be accomplished. Though each of the first two visions contains its own ironic antitheses, and though the second section directly counters the first, lines 1 through 32 are fundamentally absolutist in outlook. Section III can be seen as the grand qualification of all dogmatism in the foregoing debate. It is the "comic corrective," as Burke might say,[16] for the pessimism of the second strophe as well as for the idealism of the first.

Another grammatical feature worth noting is the predominance, in the final strophe, of the first person plural pronouns "us," "our," and "we." Almost every action in the earlier visions is performed by or upon the lovers singly, and the unilateral character of those acts reinforces the impression of their aberrancy, their inappropriateness to normal love. Now, actions are dually performed. The separate "I" and "thou" unite as one compound agent under one name, and their grammatical union corresponds to the sexual communion which this section demands.

The voice of Section III, like its grammar, is active and urgent. This strophe is pre-eminently one of dynamic images and of vigorous, kinetic verbs—"sport us," "devour," "roll," "tear," "make," "run." After the suspended animation of the preceding visions, the impression of motion and life is overwhelming. The

[16] Consult Burke's brilliant redefinitions of "comic" in *Attitudes Toward History*, esp. pp. vii, 43, 106–107, 166–175.

poem's movement may be said to duplicate the rhythm of sexual intercourse: its first two paragraphs, in which the gamesomeness of wit and the pleasure of verbal display are combined with the pain of sinister meanings, defer almost intolerably the emotional climax which occurs in the final 14 lines, yet lead to it inevitably. In any event, that strategic delay through 32 lines gives rhetorical force to the full-voiced *carpe diem* of the last strophe, just as, from the rational standpoint, the materials of Sections I and II must wait upon Section III for their synthesis. The solution to the conflict of sensual desire and mortal limitation which the speaker now overtly proposes is this: frankly acknowledging their subjection to space and time, the lovers can achieve temporary triumph, brief freedom, through a sexual consummation which makes them, for a while, oblivious to the burdens and fully sensitive to the advantages of their humanity.

Many of the images of freshness, fertility, and power which characterize this section of the argument are reversals or transposed echoes of earlier imagery. The moist, timeless dream gardens of the initial vision are now plausibly realized in the "youthful hew" which rests on the mistress's skin "like morning dew." ("Lew," or warmth, the other common emendation of the text at this point, supports the impression of a moist flush almost as well as "dew" and anticipates the "instant Fires" of line 36; but the rarity and regional quality of "lew" seem inconsistent with the diction of "To His Coy Mistress.") Similarly, "transpires" and "pore" reflect the "vegetable Love" of the first section, but without the earlier connotations of involuntary growth. Now, the succulent figure is endowed with urgency and active passion; the lady's "*willing* Soul" emits "instant Fires" as rational, sensitive, and vegetative spirits are equally aroused. No longer seen as a series of separate "charms"—eyes, forehead, breasts, *et cetera*—or as a moldering corpse, the mistress is presented as vibrantly alive and organically integral. If "the Conversion of the *Jews*" suggested a world in flames, and if the image of cold ashes depicted a love gone dead for want of fuel, the "instant Fires" of passion here create as they consume; from that sexual dying the speaker and his lady can rise again repeatedly, phoenix-fashion, as do Donne's lovers in "The Canonization."

I indicated earlier that the *carpe diem* poem differs markedly from many of the great love lyrics of the Renaissance in its advocacy of a physical, rather than an aesthetic, solution to the problem of time. In "To His Coy Mistress" art is not only subordinated to spontaneous nature; it is shown as a hindrance and a delusion. The pseudo life of the opening vision, including its superficially "natural" images of water and vegetation, is conceived, we will remember, in conventional literary terms: all is artificial, false, and stylized. Far from "immortalizing" physical beauty, the speaker's extended praise and his song ("complaint") at the Humber's banks, together with the rest of the initial supposition, are an unsatisfactory verbal surrogate for reality. His overt refutation of this fictive world in the second verse paragraph incorporates a disclaimer of the poet's ability to preserve his lady's charms: "Thy Beauty shall no more be found; / Nor, in thy marble Vault, shall sound / My ecchoing Song." It is small wonder, then, that references to poetry are absent from the final strophe, where physical life prevails.

Images of animal rapacity, used so startlingly before to describe time's fatal power over the lovers, appear again in the third verse paragraph, but in lines 37 through 40 the original relation is inverted. Time's "slow-chapt pow'r," the force of his slowly grinding jaws or beak, recalls the brutal charioteer, his viceroy death, and, more concretely yet, the things that feed on corpses. Instead of submitting helplessly to time's maw, the lovers can themselves become carnivorous creatures, "am'rous birds of prey," who "devour," in their brief present, the devourers of the future. By "sporting" themselves, taking their pleasure, they "eat up their time," as the colloquialism has it, and they feed ferociously. In this reversal of the image, as in the representation of sex as an affectionate "strife" and the seeming contradiction of the last couplet, the speaker employs a strategy of paradox not unlike Donne's "Death, thou shalt die."

The figure of the ball, in lines 41–42, is interesting on several counts. It looks back to Apollo's chariot and anticipates the sun reference in the last couplet; but further, it names the microcosm, the *sphere* of autonomous space and time, which the lovers can become through passion, and which they could not attain to in the earlier visions. A specifically erotic innuendo, furthermore, is harbored in the metaphor of the ball, though unlike the *double-*

entendres of the earlier sections it is in no wise aberrant. The speaker offers it without a leer: the rolling ball suggests the lovers, literally conjoined, exerting "all their strength" and sharing "all their sweetness" in the sexual act. By implication, then, the "Iron gates of Life" through which they "tear" their pleasures are the lady's maidenhead, as well as the restraints of space and time. Earlier, her "quaint Honour" had been associated with the cold, resistant walls of the marble vault, impenetrable by the speaker; only the grave-worm, awful proxy for the human phallus, could gain entrance and reduce the maidenhead to dust. Though the "woman's privities" are now represented by an even more inflexible image, the iron portals cannot resist the lovers' efforts.

The paradox in the concluding couplet admits of a simple resolution: though the suitor and his mistress are powerless to stop the passage of time, their acts of passion, absorbing all thought and energy, figuratively "make" time pass swiftly. Free from anxiety about time's progress as they devour their brief days in pleasure, the lovers are, for all practical purposes, time's tyrants. In a once-familiar joke, an angry father, reprimanding his insolent son, tells him to stand up in his presence. Lolling in an easy chair, the youth refuses to comply. "Sit down, then," shouts the father, "I *will* be obeyed!" The last two lines of "To His Coy Mistress" comprise a similar jest. Let us recall that the first strophe was developed as an incremental or hyperbolic joke, ending with the punch line, "Nor would I love at lower rate." Section II, with its grotesque coupling of sex and death, might be described as a sick joke, aptly culminating in the sardonic lines, "The Grave's a fine and private place, / But none I think do there embrace." The wit of the last verse paragraph is bawdy, its punch line a paradox in which the lovers cannot be losers. While sex as a stratagem for overcoming time may be a fraud, it is a necessary and comforting illusion, endorsed by the mind and body alike.

Tempted to paradoxes of my own, I will assert that the vitality and uniqueness of "To His Coy Mistress" arise from its formal discipline and underlying conventionality; and that for all its seriousness it is a comic poem, while for all its levity it is deeply serious. To account for the permanent value of "To His Coy Mistress" I think we should look to its aesthetic autonomy and distance. Neither the familiarity of the *carpe diem* materials nor the richness of Marvell's verbal patterning would give the poem special recommendation outside their controlling dramatic context. The gestures which make up this "little drama," this action complete in itself, are audibly rhetorical; every statement, every image, every turn of wit is purposive. Measured against even so lively a *carpe diem* lyric as Herrick's "Corinna," "To His Coy Mistress" impresses us as a singularly tight-knit and cleanly structured argument. And although we are not licensed to speculate about the lady's response, for the curtain descends with the speaker's final word, we will doubtless acknowledge the power of his appeal. The argument is so framed as to allow no reasonable alternative but erotic union. By persuasive no less than by poetic criteria, "To His Coy Mistress" stands the unchallenged masterpiece among lyrics of seduction.

Rhetoric and the Appreciation of Pope: *The Epistle to Dr. Arbuthnot*

ELDER OLSON

[VIEWING *The Epistle to Dr. Arbuthnot,* Alexander Pope's *apologia pro vita sua,* as an example of forensic persuasion, Elder Olson examines a number of the rhetorical devices that Pope used to vindicate himself as a poet and as a man. Paramount among these devices were, first, casting his defense in the form of a dramatic dialogue and, secondly, casting his defense not as the response of a defendant but as a bill of complaint against his enemies, so that the burden of disproof is placed upon the opposition. Of the three modes of proof that Aristotle outlined in his *Rhetoric,* Pope relies most heavily on *ethical* appeal. Consequently, his main efforts in the poem are directed toward showing that he is a man of good sense, good moral character, and good will. The dramatic form of the poem makes it possible for Pope to avoid mere assertions about his *ethos* and to exhibit himself as acting like an intelligent, moral, benevolent man. "The warrant for the credibility of the arguments," Olson says, "is the character of Pope."

Olson analyzes other rhetorical strategies that Pope adopted to support his ethical appeal—his use of induction, enthymeme, and analogy; his resort to progressively more vituperative portraits of his enemies; his use of subtle stylistic devices; his play on emotions. Olson also touches on the nature of the double audience that Pope was addressing—the friendly Dr. Arbuthnot in the poem and the eighteenth-century readers of the poem.

What Olson sought to establish with this close analysis was not only that Pope was a skillful rhetorician but that he merited the title that nineteenth-century critics denied him—the title of a great poet. For a dissenting commentary on Elder Olson's reading of the poem, see Murray Krieger's "Contextualism and the Relegation of Rhetoric," *Rhetoric and Poetic,* ed. Donald C. Bryant (Iowa City, Ia., 1965), pp. 46–58.

From *Modern Philology,* XXXVII (August 1939), 13–35.

Omitted here are the first six paragraphs, in which Olson reviewed two books on Pope that had recently been published—Geoffrey Tillotson, *On the Poetry of Pope* (Oxford, 1938) and Robert Kilburn Root, *The Poetical Career of Alexander Pope* (Princeton, 1938).]

If we are thinking of rhetoric in its truncated modern sense, as mere stylistic, the supposition that Pope is a rhetorician rather than a poet has little meaning other than of derogation; the truncation effects the substitution of a merely immediate end for the proper rhetorical one, effects, that is, the substitution of verbal ornamentation for persuasion; the result is that—since the end which alone makes intelligible the means is not regarded—the rhetorical work, which is the actualization of the means, cannot be intelligible.[1] If, however, we take rhetoric in its more ancient and more useful sense, as that faculty by which we are able in any field of discourse to induce belief or conviction in our audience,[2] the supposition enlarges the possibilities of accounting for what is present in Pope, not merely by permitting the consideration of the various devices as ordered to a more general and, it

[1] What weakens the work of Mr. Tillotson and Mr. Root is that, however much of a poet Pope may seem to them, their main concern with him, insofar as it is a literary one at all, takes the form of rhetorical explication; but the rhetoric underlying the explication is mere stylistic. It is for this reason that much which is fresh and excellent in these two books does not, after all, reach very far. Mr. Tillotson, for example, can illuminate some aspects of Pope's diction commendably, as can Mr. Root (see e.g., Tillotson, pp. 71–84; Root, pp. 37–46); neither can get much beyond the grammatical level, however, since the diction is not systematically considered as ordered to a rhetorical end. While both authors can talk rather prettily of "transitional devices" and "propriety," it is never made clear, precisely, what the transitional device effects, or what it conjoins, or why the elements of the conjunction should be so conjoined; and it is never made clear what is appropriate, or to what it is appropriate, or in what sense it is appropriate. The whole uncertainty in the consideration of the context sometimes betrays these critics into patent absurdities: Mr. Tillotson, for instance, contrasts the full treatment of Nova Zembla in the *Temple of Fame* with the bare mention of the name in *Dunciad,* I, 74, as an example of Pope's steadily developing thrift in description (pp. 60–61); Mr. Root *summarizes* poems to indicate the appropriateness of a passage, as if poetic unity were a question of material conjunction (pp. 64 ff.). Both critics leave one with the impression that what Pope does cannot be accounted for—an impression which, since the poet should have some justification for the use of his devices, is most disturbing. The justification can be only in terms of the end; here the end is not considered.

[2] Aristotle *Rhetoric* i. 2. 1.

may be, a more proper end, but by enlarging the scope of the means whereby that end might be attained.[3]

Perhaps the only way in which these statements may be substantiated is by indicating roughly, through actual analysis, what a rhetorical approach to Pope would be like. Suppose we take, quite arbitrarily, the *Epistle to Dr. Arbuthnot.* If we assume Pope to be a rhetorician, the *Epistle* (like its counterpart, the *First Satire of the Second Book of Horace: To Mr. Fortescue*) is of extraordinary rhetorical importance: these works attempt to reestablish Pope, after such attacks as the *Lines to an imitator of Horace* and the *Epistle to a Doctor of Divinity,* as a man of good moral character. To a rhetorician the appearance of having a good moral character is a first concern; as Aristotle says,[4] goodness of character is almost the most effective means of persuasion the orator possesses, since good men are more completely and more readily given credence than others, and since the possibility of persuasion is dependent upon credibility. Thus didactic and satire would have been vitiated alike, had such charges against Pope remained unanswered. The *Epistle to Dr. Arbuthnot* is, therefore, a piece of forensic in which Pope answers the accusations of his enemies; his audience consists of judges, not spectators, and they are judges of what has been done, rather than of what may be done, and because the end of the discourse is the "proof" of the justice of Pope's actions, i.e., the rehabilitation of his character.[5] One thing must be remarked at once: such questions as whether Pope's indignation is sincere, or whether Pope was actually a man of good character—questions about which his critics have troubled so much—are entirely irrelevant here. The rhetorician need not actually be sincere, need not actually be a good man; he must, however, *seem* to be these things, that is, he

[3] The preference for the second mode of consideration is best argued, I think, from the greater fruitfulness of the mode; but it might be argued as well upon historical grounds. If we hold that neo-classicism embodied much of ancient rhetorical theory, and that the doctrines of neo-classicism constituted the main direction of Pope (and these are in fact the traditional assumptions), there is some ground for supposing that Pope's own conception of rhetoric would not have been limited to stylistic. In other words, Pope was aware of the many devices suggested by Aristotle, Cicero, Quintilian, and others, and would have been likely to employ them.

[4] *Rhet.* i. 2. 4.

[5] *Ibid.* i. 3.

must through his art effect the impression that he is these things; it is far more important, from the standpoint of rhetoric, to seem to have good character when one actually does not, than to have it when one does not seem to.

Two rhetorical devices of extreme importance may be noted at the outset. First, the casting of the defense into the form of a dialogue was a stroke of rhetorical genius. By the portrayal of himself as closeted with a very close friend, Pope permits himself the most congenial and most disarming setting: the circumstance is one in which sincerity and frankness can be expected. Arbuthnot, moreover, is a great and good man, and as such serves a triple function: he can raise, as interlocutor, questions that might have been awkward for Pope himself to initiate, he serves as a warrant for the truth of the dialogue, and, most important of all, he offers a model, by his concurrence after reasonable objection, which an audience would be extremely likely to imitate; he validates, one might say, both the argument and the report of it which constitutes the *Epistle*. Again, the device of dialogue avoids the difficulties that a direct address to the audience might have entailed; it is very cunning that here the audience should seem to be not an audience, that Pope should seem to be unaware of any other hearer than Arbuthnot; the strategy obtains for Pope the opportunity of using every device of rhetoric while appearing to use none. The dramatization, moreover, sets the matter before the eyes of the audience; the audience is, in a manner, admitted as witness, and what we witness we are most assured of; and, what is more, the presentation as a kind of play insures a much sharper attention than a bare answering of charges could possibly provoke. Secondly, there is much rhetorical force in that the answer to Pope's enemies should have been drawn up, not as the response of a defendant, but as Pope himself says, as a "sort of bill of complaint." To have answered as defendant would have been to indicate the charges as worthy of serious consideration, and the defense would have been much more difficult; to file a bill of complaint, on the other hand, is to propose one's self as the wronged person and to lay the burden of disproof upon the opposition.

According to Aristotle, there are three modes of persuasion furnished by the spoken word: the first is dependent upon the personal character of the speaker, the second upon the frame of mind of the audience, the third upon the speech itself.[6] Hence the rhetorician must be able to argue well, to comprehend human character and goodness in their various forms, and to understand the emotions.[7] We may test Pope as a rhetorician, then, according to his abilities in these directions; that is, we may take for criterion the consideration of whether he has employed all the available means to his particular rhetorical purpose. Aristotle mentions three things as productive of confidence in the character of the speaker—the three, namely, that induce an audience to believe a thing apart from any proof of it: good sense, good moral character, and good will; these are all requisite because false or mistaken counsel is due to the absence of these.[8] Pope effects the characterization of himself as a man of good sense by a dozen devices: by his attitude toward flatterers (e.g., ll. 109–24), toward fools (*passim*), toward sober criticism (e.g., ll. 156–57), toward bad art (e.g., ll. 33–46), and in general by his sharp insight into character and motive, and his ready and certain evaluation of human action and production. Furthermore, he brings authority to testify to his good sense: the great have approved his studies (l. 143), and the ancients and the approved moderns (Horace, Persius, Boileau, etc.) furnish him with maxims (e.g., ll. 40, 105–6, etc.).[9] His opponents, on the other hand, are men of folly, susceptible to flattery (e.g., ll. 231–48), congenial with other fools (e.g., ll. 209–12), impatient of just criticism (e.g., l. 40), and in general the contraries of Pope. The characterization of himself as morally good is even more full: Pope has all the virtues in the calendar. He is courageous (e.g., l. 343), temperate (if we can so construe l. 263), liberal (e.g., ll. 371–72), properly ambitious (e.g., ll. 334 ff.), gentle (e.g., ll. 368–87), amiable (e.g., ll. 35, 37), sincere in self-profession (e.g., ll. 261 ff.), witty (this scarcely requires illustration), and just (e.g., ll. 283 ff.). Again his opponents are his contraries; some are vicious through deficiency, as Atticus; some through excess, as Sporus. The characterization of himself as well disposed to-

6 *Ibid.* i. 2.

7 *Ibid.* i. 2.

8 *Ibid.* ii. 1.

9 L. 3, Pers. *Sat.* iii. 5; l. 20, Boileau, *Art poétique,* Chant I, l. 22, from Mart. *Ep.* xii. 62; l. 40, Hor. *De arte poet.* 388; l. 128; Ov. *Trist.* iv. 10. 25–26; etc.

ward the audience, i.e., as having good will, Pope effects easily; his audience is those who are or who think themselves virtuous; and this generalization of the audience escapes, of course, the sharp antagonisms which might have arisen through a more specific pleading. As the matter stands, virtue is the solitary characteristic of the audience; hence Pope needs only to reassure his audience that he is a man of virtue, and that "A lash like mine no honest man need dread." The enemies of Pope, on the other hand, are haters of virtue, hence enemies also of the virtuous, hence enemies of the audience.

So far, however, we have considered only what Pope professes himself and his enemies to be; about that profession in itself there is nothing remarkable, since most people characterize themselves as having every virtue, their enemies as having every vice. The preceding discussion has served but one purpose: it has shown us that Pope has omitted nothing requisite to the character of the speaker. If, now, we can find out in what ways he is able to establish himself as possessed of these characteristics, we shall be dealing with the more properly artistic aspects of his rhetoric. And the chief device is certainly the dialogue itself; for through the dramatization Pope avoids the necessity of stating that he is morally good or sensible or well-disposed, and needs only to show himself as actually acting in such character. This is excellent for several reasons: in the first place, statement analyzes out the various attributions, making refutation or doubt much easier, whereas dramatization presents, like reality itself, complexes of characteristics in such a fashion as often to baffle analysis; secondly, statement gives the impression of hearing a report or testimony, whereas dramatization gives the impression of actually witnessing; hence the latter is clearly more credible. Notice how the attribution proceeds by dramatization; in lines 333 ff., for example, Pope breaks into a heroic declamation which has the effect of attributing extremest moral excellence to him; he does not, however, *state* that he is virtuous; he merely shows himself acting as if he were. There is not a single declarative idea in the whole speech; the whole is one subjunctive sentence. The moral indignation which he assumes in the angry interruptions (e.g., ll. 78 ff.), the ironic amusement at flattery (e.g., ll. 115 ff.), the disgust with "the whole Castalian state" (e.g., ll. 215–54), the regret at the fate of Gay (ll. 256 ff.), the apparent justice of the portrait of Atticus, the earnestness of such passages as lines 135 ff., as lines 261 ff., as lines 334 ff.—all these are speeches appropriate only to a man of distinguished virtue and prudence; the audience assumes therefore that Pope, who is saying these things, *is* virtuous and prudent, much as spectators at a play imagine an actor to be actually like the character he is impersonating. Nor can the audience take this as fiction; Arbuthnot is there, as it were, to certify that it happened. The result is something very difficult to doubt, something practically impossible to refute. Once Pope's character, moreover, is established, it tends to establish certain other things which, reciprocally, assist in the further establishment of the character; for instance, it is because we believe Pope virtuous that we believe his account of his parentage, and it is because we believe his account of his parentage that we tend to be more assured of his virtue, not merely because Pope exhibits filial piety and a wish to emulate his father's virtue, but because it is generally thought that what springs from good parentage tends itself to be good. The good will toward the audience is similarly, as I have suggested, established.

The audience here needs hardly any other characterization than that it is composed of all those, of whatever age, birth, state, or similar determination, who are virtuous or who think themselves virtuous. Their state of mind may be any state from fear and hatred of Pope [10] to mere anger with him; the rhetoric seems devised for the removal of any prejudice against him as a kind of "mad dog" satirist. It is the state of mind of the audience that orders the work: the ordering, that is, is not logical or poetical, but one determined by the stages in which such prejudice can be removed, and in which the proper conception of Pope as a man can be constructed. The most important thing is to allay the fear of the reader that he may be the next to be attacked, since such fear would make it impossible for Pope to appear as one of good will, and hence to persuade at all; consequently Pope shows himself as besieged by the rabble of bad poets; because one who is himself hard pressed is unlikely to attack new enemies, the fear is temporarily, at least, allayed. But Pope immediately proceeds to

[10] *First Sat. Bk. II. Horace: To Mr. Fortescue,* l. 41: "Ev'n those you touch not, hate you."

characterize his opponents as the mad; they, then, and not he, are the proper objects of fear. Even so, Pope is civil to them in their madness and folly; the audience is likely to judge, therefore, that he will be more than civil to the sane and wise. Indeed, Pope must be even hospitable to the mad; else the poetaster sallying forth from the Mint would not be happy to catch him "just at dinner-time." Also, Pope is apparently kind to his servant—witness "good John"; therefore it is likely that he will be kind to those who are not his servants. What is more, Pope has been wrongly accused: Arthur and Cornus impute to him what it is absurd to think he could have caused. All of these details would operate upon the minds of the audience to an obvious end; so that by line 68 it is established that Pope, far from being a mad dog satirist, far from being a perpetrator of unprovoked literary outrages, is a man of civility and humanity, as well as of acumen, who has borne the extremest provocation that a character so constituted can bear. His enemies, on the other hand, are men of the opposite stamp; they fit the description of those whom Persius, Martial, and Boileau had satirized,[11] and they will not in their literary folly profit by the advice even of Horace;[12] thus the authority of the ancients and moderns is invoked against them. It is to be noted that as the speech progresses, as Pope obtains increasing control over his audience, the satire sharpens with more and more serious allegations: thus, for example, the portrait of Atticus is sharper than the ridicule of the fools at the beginning, and the portrait of Sporus is sharper than that of Atticus.[13] The jesting tone of the opening lines, moreover, permits exaggerations which a more serious statement might have made to appear falsity; in addition, the pleasantry is most disarming.[14]

The fear of the audience is perhaps, for the moment at least, sufficiently allayed; but certain possible prejudices against Pope's character must be removed. For example, the audience may feel that while Pope's satire is certainly not unprovoked, the punishment may be excessive, and Pope, consequently, may be cruel. This charge is answered in lines 83–101, and it is notable that

[11] See n. 9, above.

[12] L. 40.

[13] Cf. the increasing sharpness in the speech of Mark Antony in Shakespeare's *Julius Caesar*, III, ii, 74–260.

[14] Arist. *Rhet.* iii. 18.

Pope himself raises the question rather than Arbuthnot: as one who punishes justly, Pope must himself have weighed the punishment; for Arbuthnot to have raised the point would have been to suggest that it was an issue overlooked by Pope. The charge is, of course, answered casuistically; but while the argument itself is fraudulent, it is posed in such a fashion as to provoke laughter; and laughter, as Pope himself once said,[15] is a kind of assent. The anger of those who might object to Pope's attacks upon royalty, as arising from the most serious prejudice, has been removed previously: in lines 70–72 Pope's reference to "queens, ministers, and kings" had been innocent and accidental; and the fear of Arbuthnot that such a reference might be turned against Pope suggests in the most cunning fashion that all such charges had had similar origin.[16] Lines 101–24 remove any prejudice which the audience may have against Pope on the score of imprudence; lines 115–24, any which the audience may hold on the score of vanity. Following this, Pope attempts to move the audience into a positive conception of him; the appeals to the authority of nature (ll. 125–28) and of the great who had approved his labors (ll. 135–46), together with the brief appeal to the pity of the audience (ll. 131–33), signalize the beginning of this attempt. Certain of the minor enemies can be discredited now that the audience has been fairly caught; but the attack must begin mildly, or the old prejudices will revive. Accordingly Pope, while apparently illustrating his restraint, discounts Gildon and Dennis (ll. 146–56) by adumbrating the causes of their attack upon him. Similarly, the momentary fury of the attack upon his "more sober" critics is made pardonable by the apparent aptness of the metaphor in lines 169–72, although the punitive force of the passage is thereby increased and not lessened; and similarly, too, the treatment of the "others angry" moves assent by the inclusion of aphorisms on the difficulty of pleasing the proud (ll. 175–78). Immediately thereafter we have Atticus. A good deal has been said on the apparently nice justice of these lines,[17] so that any extended treatment here is unnecessary; however, it may

[15] *First Sat. Bk. II. Hor: To Mr. Fortescue,* ll. 155–56.

[16] Note other attempts to remove the same charge in this epistle; e.g., the canceled verses after l. 282 in the MS; ll. 356–59, etc.

[17] Mr. Root has some excellent suggestions; see *Poetical career,* pp. 201–5.

be noted that in the character Pope is professing himself to be, any purely scurrilous treatment of Addison would have been inappropriate, and that, at the same time, some treatment of Addison was requisite: Addison was too distinguished an adversary to be ignored. He must, moreover, be removed as early in the argument as would be consistent with safety, since to reserve him for later answer would have been to effect in the audience only a tentative acceptance of the greater part of Pope's argument. Hence Pope, using what Aristotle calls a "method of thoroughly skillful and unscrupulous prosecutors,"[18] mixes the virtues and vices of Atticus in such fashion as to disguise perfectly that this is special pleading. The statement is not even plain and flat; as Mr. Tillotson admirably suggests, the whole "hangs on a condition."[19] Even so, the attack may have been too daring; hence, lest the audience feel that it has proceeded from literary envy, Pope hastens, in lines 215–70, to indicate himself as one quite without ambition of the worldly kind, whether literary or otherwise; the portrait of Bufo the patron is introduced to show the kind of character to whom "the Castalian state" would be desirable, to provide an object for the contempt of Pope, and so to disclaim any similar ambition. This is followed by several self-characterizing speeches in which the audience is further impressed with Pope's good will: if certain works attributed to Pope have given offense, the attribution is questionable;[20] Pope is a friend of the virtuous, hence of the audience. Thus the shocking portraiture of Sporus—in this instance the main enemy, since he and Lady Mary[21] had brought the charges—is prepared for: at the precise moment when the identification of Pope with the audience is most complete, Pope turns on Sporus; and the assent of the audience is a foregone conclusion. The contemptuous interruption of Arbuthnot reinforces the ferocity of the attack; and the coincidence of the audience is counted upon to such an extent, now, that Sporus' very best parts—his "eternal smiles," his personal beauty, his evident charm, his wit, his possession of royal

[18] *Rhet.* iii. 15.

[19] *On the poetry of Pope,* p. 38.

[20] Cf. ll. 279–82 and 351.

[21] Lady Mary is mentioned by name only in l. 101 and, still with considerable reticence, in l. 369—probably because a too furious attack might have been out of character here.

favor—all suffer a horrid inversion. That removes all charges against Pope; and Pope proceeds to stamp home, once and for all, the impression of himself which he wishes to create: all his acts have virtue as their source (ll. 334–59); his very enemies can give evidence of that (ll. 368 ff.); he is good in origin (ll. 382–403) and he will so continue (ll. 404–17). Arbuthnot acquiesces completely, closing the dialogue. What is left last of all with the audience is, therefore, a proper picture of Pope, duly approved by Arbuthnot, to bear in mind against any further attacks.

The argument itself is relatively simple: it must first be shown that Pope's action in the present instance is just retaliation; next, that he did not initiate the literary war; and finally, to provide against further charges of a similar nature, that Pope's intentions are virtuous and that it is improbable that he will depart from those intentions. Accordingly the argument falls into three parts: the first (ll. 1–124) arguing the present charges (i.e., of the *Verses to an imitator of Horace* and the *Epistle to a Doctor of Divinity*), the second (ll. 125–248) arguing that Pope was not the original aggressor, the third (ll. 249–end) arguing the guarantee of Pope's future conduct.

In the first part Pope spends lines 1–68 in establishing, by rhetorical induction, his minor premise, namely, that his case is worse than that of Midas' minister, since every coxcomb perks asses' ears in his face; the major, that all who have secrets similar to that of Midas' minister cannot retain them, is suggested in lines 69–74; and the conclusion appears in lines 79–80 through the false *a fortiori:* Pope is "forced to speak or burst," hence "Out with it, Dunciad! Let the secret pass." Two objections are posed, one with respect to the possible cruelty, the other with respect to the possible imprudence of retaliation; each of these meets a threefold argument of counter-objection. The first objection is answered first by enthymeme; the major is "Fools do not suffer pain" ("No creature smarts so little as a fool"); the minor, that these are fools, is taken as *ex concesso* and is suppressed; the conclusion, that these do not suffer pain sufficiently to constitute the infliction of it a cruelty, then follows.[22] Next, the objection is refuted by analogy (ll. 89–94): if a scribbler is like a spider and

[22] Depending upon grammatical interpretation, the argument is either maxim or enthymeme. For the distinction see Aristotle *Rhet.* ii. 21–22.

it is no cruelty to destroy the fabrication of the spider, then by analogy it is no cruelty to destroy the fibs or sophistries of the scribbler. The analogy is so skilfully drawn as to command the assent of the audience; but with the assent to the analogy the conclusion apparently follows. Thirdly, Pope refutes, by seemingly perfect induction ("Whom have I hurt?") for the last time the objection of cruelty (ll. 95–101). In turn the objection of imprudence is answered by enthymeme or maxim (l. 104), by analogy (ll. 105–6) fortified by an appeal to authority ("if the learned are right"), and finally by induction (ll. 109–24).

The second part of the argument establishes the innocence of Pope's conduct previous to the present warfare. The cause of his writing is nature ("the numbers came"), not vanity, since he wrote as a child, when he was not yet "a fool to fame"; and the natural capacity was realized in accordance with duty, piety, and friendship; hence his writing is in origin and in actualization good. The cause of his publication is authority; and the *ad verecundiam* argument serves the double purpose of supporting the contention and of characterizing Pope as amiable, sensible, modest, and talented, as indeed does most of the argument. The writing so generated, so developed, and so published could have given no offense; yet he was attacked by Gildon and Dennis, who wrote not through nature but through want, and who published not by authority but through madness; Pope is not, then, the first aggressor. Indeed, he did not act even then; though he may have angered some (l. 173), it was only an attempt upon his part to evaluate them justly; and since the evaluation was truthful, it could have given anger only to the proud (ll. 173–78). It is notable that nowhere in this part does Arbuthnot pose an objection; these are matters that Arbuthnot could not have called in question without ruining the rhetorical effect. For the most part the argument has proceeded by enthymeme and induction; but the analogy in lines 169–72, like that of the spider, is of telling force.

In the third part the argument is of extremest simplicity; here Pope for the most part falls back, quite properly,[23] upon moral discourse; his future conduct is suggested from his wishes (e.g., ll. 249–62) and his present virtue (ll. 283 ff.), the latter being in

[23] Cf. *ibid.* iii. 17.

fact the reason why his genius, by nature literary, should have been given a satiric determination.[24] The piece closes with the purely rhetorical exhibition of Pope, as it were, in the bosom of his family.

Space has not allowed more than the adumbration of an analysis; but even from this it would be easily possible to show how the style, the prosody, and even the grammatical constructions are appropriate to the rhetorical work we have outlined. The style, for example, is excellent if for no other reason than that it is in the great rhetorical tradition of Horace, Juvenal, and Persius; to write in that fashion is in a manner to invoke the authority of these writers; and to write so, furthermore, would be rhetorically justifiable if only upon the ground that such a style was demanded by the audience. More specifically, however, the appropriateness of the diction can be seen from the manner of its exhibition of character and emotion and from its suitability to the subject matter. For example, in the passage describing the simplicity of Pope's life (ll. 261 ff.) the diction itself is simple; the words are among the commonest in the language and they are used in their literal sense; mostly, indeed, the speech is monosyllabic; there are almost no epithets, and there are no ambiguous or unusual grammatical constructions. That simplicity of diction of course makes for clarity; but to appreciate how it exhibits character and emotion we have only to consider what a more fanciful or elaborate diction would have effected; any such departure from the simple would have belied the simplicity of taste that Pope was attempting to establish as characteristic of him, and furthermore, would have given a flavor of artificiality to his professions, since people tend to believe that sincerity is attended by simplicity of speech. I think the very grammatical structure here is defensible; the subjunctive sentence, particularly when exclamatory, as here, is much more effective than a declarative sentence could have been, since it has an emotional tone; we have only to substitute "I wish to live my own and die so too" for "Oh, let me live my own and die so too!" to observe how the emotion disappears. The exhibition of emotion is particularly important here; the good man ought not merely to wish a good life but to feel strongly about it, so that all his emotions are ordered to it; and

[24] Ll. 334–59.

the best argument that one has such and such desires is the exhibition of one's self as actually moved by the contemplation of them. The use of the verbs "maintain," "see," "read" without the auxiliary construction (i.e., without "let me") is also defensible; it gives the passage a rational tone through grammatical coordination, where a series of short exclamatory sentences would have made but hysterical declamation. It is proper, too, that the analysis of what it is to "live my own" should be brief; a long series of statements about the simple life would have made the life seem not simple but complex. The entire absence of grammatical inversion in this passage was almost necessitated by the need for an air of plainness and simplicity; hence, once the kind of sentence has been determined, the organization of the words is according to normal order; and although ellipsis is employed, it is normal ellipsis only: the omission of a subject before predicates in series, or of verbal auxiliaries. Wit could have no place in this passage; it could but make suspect Pope's sincerity. Simple though the verses are, the diction is saved from meanness through its employment in moral discourse, through the absence of any low referents, and through the verse.

Viewed generally, even in this crude sketch of an analysis, the *Epistle* presents certain striking peculiarities of form. Not the least striking of these is the circularity of the rhetoric; the work is intended to establish the character of Pope through argument, but the warrant for the credibility of the argument is the character of Pope, and, strangely enough, the particular arguments establishing each trait of character depend upon the previous assumption that Pope *has* the very trait in question; for instance, we can grant the argument establishing truthfulness as a characteristic only if we already believe in the truthfulness of the speaker advancing the argument, and we can grant the thesis of his prudence only if we have previously ceded that characteristic as present in him. There is a reciprocal relation, consequently, between the principles and the conclusion of the rhetoric, a circularity not even broken by the presence of Arbuthnot as witness, since in the end we have only Pope's word for that. But the peculiarities do not cease here; the internal rhetoric is one in which speaker, audience, and speech are one: Pope is the speaker, Pope is the thesis in question and the argument supporting it, and finally, since Arbuthnot, the apparent audience, is nothing more than the creature of Pope, Pope is the audience as well. The effect on the actual audience, i.e., the readers for whom the rhetoric is designed, is most curious; it is as if they were overhearing one more *Débat de cuer et de corps,* one more A *son esprit.*[25] What is more, there is here, in a sense, rhetoric within rhetoric; there is the rhetoric by which Arbuthnot becomes convinced of the propriety of Pope's satire, and there is the rhetoric effecting conviction in the reader through the example of Arbuthnot's conviction. Here again a circle is evident; the first can be effective only if the second is effective, and the second can be effective only if the first is.

The rhetoric is not thereby vitiated, strangely enough; it is saved by Pope's lively simulation of virtue, which is sufficiently impressive to establish part, and hence all, of the circle. As Aristotle remarks, an audience generally tends to commit the fallacy of the consequent, to suppose, in other words, that because the speaker acts just as virtuous men do under the circumstances, he is himself virtuous.[26] In appraising the *Epistle* as forensic, then, it should be sufficient for us that the semblance of virtue is good, that the part is well acted; to judge the work as demonstration there would be requisite a certitude, which no historical information could provide, that Pope was in fact virtuous. If we assume that Pope is dissembling here, the rhetoric is much like that of the first speech of Socrates in the *Phaedrus;*[27] unlike the speech of Lysias,[28] it has an ordering principle, and unlike the second speech of Socrates,[29] which is the true rhetoric, i.e., dialectic, it does not possess truth. The conception of rhetoric which is exemplified in the first speech of Socrates approximates to Aristotle's conception of rhetoric; it is an art of uttering semblances of truth rather than truth itself; and it bears that relation to the true rhetoric, dialectic, which in Aristotelian statement rhetoric would

[25] It was apparently Warton who first mentioned this latter, the ninth Satire of Boileau, as strongly influencing the *Epistle to Arbuthnot* (*Essay on the genius and writings of Pope,* II [London, 1782], 264). Certainly there are important similarities.

[26] *Poetics* xxiv.

[27] 237 C ff.

[28] *Ibid.* 231 A ff.

[29] *Ibid.* 244 A ff.

bear to demonstration; it seeks, that is, its warrant in the opinions and emotions of the audience rather than in principles of scientific demonstration.

I have suggested, thus roughly, a possible approach [30] to the *Epistle to Dr. Arbuthnot;* I think that a similar treatment of the *Moral essays,* the *Essay on man,* the *Essay on criticism,* the *Dunciad,* and in general the rhetorical works of Pope, might prove not unprofitable. Such works as the *Pastorals,* the *Temple of Fame,* the *Rape of the lock,* and the translations of Homer, Statius, and Donne are not, on the other hand, likely to yield much in such analysis; these seem to me rather to be translations in the sense in which any attempt to construct a literary analogue of a given work is a translation, and must be approached accordingly. Whatever approach be adopted, however, it will tend to be more fruitful if it examines systematically the nature of the equivalences which may exist between literary analogues. The problem of Pope's Homer, for instance, is not touched, much less solved, when we point out that Pope is or is not Homer, or when we underscore similarities or dissimilarities of diction; we cannot operate properly apart from a clearly formulated theory of translation if we are to make any literal statements concerning a work *qua* translation. In the case of Pope we have been provided with a statement of what he considered translation to be; the danger has been that we have interpreted that statement too easily, too naïvely; the larger critical doctrines in which it was included, and

[30] Since literary analysis, like any analysis, involves variables (e.g., the sensibility or erudition of the reader, the certainty of the text, etc.), its status is that of hypothesis. There can, consequently, be no proof positive of the present analysis, if by proof positive we mean something of the order of demonstration; but there may be derived from the definition of the term *hypothesis* eleven topics which can be taken as criteria for the evaluation of hypotheses. If we define *hypothesis* as a supposition explaining data, it is clear that (1) the hypothesis must be more intelligible than the data (since explanation is always of the less well known in terms of the better known); (2) the hypothesis must be clearly formulated; (3) it must have a single principle governing the admission of data as evidence; (4) it must take into account all the evidence resulting from the application of that principle; (5) it must imply all the admitted evidence; (6) it must in that implication have systematic unity; (7) it must be self-consistent; (8) it must rest upon no hypotheses less probable than itself; (9) it must be economical; (10) it must constitute an explanation of the data, i.e., the data must be intelligible through it; and (11) it must be consistent with known truths.

The present analysis is intended, thus, not as a final and absolute explanation of the poem, but as an illustration of a critical method.

without reference to which it is unintelligible, have in a similar fashion been construed too readily, or ignored. In the main the concern of Popian critics has been with the conventions that are considered to have limited, fortunately or unfortunately, the genius of Pope; it might be profitable to remember that if convention, as a postulate, constitutes a limitation, it is also the source of a structure the realization of which is possible only through it. If we are to study Pope, that study might include what the works of Pope are, as well as what they are not. In such fashion alone are we likely to comprehend how, in the judgment of a whole century, and by no means without reason, Pope must be reckoned among the few first figures of English literature.

The Rhetoric of Newman's *Apologia*

LEONARD W. DEEN

[WE HAVE SEEN how Alexander Pope managed, in a poetic medium, the defense of his life and character in *The Epistle to Dr. Arbuthnot.* We will see now how John Henry Newman managed his defense in a much longer work written in prose. The immediate occasion of *Apologia Pro Vita Sua* was Charles Kingsley's published indictment of Newman's honesty and integrity. But Newman made the *Apologia* something more than just an answer to Kingsley's specific charges: he attempted to vindicate himself in the eyes of his fellow countrymen—and ultimately in the eyes of all English-speaking people. History attests to how well he succeeded. As Newman himself said, in his journal for October 30, 1867, "I never was in such happy circumstances as now. . . . My reputation has been cleared by the *Apologia.*"

Newman's life and letters were one long exercise in rhetoric. He had a thorough-going knowledge of Aristotle, Cicero, and Quintilian, and he played a part in the preparation of Richard Whately's *Elements of Logic* (1826) and *Elements of Rhetoric* (1828). Leonard W. Deen shows us to what good use Newman put this expertise in the climactic work of his public career. Because the *Apologia* is a long work, Deen has to analyze it in large sections. So he marks off the main stages of Newman's argument and analyzes the rhetorical strategies operating in those sections. "In thus summarizing the change in Newman's faith," Deen says, "I am of course closely paralleling Newman's own rhetoric." Written in haste and under great emotional strain, the *Apologia* proved to be a rhetorical *tour de force*—perhaps the greatest of its kind since the *Confessions* of another great practicing rhetorician, St. Augustine.]

From the *Journal of English Literary History,* XXIX (June 1962), 224–38. Reprinted by permission of The Johns Hopkins Press.

When, in 1864, Charles Kingsley pointedly suggested that John Henry Newman was a liar and a hypocrite who, even before his conversion to Roman Catholicism had been secretly a "Romanist" mining the English church from within, he added open charges to the more diffuse and hidden suspicion from which Newman and the Catholic clergy had suffered for years. Kingsley's personal attack created a real issue—a plaintiff and defendant and a clear-cut question of justice. That Kingsley had insulted him personally gave Newman a rhetorical opportunity that a more abstract or theoretical attack—on the Church itself, say, or on its doctrine and practice—would not have given him.

To defend oneself publicly against public accusations is of course a rhetorical problem; Aristotle lists it as one of the primary functions of rhetoric in the first book of his *Rhetoric,* and Newman himself obviously considered his defense a problem of rhetorical means and ends. In solving the problem, he used both the principles and the particular devices of classical rhetoric. He did not object to using such devices, but he did not want to persuade by them alone, or did not think them sufficient. The effectiveness of the *Apologia* depends on Newman's using the basic *principles* of classical rhetoric in a way that virtually transformed them. He gives an account of how his mind "moved" (and was moved) to conviction, so that his readers can be persuaded of his sincerity by being brought as close as possible to reliving Newman's experience. This purpose required him to show a unique, living, and growing mental life which, although unique, could claim to be human and available to ordinary human understanding. "Be large-minded enough to believe that men may feel and reason very differently from yourselves" (Since 1845, p. 240).[1] Rhetoric has too often been separable from substance, but this is not so of the *Apologia;* its rhetoric can be discussed adequately only by showing its relation to Newman's subject—the growth of his own mind—and to the structure which the *Apologia* gives to that subject.

[1] I have used the Houghton Mifflin Riverside edition of the *Apologia,* ed. A. Dwight Culler, which follows the text of the last edition published in Newman's lifetime. Since this text differs not only in material but in arrangement from some popular editions (the Everyman, for example), I will cite brief chapter titles as well as page numbers for most quotations.

At the beginning, I should acknowledge my debt to Walter Houghton's fine study, *The Art of Newman's "Apologia."*

The more obvious rhetorical devices tend to come early in the *Apologia*, as preparation for Newman's more original mode of defense. In the Preface, his characterization of his judges—the English public—is ingratiating; he expects justice from Englishmen, who, if they are quick to judge, are also "generous," and Newman is careful to identify himself with the English: "I had rather be an Englishman, (as in fact I am,) than belong to any other race under heaven" (Preface, p. 12). It is not difficult to praise Athenians in Athens, but Newman had also to take account of the fact that he belonged to a "most un-English communion." Conscious of his reputation for the Italian or Mediterranean vices of subtlety and economy, or reservation of the truth, he quickly establishes the "English" quality of his virtues. The character Newman displays, and its points of leverage on the English national character and the moral "maxims" admired by Englishmen, can be seen in the passage that follows, where he reveals his frankness, his fairness, his willingness to confess faults, his generosity, and his devotion to truth:

> I have no misgiving at all, that [Englishmen] will be ungenerous or harsh towards a man who has been so long before the eyes of the world; who has so many to speak of him from personal knowledge; whose natural impulse it has ever been to speak out; who has ever spoken too much rather than too little; who would have saved himself many a scrape, if he had been wise enough to hold his tongue; who has ever been fair to the doctrines and arguments of his opponents; who has never slurred over facts and reasonings which told against himself; who has never given his name or authority to proofs which he thought unsound, or to testimony which he did not think at least plausible; who has never shrunk from confessing a fault when he felt that he had committed one; who has ever consulted for others more than for himself; who has given up much that he loved and prized and could have retained, but that he loved honesty better than name and Truth better than dear friends . . . (Preface, p. 11).

But this is only preparation for the real work of the *Apologia*, which was considerably more difficult.

In what Cicero would call "consultation" (*deliberatio*) with his audience, Newman demonstrates the unfairness of Kingsley's rhetoric, and confesses his dismay at the prospect of trying to answer all of Kingsley's innumerable charges and innuendoes. At the same time he decides on an "antagonist unity" of defense which will answer Kingsley's all-purpose tactic of "*poisoning the wells*" by insinuating in advance the deceptiveness of whatever Newman might say in his own defense. Since he is misunderstood Newman will explain himself; he will trace the events and influences and thought which account for his conversion to Catholicism, and in the process show that he had *not* all along been a Romanist in Anglican vestments. He had changed, and it became his business to make this change understandable and credible. His procedure, then, will be to write the "history of [his] mind." In doing so, Newman says, "I wish, as far as I am able, simply to state facts, whether they are ultimately determined to be for or against me. Of course there will be room enough for contrariety of judgment among my readers" (Preface, p. 18). The *Apologia* is largely what Cicero or Quintilian would call *narratio*—statement of facts, which might take the form of narration—and Newman, following classical advice, calls attention especially to the "instructive" or factual nature of his history.

Newman's facts or witnesses—letters and documents of the past, as well as the testimony of friends—were materials extrinsic to rhetorical art, but they could be turned to rhetorical uses. They became the instrument of Newman's self-characterization. The "history" in the *Apologia* does not pretend to be *simply* factual, but describes Newman's experience and thought, establishing his sincerity, and arousing, through Newman's personal response to this experience, sympathetic feeling in the reader. Given this narrative, Newman's misunderstood words, as he says in the *Lectures on the Present Position of Catholics in England* (1851), could be seen as "the words of a particular speaker, in a particular state of mind, which must be experienced, or witnessed, or explored, if it is to be understood" (Lecture VIII). Newman's strategy, in his most precise definition, is to defend himself by portraying "that living intelligence, by which I write, and argue, and act" (Preface, p. 16).

This strategy turns the *Apologia* away from the usual structure of autobiography. The subject of the *Apologia* is Newman's conversion—his essential beliefs and the experience and inner struggle through which they changed and developed. The

Apologia's closest model is perhaps Augustine's *Confessions*.[2] Like the *Confessions*, the *Apologia* concentrates on the developing convictions of the writer; and the almost inevitable stages of this development are ignorance (or sinfulness); an extremely complex period of awakening, growth, and struggle; and final conviction, or conversion. The dramatic center of both the *Apologia* and the *Confessions* is in the "hero's" struggle towards inner wholeness and harmony, and in his effort to turn thought into conviction and conviction into principles and consistent action. (Augustine's wrestling between the new will and the old, however, is considerably more dramatic and "gigantic" than Newman's, and his paradoxes more frequent and violent). The fundamental conversion-pattern of both books recurs as the pattern of individual passages, chapters, and sections; and this recurrent pattern contributes to the unity and structural clarity of both.

From the confessional aspects of the *Apologia* Newman gains considerable rhetorical advantages. As an account of religious experience, which presents the writer as a man speaking to men, bearing witness to the truth that is in him, the *Apologia* would find immediate response in an age characterized as much by religious longing as by religious doubt. As a confession of error (and it is sometimes that), it claims the suspension of judgment due to the human limitations which we all share. As a violation of the writer's privacy (an apparently inescapable aspect of confessions), it claims our sympathy. Newman quotes Pascal: "*Je mourrai seul*"; and he insists that his faith is a matter between himself and God. But he reveals it nevertheless, and prefaces his history by complaining of the difficulty of violating the law "*Secretum meum mihi*"—my secret is my own. Thus (while almost unavoidably stimulating a certain appetite for private revelations in the reader), he underlines the bitter necessity which forces him to do what he is so reluctant to do. From the beginning of the *Apologia*, Newman appears as a man who has suffered grievous misunderstanding, and he continues throughout his narrative to direct our attention to the man writing, and to the

[2] Northrop Frye has pointed out the confessional aspects of the *Apologia* in the essay "Rhetorical Criticism: Theory of Genres," in *Anatomy of Criticism* (Princeton, 1957).

conditions under which he writes, as well as to what he writes. In spite of Newman's reluctance to reveal himself, the *Apologia* does not entirely escape the influence of Rousseau, whose *Confessions* are also an apology, and one in which the personality and sufferings of the writer are even more central. But we should not exaggerate this quality: the larger part of the *Apologia* is a factual account of opinion and controversy.

Newman begins his history by establishing a unique temperament and experience, and describing the growth of thought in a particular personality. Two memories are crucial: "I used to wish the Arabian Tales were true: my imagination ran on unknown influences, on magical powers, and talismans . . . I thought life might be a dream, or I an Angel, and all this world a deception, my fellow-angels by a playful device concealing themselves from me, and deceiving me with the semblance of a material world" (To 1833, pp. 21–22). The second is a specifically religious experience at the age of fifteen: "I received [the doctrine of final perseverance] at once, and believed that the inward conversion of which I was conscious, (and of which I still am more certain than that I have hands and feet,) would last into the next life, and that I was elected to eternal glory" (p. 24). This conviction confirmed the "mistrust of the reality of material phenomena" mentioned in the first passage, and caused him to "rest in the thought of two and two only absolute and luminously self-evident beings, myself and my Creator" (p. 25). The fundamental elements with which Newman begins his account of his early religious experience recur, becoming increasingly complex. They dominate the remainder of the first chapter, and the *Apologia* as a whole.

With the first "note" about his childhood, Newman allows us to see that his temper of mind ran counter to the rationalism and commonsense of the time. Realizing that his self-explanation and defense depended on his clearly establishing this difference, which would go a long way towards explaining the suspicions he aroused in others, Newman again calls our attention to the crucial point near the end of the chapter:

> I am aware that what I have been saying will, with many men, be doing credit to my imagination at the expense of my judgment—'Hippoclides doesn't care;' I am not setting myself up as a pattern of good sense or of anything else; I am but giving a history of my

> opinions, and that, with the view of showing that I have come by them through intelligible processes of thought and honest external means (p. 48).

Though the singularity of character and experience which the *Apologia* establishes in the beginning is, logically speaking, no argument at all, it is one of the most powerful "arguments" for Newman's sincerity. In describing the angels and the undeniable religious intuitions of his childhood and youth, Newman provides an explanation of how in later life he could sincerely believe in a continuing supernatural influence on the physical world and on human affairs—how he could believe in what he calls the "sacramental principle." The early "notes" suggest that Newman's world was not the same as that of his critics, who were judging him by their own unproved and perhaps unexamined assumptions—by invalid or irrelevant criteria. They are Newman's attempt to add another dimension to the reality assumed by his critics, and thus to remove his case from the court of rationalism and everyday factuality.

Besides persuading us that he did not need to be a hypocrite to profess "Catholic" faith in miracles and saints, Newman had also to account for his conversion from one faith to another. He does so partly by stressing the internal contradiction of his early beliefs and feelings, and thus prepares and gives a reason for the change and struggle to come. He finds in his youth the "seeds" of a conflict between inconsistent ideas which "disables" him for years: at the age of fifteen, during the year of his first conversion, he reads simultaneously "Milner's Church History," and is "nothing short of enamoured" of the extracts from the Fathers of the Church, and "Newton on the Prophecies" and concludes that the Pope is Antichrist:

> My imagination was stained by the effects of this doctrine up to the year 1843; it had been obliterated from my reason and judgment at an earlier date; but the thought remained upon me as a sort of false conscience. Hence came that conflict of mind, which so many have felt besides myself;—leading some men to make a compromise between two ideas, so inconsistent with each other,—driving others to beat out the one idea or the other from their minds,—and ending in my own case, after many years of intellec-

> tual unrest, in the gradual decay and extinction of one of them,—I do not say in its violent death, for why should I not have murdered it sooner, if I murdered it at all?
>
> (To 1833, pp. 27–28).

This passage precisely defines Newman's temperament and the whole process of religious conversion which is described in the *Apologia.* It recognizes the complexity of the mind; it suggests, for example, that his suspicion of Rome went underground—faded from his reason and judgment—and remained as an almost inaccessible prejudice, and that for this reason Newman was unable to "murder" it even if he had wanted to. It endows ideas as they exist in a living mind with potentialities for development or decay; it insists on a rigorous consistency of ideas, and forecasts the struggle between inconsistent ideas and the attendant "unrest of mind" which are, succinctly, the entire matter of the *Apologia.*

The first chapter of the *Apologia* (To 1833) sets forth Newman's fundamental beliefs and the influences he felt almost as axioms. His early delight in reading the Bible; his "imaginative" doubts of a material world; the crucifix he inexplicably draws in an early school book; the "impressions of dogma" (mostly Calvinist but not entirely unCatholic) which he receives at the age of fifteen; his "preference of the personal to the abstract," and his love for the Fathers of the Church prepare for additional convictions at Oxford. These and later elements of the first chapter are the given material of the *Apologia,* on which the following chapters are of course based, and with which we can hardly quarrel, since the point in question is not the validity but the sincerity and intelligibility of Newman's beliefs.

What emerges from this chapter, though Newman refrains from pointing it out, is that his beliefs were at this point in an unformed state. They were the elements of a faith, not yet clearly interrelated and organized. The first chapter is to be contrasted with the last, which presents Newman's convictions in their final and ordered form. The *Apologia* as a whole describes and "imitates" the struggle by which they were organized.

This process of growth, expression, analysis, and arrangement of ideas Newman described in the *Essay on the Development of Christian Doctrine:*

> An idea . . . grows in the mind by remaining there; it becomes familiar and distinct, and is viewed in its relations; it leads to other aspects, and these again to others, subtle, recondite, original, according to the character, intellectual and moral, of the recipient; and thus a body of thought is gradually formed without his recognizing what is going on within him. And all this while, or at least from time to time, external circumstances elicit into formal statement the thoughts which are coming into being in the depths of his mind; and soon he has to begin to defend them; and then again a further process must take place, of analyzing his statements and ascertaining their dependence one on another. And thus he is led to regard as consequences, and to trace to principles, what hitherto he has discerned by a moral perception, and adopted on sympathy; and logic is brought in to arrange and inculcate what no science was employed in gaining.[3]

The growth into thought of what was at first "moral perception" and "sympathy" by its expression or its "elicitation" and its ordered, logical arrangement is the basic pattern of the *Apologia*.

This pattern might be illustrated by the history of Newman's attitude towards liberalism. The Tractarian Movement began in opposition to liberalism, the "anti-dogmatic principle," which Newman considered the greatest threat to Christianity in his time. The "external circumstances" which "elicited" Newman's opposition to liberalism, and forced him to clarify and justify what had previously been latent were the 1830 revolution in France and the concurrent agitation for reform in England. They "brought out into form and passionate expression the various beliefs which had gradually been winning their way into my mind." The "vital" necessity was to prevent the liberalization of the church, and Newman felt compelled to make a rigorously consistent choice between warring systems of ideas. During the battle against liberalism he became convinced that Anglicanism was itself vitiated by the anti-dogmatic principle and that it lacked the force and consistency that he considered to be crucial tests of an idea or a system of ideas. He found this force instead in Roman Catholicism.

In the last chapter ("Position of My Mind Since 1845") the great antagonism on which Newman's thinking is based, and

[3] *An Essay on the Development of Christian Doctrine* (New York and Toronto, 1949), ed. Charles Frederick Harrold, p. 176.

which had been kept under fairly rigorous control throughout the *Apologia*, finally reveals itself clearly, and takes its position of real importance. What is essential and unchangeable in Newman's belief is the authority and necessity of belief; and the collision of that necessity with the world, with skepticism, unbelief, anarchy, liberalism, rebellion, and sin—with the "wild living intellect of man" and "the energy of human skepticism"—generates Newman's expanded faith. In Newman's final analysis, the necessity for guiding and protecting the spontaneous religion of the conscience accounts for revelation, dogma, authority, and an infallible church; and later developments are confirmations and protections of original intuition and revelation. They are necessary "to preserve religion in the world, and to restrain that freedom of thought, which of course in itself is one of the greatest of our natural gifts, and to rescue it from its own suicidal excesses" (233).

Presenting his later Roman Catholicism as a development, not a rejection, of his basic convictions and of his earlier Anglicanism, Newman describes his conversion as a progress from a relatively simple faith to a more complex one. The principles with which he began developed unforeseen conclusions. The necessity of adjusting one principle to another, and of determining their relative importance, generated other conclusions. The parts fitted into a complex and interdependent system, and this consistency itself seemed to Newman to constitute an argument in favor of his developed convictions. He became convinced that ideas and principles must be held not only purely, but in their mature and perfect form, and that the same reasons and kinds of argument which had led him to believe as much as he had in the past, must, if consistently carried out, lead him to believe more. To be correct as far as he went was not to be correct.

In thus summarizing the change in Newman's faith I am of course closely paralleling Newman's own rhetoric. Throughout the *Apologia*, both implicitly (in image and metaphor) and explicitly, Newman claims for his conversion to Rome that it was a growth contained in potency in the seeds from which it was developed. He claims furthermore that it was an ordered development consistent with the demands of logic. In describing his thought as both growth and systematic deduction, Newman seems to be true to the actual complexity and obscurity of mental processes; at the same time he persuades us of the logical consistency of his conclusions. Though its "axioms" are rooted in individual temperament and personality, Newman's demonstration of the internal consistency of his development employs in a very subtle way one of the primary instruments of classical rhetoric: "argument." The argument demonstrates not only the controversial considerations which led to Newman's conversion, but his faithfulness to the inner voice with which he began his history.

In setting forth the essential consistency of his beliefs, Newman's concern is still reason as it operates "concretely," in union with feeling and imagination and conscience, and in response to particular experience. Correspondingly, since rhetoric is the persuasive form of substance, his appeal is as much to feeling and imagination as it is to logic.

Newman's use of emotional-imaginative devices of rhetoric in the history of his mind might perhaps best be demonstrated by the rhythmic recurrence in the *Apologia* of "sufferings" which are at the same time awakening shocks or conversion experiences. One such series of shocks is formed by the repeated appearance of what Newman calls a "ghost" or "spirit"—the logical-intuitive conviction that Roman Catholicism would be "found right after all"—which struck him during his study of the Monophysite heresy and the Arian heresy, and in the Augustinian formula "*Securus judicat orbis terrarum*" (the whole world judges rightly), which Newman interpreted to mean that the deliberate and eventual judgment of the whole church was the decisive principle that settled doctrinal questions. In each of the visitations he saw "Antiquity . . . deciding against itself," and destroying the basis of his own attempt to equip the Church of England with a theology that would be neither Protestant nor Roman.

> '*Securus judicat orbis terrarum!*' By those great words of the ancient Father, interpreting and summing up the long and varied course of ecclesiastical history, the theory of the *Via Media* was absolutely pulverized. . . . After a while, I got calm, and at length the vivid impression upon my imagination faded away. What I thought about it on reflection, I will attempt to describe presently.

> I had to determine its logical value, and its bearing upon my duty. Meanwhile, so far as this was certain,—I had seen the shadow of a hand upon the wall. It was clear that I had a good deal to learn on the question of the Churches, and that perhaps some new light was coming upon me. He who has seen a ghost, cannot be as if he had never seen it. The heavens had opened and closed again. The thought for the moment had been, 'The Church of Rome will be found right after all;' and then it had vanished. My old convictions remained as before (1839 to 1841, pp. 124–125).

Newman describes the force of Augustine's *Securus judicat* as a "vivid impression upon [his] imagination," and a mystery which he is unable to analyze. In the climax of the passage, it attains the status of a vision, with suggestions of an obscure revelation. The revolution it made in his mind turned out to be a great stride forward in his conversion.

The mind, as Newman describes it, moves forward by leaps, and the intervening territory later has to be filled in. Newman's response to Augustine's words is only one of several complex knots of meaning and feeling, intersections of reason, conscience, and imagination, which take him years of analysis to unravel. Their force and their general control of the direction of movement is felt; their significance is only gradually discovered, and it continues to vibrate in the mind. Such points of significance overlook, like mountain peaks, long pages of factual description of controversy. These sudden ascents to emotional peaks or sudden expansions into elaborate patterns of rhetorical development involving a complex interplay of rhythm, metaphor, and the language of the heart are so many eruptions of Newman's "preference of the personal to the abstract," and they appeal to the same sense in the reader. They invite us to identify ourselves with Newman's feelings and intuitions and to participate in his experience. At the same time, their power is very much increased by their organic-structural importance as the seeds and materials of long processes of analysis and clarification, and by their rhythmical recurrence. The world of Newman's experience—the sense of himself which he counts on to dispose us favorably towards him —becomes familiar to us by a series of repetitions each of which leaves its increment of understanding.

The same process increases the pathos of Newman's experience, without his openly claiming our pity or obviously working on our feelings. Through a series of hard but (from Newman's later point of view) salutary shocks, the *Apologia* dramatizes the reaction of time and the unexpected against abstract, untested conceptions. The first chapter refers elliptically to Newman's near defection to the enemy—liberalism—and to two blows which cut off his incipient error: "The truth is, I was beginning to prefer intellectual excellence to moral; I was drifting in the direction of the liberalism of the day. I was rudely awakened from my dream at the end of 1827 by two great blows—illness and bereavement" (p. 34). This incident (besides disarming suspicions that Newman was excessively clever and Jesuitical) sets the pattern for a series of later blows. The second chapter (1829–1841) leads up to three blows which shattered Newman's faith in the Anglican Church, and is followed by the long account of his suffering. By emphasizing the "supreme confidence" with which Newman undertook the Tractarian Movement, and following this by a series of unexpected blows which reduce him first to doubt and then to despair, the *Apologia* evokes what might be called a tragic rhythm of exaltation and reversal.

The central section of the *Apologia* is a history of doubt—of "growing doubt" about the Anglican Church and of "waning doubt" about the Church of Rome. Newman's uncertainty and confusion reach their climax in the next-to-the-last chapter (1841–1854). By far the longest chapter in the *Apologia,* it is entirely a history of despondency and uncertainty. It is the nadir of Newman's history—"a tedious decline, with seasons of rallying and seasons of falling back." As Newman says, "the sick man neither cares nor is able to record the stages of his malady," and "in consequence, my narrative must be in great measure documentary, as I cannot rely on my memory, except for definite particulars, positive or negative" (p. 151). This chapter describes the temporary tactics and shifts of ground to which Newman was forced by his position between two faiths, neither of which was acceptable. It contains fragments and loose ends, documentary evidence and relics of Newman's former life, which he allows to stand as a kind of mute evidence of his struggle and suffering. The representation of disorder is a risky process, but it is justified by the fact that through it the *Apologia* gains in rhetorical power what it loses in "classic" artistic concentration and order. It wins the reader over to a sympathetic participation in Newman's experience.[4]

Much of the emotional effectiveness of the next-to-the-last chapter depends on its bringing to a focus one of the recurrent episodes of the *Apologia*—sickness—which connects the intellectual crises and turns of faith and doubt with the physical crises of life. The illness in Sicily which Newman mentioned in the first chapter prepared for his writing the Tracts which began the Tractarian Movement. The phrase which he kept repeating during his illness—"I have not sinned against light"—perhaps revealed his half-suppressed recognition that he did not know why he believed, nor what he believed, and caused him to throw himself into the writing of tracts in order not only to defend but to clarify this faith. Newman is unable to explain the significance of the Sicilian illness, but he sets it down as a fact whose relevance and importance he feels, though he is unable to explain it, and the *Apologia* continues to recall it. Partly because it is accorded an unexplained importance, it takes on metaphorical or symbolic qualities. It seems to be connected with the later "spiritual" sickness of 1841–1854: both appear to be one sickness, which is alternately quiescent and active, and which returns in full strength after Newman suffers the three "blows" which destroy his faith in the Anglican Church. After this, as Newman says, "I was on my death-bed, as regards my membership with the Anglican Church,

[4] Here, someone may object that the "disorder" of the *Apologia* (it is difficult to talk about it without exaggerating it) is to be explained by the haste with which Newman wrote it. But whatever caused the disorder, Newman turns it to account as a reflection of his state of mind. He does so in the passage quoted above, when he remarks that "the sick man neither cares nor is able to record the stages of his malady," and that "in consequence, I cannot rely on my memory. . . ." Furthermore, the *Apologia* went through several editions in Newman's lifetime. The edition I am using is the last one Newman was responsible for, and it is considerably changed from the first edition. If Newman had been particularly dissatisfied with, for example, the next-to-the-last chapter, which is particularly fragmentary, he might have rewritten it or at least shortened it (as I said, it is much the longest chapter in the *Apologia*). But he did not. Instead, he announced his satisfaction, on the whole, with the *Apologia,* and perhaps refers to the peculiarity of method which I am discussing: "Nor is it the least part of my trial, to anticipate that, upon first reading what I have written, my friends may consider much in it irrelevant to my purpose; yet I cannot help thinking that, viewed as a whole, it will effect what I propose to myself in giving it to the public" (To 1833, p. 21).

though at the time I became aware of it only by degrees" (1841–1845, p. 151). By this time, "sickness" has been laden with emotional significance. At the same time, it is part of Newman's unanalyzed experience, and it expands for what one wants to put into it. Newman does not force its mysteriousness on us. He is content only to suggest that it is meaningful, and allows the reader to discover its significance for himself. Newman apparently aims to satisfy the reader's skeptical mind partly by stimulating his imagination.

In the final chapter, Newman's sickness gives way to health restored. The "tragic" descent of the central chapters of the *Apologia* is balanced, as in all accounts of conversion, by an ascent to certitude. The last chapter, which begins by announcing the sense of "intellectual satisfaction and repose" which is one of the tests of certitude (the phrase is from the *Grammar of Assent*), imposes on the *Apologia* its final and delayed pattern of significance. It is summary and reflexive; in contrast to the chronological organization and historical view of preceding chapters, it succinctly states the organized and logical form of Newman's final assent. By extracting the essential and permanent significance of the preceding history, the last chapter achieves a release from historical and mutable record. Its force depends not only on the calm assurance with which Newman describes his faith, but on our knowledge of the doubt and struggle through which it was achieved. It has a kind of existential force of commitment behind it.

As Newman has described them, his beliefs began in the mysterious roots of innate character and early experience and imagination. They were personal and unique, and could live only in their source of nourishment—in the images and feelings and bent of mind they started from. They grew largely in darkness; they had to be clarified, and their reasons determined. The process of this clarification was like exploring and conquering a newly discovered country. Temporary resting points were gained, and later had to be abandaned, and the whole struggle involved intense suffering. When a final conviction was reached, it had to be made certain. The certitude which puts an end to conflict and doubt gives the *Apologia* both its historical and its rhetorical finality. Newman no longer has any revolution of opinion to record, because he rests in his conviction of the truth.

To generalize from the particular history of the *Apologia,* as Newman seems to do in the *Grammar of Assent,* the "notes" of living thought are the marks it bears of a unique personality and experience, its "development" (which includes growth and increasing consistency of organization), and its mysterious and unpredictable changes and complexities. These are the main emphases of Newman's self-analysis in the *Apologia.* His conception of the life of thought is the key to the *Apologia's* structure, the focus of its varied materials, and it gives it its power of employing facts and documents, logic and feeling, confession of religious faith and "apologetic" self-justification, to such telling rhetorical effect.

The *Apologia* reveals the mind's movement in arriving at conviction, and we accept as a true description and a faithful psychological record what we might not accept as valid argument. The *Apologia* does not demonstrate the truth of Newman's conclusions, but persuades us of their consistency, and conveys the force of internal conviction with which he holds them. It presents the image of Newman's mind—his *sense* of the truth, as Pater would say. It is perhaps enough for Newman's purposes (though far from ideal) if we interpret the *Apologia* as conveying a relative or personal truth, a world-view which is an aspect of the writer's personality. Newman's own emphasis on personality and feeling, and his dependence on the persuasiveness of self-expression or self-revelation, are perhaps partly to be explained by his living in an age which had felt the influence of Rousseau and Goethe and Byron. If such an emphasis is indeed Romantic, it nevertheless makes use of classical principles of rhetoric, with their inculcation of the persuasive possibilities of the "speaker's" self-characterization or persona, and of the necessity of his feeling and expressing the emotions which he wishes to kindle in his audience.

ARRANGEMENT

Rhetoric and Meaning in *Religio Laici*

JIM W. CORDER

[RELIGIO LAICI, which presents and attempts to justify a layman's religious position, straddles the line between what Northrop Frye calls "real assertion" and "*mimesis* of assertion." The resolution of the question whether this discourse is merely John Dryden's statement, in rhymed couplets, of his religious position or whether it partakes enough of *mimesis* to be considered an instance of *belles lettres* depends partly on whether the "voice" we hear in the poem is Dryden's or some persona's. Jim Corder makes clear how he would answer the question, when, toward the end of his article, he says that with the aid of the rhetorical structure imposed on the work, Dryden was able "to transform what in lesser hands would be private confession into a public ritual given authority and more widely shared meaning."

The rhetorical structure that Mr. Corder sees in the work is that of a classical oration. The effect of this particular organization, Corder maintains, is not only to clarify the meaning of the poem but to point up the debate-movement in the dialectic going on at the time among the Deists, the traditionalists, the enthusiasts, and the proponents of Dryden's persuasion. As Lillian Feder demonstrates in her article "John Dryden's Use of Classical Rhetoric" (see footnote 3), Dryden was thoroughly schooled in ancient rhetoric and did not hesitate to employ rhetorical techniques in the composition of his poetic works when he saw that such techniques could contribute to the aesthetic and didactic effectiveness of his work. Positing that *Religio Laici* has the six-part structure of a judicial oration, Corder marks off the successive parts of the poem, shows that these parts do indeed conform to the pattern of a classical oration, and explains the functions and relationships of those parts in the general debate-movement. There are other ways, certainly, in which the poem might be outlined, but this exposition of the form that Dryden himself chose for his work can perhaps bring us closer to an understanding and appreciation of how this particular piece of occasional literature "works."]

From *Publications of the Modern Language Association*, LXXXII (May 1967), 245–49. Reprinted by permission of the Modern Language Association and Jim Corder.

ANALYSIS of the rhetorical structure of *Religio Laici,* by directing attention to the form and development of the poem, clarifies its meaning. Such an analysis, further, enables us to accommodate equally appealing but apparently contradictory readings of the poem.[1]

Dryden indicates the rhetorical provenance of *Religio Laici* in his marginal notes marking the progress of the controversy. Of the questions for oratory, there are in most rhetorics two types, the thesis, or *quaestio infinita,* a general question, and the cause, or *quaestio finita,* a specific question. Only the latter is given full consideration in treatises on rhetoric, and most such considerations name three kinds of cause. These include the epideictic, the deliberative, and the judicial. The epideictic speech is an occasional speech, designed to praise virtue or to discountenance vice in the present. The deliberative exercise is designed to persuade or dissuade in regard to some future action; the final rhetorical exercise in deliberation is the *suasoria,* which is a weighing of one side against another. The third of these kinds of cause, the judicial, is most pertinent to the discussion at hand. Specifically designed to celebrate virtue or to castigate vice in the past as Dryden does in *Religio Laici,* judicial oratory seems to have been regarded by rhetoricians as the most important of the three types. The final exercise in judicial oratory is the *controversia,* which, far from being limited to the court, is the rhetorical means by which the speaker or writer can plead before public opinion, as in Newman's *Apology* or Milton's *Defensio pro se.*[2] Dryden's *Religio Laici* is an exercise of this type.

Dryden is working not only with a recognized rhetorical type, but also with a recognized rhetorical structure. A standard feature of all rhetorics used in England in the sixteenth and seventeenth centuries, whether Ciceronian, Ramist, or whatever, is instruction in the fundamental parts of an oration. While some rhetorics list and discuss other parts such as the digression and the proposition, the most common listing gives six basic parts: *exordium, narratio, partitio, confirmatio, confutatio,* and *peroratio.*

[1] See Louis I. Bredvold, *The Intellectual Milieu of John Dryden* (1934); Thomas H. Fujimura, "Dryden's *Religio Laici:* An Anglican Poem," *Publications of the Modern Language Association,* LXXVI (September 1961), 205–217; and Victor M. Hamm, "Dryden's *Religio Laici* and Roman Catholic Apologetics," *Publications of the Modern Language Association,* LXXX (June 1965), 190–198.

[2] Donald L. Clark, *Rhetoric in Greco-Roman Education* (1957), p. 228.

It is to this plan we should look now, for *Religio Laici* is organized in the manner of a classical oration.

The *exordium,* or introduction, achieves its purpose through *benevolem, attentum,* and *docilem,* respectively the author's effort to make his audience well disposed toward him, to catch its attention, and to awaken sufficient trust to make the audience willing to listen to him. The *narratio* is given to necessary background information. The *partitio,* sometimes combined with *narratio,* forecasts the stages of the oration or written discourse to follow. This is followed usually by the *confirmatio,* the burden of the discussion, the proof of the argument. The rhetorician could rely on several modes of confirmation; he could depend, for example, on *ethos, pathos,* or *logos.* That is to say, he could depend on establishing his own character as sufficiently trustworthy to give his words authority. Or he could depend upon arousing feelings in his audience. Or he could depend upon apparent proof of his position. He could, further, seek this proof both outside and inside his rhetoric. From outside, he could bring to bear laws, witnesses, and the like. From inside, from the nature of his presentation, he could establish apparent proof, for example, by judicious use of the enthymeme and illustration. Following the *confirmatio* is the *confutatio* or *reprehensio,* the refutation of opposing views. This was followed in turn by the conclusion, or *peroratio,* an opportunity for recapitulation or amplification or for a last appeal to feeling. Most rhetorics allow *digressio,* or digression.

This is the plan Dryden follows in *Religio Laici.* His wise use of this structure illustrates what Lillian Feder has suggested:

> . . . it can be shown that he developed as a poet from the student writing epideictic declamations [many of his early poems] to the *orator* inspiring men by reasonable and moving argumentation. A brief survey of Dryden's progress from *declamatio* to *oratio* will demonstrate how he adapted certain oratorical techniques to poetry and will indicate how this discipline helped him to find his "true vein" as a poet.[3]

The shape of his "reasonable and moving" discourse does indeed depend upon these rhetorical techniques. The Preface itself is an

[3] Lillian Feder, "John Dryden's Use of Classical Rhetoric," *Publications of the Modern Language Association,* LXIX (December 1954), 1271.

incipient oration, its opening having all the qualities of the *exordium,* its closing with an account of the occasion and a defense of the mode of the poem suggesting the *peroratio,* and its long middle section providing extensive background information and some foreshadowing of the points to be argued in the poem.

In the poem itself the famous opening is Dryden's *exordium.* Extending through line 24 and separated from what follows by Dryden's notes, the *exordium* effectively accomplishes the three goals named earlier.[4] It catches the reader's attention with the withheld subject that suspends sense until the third line, and with the perfect simile that foreshadows Dryden's treatment of reason and embodies an enthymeme, one of the customary resources for proof in discourse. The self-denial and the qualified and unassuming trust in reason of lines six and seven help to make Dryden's audience benevolently disposed toward him, as does his assertion in lines ten and eleven of the predominance of "Supernatural Light." The series of example-questions (ll. 16–24) on the nature of "that one first great principle" helps to accomplish the purposes of both *benevolem* and *docilem,* for the examples reveal that the author is open-minded at this point and that he has considered other views than his own.

The first glossed section of the poem, lines 25 through 41, forms the *narratio.* These lines provide background for the discourse to come, explaining "Opinions of the several Sects of Philosophers concerning the *Summum Bonum.*" Against this background in the lines that follow, Dryden begins the explanation of his own position, initiating the explanation with the Deists, one of the "several Sects of philosophers" and one of the principal antagonists to whom he will address himself throughout the rest of the poem. The *narratio,* in its provision of background, prepares for the discourse to come and explains the occasion of the poem, the problem to be resolved there:

> Thus, *anxious Thoughts* in *endless Circles* roul,
> Without a *Centre* where to fix the *Soul.*
>
> (ll. 36–37)

The *narratio* also serves a further purpose. The conclusion of this section serves as the *partitio* for Dryden's poetic discourse,

[4] James Kinsley, ed., *The Poems of John Dryden* (1958), I, 311. All further references are to this edition.

forecasting the mode of development for the rest of the poem. The various opinions mentioned in this section, Dryden explains in the closing lines, are confused and baseless:

> In this wilde Maze their vain Endeavours end.
> How can the *less* the *Greater* comprehend?
> Or *finite Reason* reach *Infinity?*
> For what cou'd *fathom GOD* were *more* than *He.*
> (ll. 38–41)

These lines, contained within the *narratio,* do not specifically state the steps Dryden is to follow in the rest of the poem, but by means of the rhetorical strategy known as dialysis, they nevertheless foreshadow the plan of what follows. The lines above, with their suggestion of the futility of previous quests for the *summum bonum,* in effect pose the problem, alternative solutions to which are the primary topics of the poetic debate that forms the major part of the poem. The problem is that the "less" cannot "the greater comprehend." Alternative forms of the quest for the greatest good, the Deistic and the traditionalist, are considered in that order in the lines following this *partitio.*

The central portion of the poem, lines 42 through 426, because of the debate framework, constitute a combined *confirmatio-confutatio,* offering both Dryden's cardinal belief and his rebuttal of the antagonists foreshadowed in the *partitio* where he names their shared failing, the incapacity of their finiteness to reach infinity. In this combined *confirmatio-confutatio* he relies on the modes of confirmation and on the kinds of proof traditionally recommended for discourse.

Among the accepted modes of confirmation is the achievement of such rapport between the audience and the speaker (*ethos*) that the audience will think him reliable. Dryden's Preface and the unassuming tone of the entire poem help to accomplish this end, and his parting words to the audience further establish his openness:

> Thus have I made my own Opinions clear;
> Yet neither Praise expect, nor Censure fear:
> And this unpolish'd, rugged Verse, I chose;
> As fittest for Discourse, and nearest Prose.
> (ll. 451–454)

The rhetorician may proceed also through *pathos,* in an effort to stir the emotions of his audience. Evidence of Dryden's efforts to this end is ample. He enlists the audience on his side frequently, for example, by employing the plural form instead of the singular, as in lines 186 and 430, and in the opening figure. He elicits their sympathy early in the poem by showing the futility of man's other quests for the great good, and by sharing with them the incapacity of man to soar to heaven by his own strength. Finally, the rhetorician may depend also on the words of the speech itself, the *logos,* as Dryden does, for example, in his account of the Bible's efficacy in lines 121 through 167.

Certain kinds of proof useful to the rhetorician—witnesses, laws, oaths, for example—lie outside rhetoric itself. Dryden calls to his aid various sources outside rhetoric, most notably Scripture:

> If then *Heaven's Will* must needs be understood,
> (Which must, if we want *Cure,* and *Heaven,* be Good,)
> Let all *Records* of *Will reveal'd* be shown;
> With *Scripture,* all in equal ballance thrown,
> And *our one Sacred Book* will be *That* one.
>
> (ll. 121–125)

He also relies on kinds of proof which do belong to the art of rhetoric; of these, perhaps the most frequently cited in rhetorics are two, the enthymeme and the example. In his praise of the Bible Dryden employs the enthymeme, drawing a conclusion not from a major premise, but from opinions generally accepted with no intermediate minor premise involved:

> Then for the Style; Majestick and Divine,
> It speaks no less than God in every line.
>
> (ll. 152–153)

Or again, supporting the Bible as revelation:

> Whence, but from *Heav'n,* cou'd men unskill'd in Arts,
> In several Ages born, in several parts,
> Weave such *agreeing Truths?*
>
> (ll. 140–142)

Examples Dryden uses frequently. Indeed examples provide the bulk of the poem, for the lines on Father Simon's history and the speeches of the Deist and of the traditionalist are specific examples for the argument Dryden offers.

The development of this combined *confirmatio-confutatio* is quick and continuous, depending not on logical step-by-step sequence, but upon responses aroused by antagonistic views, both the antagonistic views and the responses being introduced and connected by simple, natural transitions. When the Deist's view is introduced at line 42, for example, his assumption that he stands on *firmer* ground immediately connects his with foregoing quests for the great good by the explicit comparison. Dryden's initial answer, running as the notes testify, from line 62 through line 167, is a two-stage development. He first amplifies and solidifies the position he has already taken implicitly in lines 39 through 42 to assert that "finite reason" cannot reach infinity:

> Thus Man by his own strength to Heaven wou'd soar:
> And wou'd not be Oblig'd to God for more.
> Vain, wretched Creature, how art thou misled
> To think thy Wit these God-like notions bred!
> These Truths are not the product of thy Mind,
> But dropt from Heaven, and of a Nobler kind.
> *Reveal'd Religion* first inform'd thy Sight,
> And Reason saw not, till *Faith* sprung the Light.
>
> (ll. 62–69)

With his insistence on revelation, he introduces the second stage of his answer to the Deist, that relevation as given in the Scripture is ample to man's needs:

> If then *Heaven's Will* must needs be understood,
> (Which must, if we want *Cure,* and *Heaven,* be Good.)
> Let all Records of *Will reveal'd* be shown;
> With *Scripture,* all in equal ballance thrown,
> And *our one Sacred Book* will be *That one.*
>
> (ll. 121–125)

Arguing the efficacy of Scripture on the grounds of its "agreeing Truths" and its "Style, Majestick and Divine," Dryden concludes this initial response:

> To what can *Reason* such Effects assign,
> Transcending *Nature,* but to *Laws Divine?*

Which in that Sacred Volume are contain'd;
Sufficient, clear, and for that use ordain'd.
(ll. 164–167)

The objection of the Deist that follows takes its source directly from these lines. When Dryden urges that the Scripture is "sufficient, clear," the Deist will "urge anew" that it is insufficient, for it provides no general law, "Which must to *all*, and every *where* be known" (l. 171).

When the objection is concluded, at line 183, Dryden's second response begins as a direct answer to it:

Of all Objections this indeed is chief
To startle Reason, stagger frail Belief:
(ll. 184–185)

This second answer, lines 184 through 223, is sufficient to quell the objections of the Deist, for it depends on a balanced and moderate account of the uses of reason to support revelation, as the opening enthymeme had forecast. The Deist's objection, that revelation through Scripture provides no solace for those unaware of its message, finds its answer here:

Then those who follow'd *Reason's* Dictates right,
Liv'd up, and lifted high their *Natural Light;*
With *Socrates* may see their Maker's Face,
While Thousand *Rubrick-martyrs* want a place.
(ll. 208–211)

The *confirmatio-confutatio* is interrupted at this point by a *digressio,* so designated by Dryden in the gloss. Not immediately germane to the issue at hand, the subject of the digression, the translation of Father Simon's work, is introduced through Dryden's answer to the Deist. In the first place, Dryden's reference to the "Egyptian bishop," Athanasius, in his answer, is a source for the digressive reference to the priest. In the second place, there is a connecting parallel between the bishop and the priest: as Athanasius had argued that the pre-Christian could find no salvation because he could have no access to the teachings of Christ, so the priest argues that those who depend solely on the Scripture can find no salvation because they can have no access to the other necessary teachings of the church.

The digression, in turn, provides the transition necessary for Dryden to move into the second major stage of his *confirmatio-confutatio,* where the second major antagonist is introduced. Dryden's attack on the non-scriptural resources of the church, as represented by Father Simon's work, arouses the traditionalist, who argues (ll. 276–281)that if tradition be set aside, "Where can we hope for an unerring guide?" Dryden's initial response to this new opponent (ll. 282–304), conceding that "an omniscient Church we wish indeed," but do not have, is that

> . . . MY Salvation must its Doom receive,
> Not from what Others but what I believe.
> (ll. 303–304)

This positive statement elicits then the first full objection in behalf of tradition (ll. 305–315); this, in turn, elicits Dryden's answer (ll. 316–355). It is here, in answer to the traditionalist's insistence upon the necessity of non-scriptural resources to explain Scripture, that Dryden urges one of his key points: many have been saved, he argues, who never heard fine points analyzed.

The traditionalist then objects a second time (ll. 356–357). Dryden has insisted that the written tradition of Scripture itself

> Rouls down to us the Sacred History:
> Which, from the *Universal Church receiv'd,*
> Is *try'd,* and *after,* for its *self* believ'd.
> (ll. 353–355)

The traditionalist, seizing on these last words, insists then that "*Their* Church, in last resort, shou'd Judge the *Sense.*" Dryden's answer to this second objection concludes the *confirmatio-confutatio,* running from line 358 through 426.

His answer reminds the traditionalists that "Their Church" is only part "Of that vast Frame, the Church," while "The *Book's* a *Common Largess* to *Mankind.*" The brief history of the church that follows explains how the Bible was made available to mankind. This history leads Dryden to make a concession in his argument that is important to the meaning of the poem. The good done when the Bible was given to all "had full as bad a consequence":

> The Book thus put in every vulgar hand,
> Which each presum'd he best cou'd understand,
> The *Common Rule* was made the *common Prey;*
> And at the mercy of the *Rabble* lay.
> The tender Page with horney Fists was gaul'd;
> And he was gifted most that loudest baul'd.
>
> (ll. 400–405)

As a result,

> Each was ambitious of th'obscurest place,
> No measure ta'n from *Knowledge,* all from *GRACE.*
> *Study* and *Pains* were now no more their care;
> *Texts* were explain'd by *Fasting,* and by *Prayer:*
> This was the Fruit the private *Spirit* brought;
> Occasion'd by *great* Zeal, and *little Thought.*
>
> (ll. 411–416)

The *peroratio,* to which I shall return in a moment, begins at line 427 and ends the poem.

Analysis of the rhetorical structure of *Religio Laici* is interesting enough in its own right, and as it reminds us of the provenance of the poem, needs no further justification. Aware of the marriage of poetic and rhetoric, we can see something of how the poet operates in his poem and be thus reminded of his craft. With the aid of this established rhetorical form, Dryden is able to transform what in lesser hands would be private confession into a public ritual given authority and more widely shared meaning.

But rhetoric is not its own end. Knowledge of the rhetorical structure clarifies the poem's meaning. The shape of the poem indicates that it is neither systematic theology nor codified philosophy, as the well-known and valuable exegeses of Bredvold and Fujimura suggest. It is, rather, as we have seen, a debate-movement brought to a conclusion by thematic and tight transitional developments. This debate-movement, by its rhetorical organization, directs our attention to the primary antagonists and to Dryden's calm and moderate response. As these are brought together in the *peroratio,* we discover the efficacy of Dryden's golden mean.

The Deist and the traditionalist are obviously the first two major antagonists and are so designated by Dryden. But he also designates a third antagonist by the rhetorical movement of the poem. In his answer (ll. 358–426) to the second objection of the traditionalist, as we have already seen, Dryden makes a concession, granting that when the Scripture was made available to all mankind, this great good "had full as bad a consequence" when

> This was the Fruit the *private Spirit* brought;
> Occasion'd by *great Zeal*, and *little Thought*.
> (ll. 415–416)

Thus he names as a third antagonist the fanatic, the enthusiast, to whom our attention should be directed when we see Dryden conceding the weakness in his argument.

The three antagonists, each refuted for peculiar follies in the *confirmatio-confutatio*, are brought together in the *peroratio* and dismissed for shared follies:

> What then remains, but, waving each Extreme.
> The Tides of Ignorance, and Pride to stem?
> Neither so rich a Treasure to forgo;
> Nor proudly seek beyond our pow'r to know:
> Faith is not built on disquisitions vain;
> The things we *must* believe, are *few*, and *plain*.
> (ll. 427–432)

Waiving "each extreme"—and he has named three extreme positions—Dryden sought to stem the "Tides of Ignorance and Pride." His separate accounts of the three antagonists have already convicted each of ignorance and pride. The Deist "by his own strength to heaven would soar." The traditionalist would impose his vision of salvation upon a mind which must receive its own doom. And the fanatic assumes that the "spirit gave the doctoral degree."

To these follies, the "Tides of Ignorance and Pride," Dryden opposes himself throughout the poem and especially in the *peroratio*. His spiritual goal is the repudiation of ignorance and pride, repudiation, indeed, of his very self. To the Deist's proud reasons, he says "Look humbly upward." To the traditionalist's reasoning pride he replies, "The *Book's* a *Common Largess* to *Mankind*." To the fanatic's prideful ignorance he remarks how he seemed "gifted most that loudest baul'd."

Steering a course among extremes, among versions of self-love, Dryden finds his way. Each of the antagonists goes astray when proponents allow self-love—ignorance and pride—to convince them that their version of religious truth is sufficient. In his *peroratio,* Dryden accepts what is good in the two fully developed extreme positions. To the traditionalist he concedes that

> In doubtfull questions 't is the safest way
> To learn what unsuspected Ancients say.
> (ll. 435–436)

To the reason of the Deist he concedes that

> Nor can we be deceiv'd, unless we see
> The *Scripture,* and the *Fathers disagree.*
> (ll. 439–440)

But in his last repudiation of the enthusiast, he denies again the exaggerated claims of all his opponents:

> 'T is some Relief, that points not clearly known
> Without much hazard may be let alone:
> And, after hearing what our Church can say,
> If still our Reason runs another way,
> That private Reason 't is more Just to curb,
> Than by Disputes the publick Peace disturb.
> (ll. 443–448)

In the overwhelming matter of the spirit, even though what each man believes is the condition of his doom, *no* strident, self-proclaimed version of the truth is sufficient.

Knowledge of the rhetorical structure of *Religio Laici* can enable us to see that readings of the poem that contradict each other are yet quite likely to be right. Bredvold argued that Dryden was a philosophical skeptic, and he was right, for Dryden marshals the arguments of philosophical skepticism against the claims of the Deist, and most of the passages Bredvold cites to illustrate his point are from those sections of the rhetorical structure where Dryden is answering his deistic antagonist. Fujimura argued that Dryden is after all an orthodox Anglican, and he was right, for Dryden marshals the arguments of orthodox Anglicanism against the claims of the traditionalist, and most of the passages Fujimura cites to illustrate his point are from those sections of the rhetorical structure where Dryden is answering his traditionalist opponent. His rendition of the last opponent, the enthusiast, and his folly of ignorant, prideful zeal, dramatizes the need for accepting what is good in the claims of the Deist and traditionalist and for repudiating what is bad, the exaggerated claims of partial insight.

Religio Laici is the poetic statement of a layman's religious attitudes. Its rhetorical ordering makes clear that its principal purpose is the resolution of an argument of faith. Dryden addresses himself to what he considers the necessities of faith by rhetorically and poetically rendering the inefficacy of the common versions of religious truth. The necessities of religion are unsatisfied by the claims of reason, by the authority of tradition, and by the zeal of private fire. What remains, these extremes denied, is a layman's religion. And that, perhaps, is no question for argument.

Order and Emphasis in Chapter XV of Gibbon's *Decline and Fall of the Roman Empire*

WILLIAM A. GIBSON

[WILLIAM A. GIBSON analyzes the strategies of arrangement in the famous Chapter XV, "The Progress of the Christian Religion," of Edward Gibbon's *Decline and Fall of the Roman Empire,* an ambitious historical work which because of its singular artistry has come to be regarded as a monument of English literature. In this chapter, Gibbon is not just giving an exposition of historical events; he has to persuade his audience to accept his presentation and interpretation of events. The task of persuasion is complicated in this instance by the fact that his largely Christian audience is not going to be favorably disposed to the aspersions he casts on the actions of the early Christians. So Gibbon has to tread delicately through a heavily mined field.

Mr. Gibson examines the rhetorical skill with which Gibbon selected and arranged his materials in order to make his readers aware of the contradictions among their religious and humanistic values and yet not to alienate his audience. Gibbon perceived that the order in which he disposed his arguments could help him in effecting his persuasive purpose, and Mr. Gibson demonstrates what that strategic disposition is. We have seen in the Introduction that arrangement (*dispositio*) was the second rhetorical process, coming after invention (*inventio*) and before the verbalization of the discourse (*elocutio*), but Gibson manages his analysis without using any of this technical terminology from classical rhetoric and without resorting to the framework of the classical oration that Jim Corder used in his analysis of the organization of Dryden's *Religio Laici.* What Gibson makes particularly clear in this analysis is that audience was the chief determinant of the means Gibbon adopted to achieve his end.]

This analysis was written especially for this collection. Reprinted by permission of William A. Gibson.

EDWARD GIBBON'S *The History of the Decline and Fall of the Roman Empire* (1776–88) has earned him the name of "Infidel," the clumsy blows of some of Christianity's pious defenders, and the criticisms of some well-meaning scholars insensitive both to his rhetorical strategies and his humanistic values; it has also long assured his reputation as historian and man of letters, and recently has earned him much-deserved credit for being a literary artist as well.[1] To call Gibbon an "artist" is surely to praise him, but the word is so vague as to suggest few of his particular skills. I should like to suggest that his skills, as especially well illustrated in his famous (or notorious) Chapter XV, "The Progress of the Christian Religion—Sentiments, Manners, Numbers, and Conditions of Primitive Christians," include those of a superb rhetorician, making Gibbon worthy of a place in the company of the other great rhetoricians of his age—Jonathan Swift, Alexander Pope, Samuel Johnson, and Edmund Burke. Indeed, the outbursts against Gibbon's attack on Christianity give evidence of the success of Gibbon's rhetoric, of his attackers succumbing to his strategies while remaining unaware of the methods he uses to evoke their responses.

Gibbon's admirers often delight in his *irony* or, like Lytton Strachey, in his ability to turn his back on religion "with a withering smile," but for understanding Gibbon's manipulations of his materials these appreciations are no more adequate than his detractors' objections to his *sneers* and *sarcasms.* In calling attention to *sneers* or *ironies* one shows his understanding of a writer's attitudes or intentions, but this understanding does not necessarily imply that he recognizes the means (linguistic, rhetorical, logical, etc.) by which the writer has achieved his effects. In complaining that Gibbon "is as incapable of understanding the spiritual significance of the phenomenon [Christianity] as of assigning a cause for it," [2] Sir Leslie Stephen confounds Gibbon's attitude toward religious experience with one of his rhetorical tactics. Yet this remark anticipates Strachey's helpful suggestion

[1] Especially helpful are William R. Keast, "The Element of Art in Gibbon's History," *ELH*, XXIII (1956), 153–62, and Harold L. Bond, *The Literary Art of Edward Gibbon* (Oxford, 1960).

[2] Sir Leslie Stephen, *English Thought in the Eighteenth Century,* 3rd ed., 2 vols. (London, 1927), I, 449.

that "Gibbon's style is probably the most exclusive in literature,"[3] for exclusion does not necessarily imply either indifference to or total ignorance of a subject. What Gibbon has chosen to exclude from his discussion is almost as significant as what he includes, especially since his irony often depends on a disparity between what his readers expected to be shown in a history of the Church, and what, in fact, his arguments and examples demonstrate or imply. How well Gibbon understood his readers' beliefs, assumptions, prejudices, and values is evident from their sensitivity to his "style," "tone," or "dark colourings." Gibbon could predict the effects of his verbal subtlety only if he knew his readers' expectations. But Gibbon's understanding of his audience is also evident from his selection and arrangement of his materials, and these, I believe, contribute as much to his success in coercing or enticing his readers into drawing the conclusions he desires as any other feature of his style. I shall try in this paper to suggest some of Gibbon's strategies in arranging his materials, and some of their effects on his audience.

I

The rhetorical problems Gibbon faced in "The Progress of the Christian Religion" were as great as those he faced anywhere in the *Decline and Fall*, but they were nevertheless representative of those that directed his strategies throughout the work. In this chapter and in the next (on the Christian martyrs), perhaps more so than in those of straight narrative, he had to pay particularly close attention to his audience. Most of his readers believed, or professed to believe, in the holiness, truth, and divine origins of the Christian religion, yet Gibbon was addressing to them a work implying, among other things, that Christianity helped to undermine the political foundations of the much-admired Roman Empire. In an age of growing religious enthusiasm and widespread evangelizing, Gibbon was himself incapable of spiritual ecstasy, and tended to dismiss such experiences as the products of an addled imagination—or perhaps of indigestion. He was deeply skeptical about the piety, innocence, and selflessness of Chris-

[3] Lytton Strachey, "Gibbon," in *Portraits in Miniature* (New York, 1931), p. 161.

tianity's first adherents, and of those who created the Church's organization and institutions. He perceived much more clearly than most of his contemporaries the assumptions essential to Judaeo-Christian views of history, and the limited perspectives that resulted from them. Consequently, he rejected the idealization of the primitive Church that had, since the sixteenth century, been an essential part of religious disputations, including Anglican apologetics.[4] Not even the merely nominal Christians who valued the Church mainly for its political usefulness would applaud the revelations of cupidity, ambition, pride, and hypocrisy that Gibbon made in the name of historical detachment.

Gibbon also believed that his readers shared most of his humanistic values, even if their piety prevented them from accepting completely his estimate of Christianity. Their very shock at the suggestion that Christianity undermined the Roman Empire implies a veneration for ancient culture—and for the values it was believed to represent—little different from Gibbon's. He could assume—or at least profess to assume—that they shared his confidence in the sophistication of their own society, in the necessity for and worth of toleration, charity, and justice. He accepted as self-evident their devotion to the idea of an orderly society and of every citizen's doing his part to preserve that order. Finally, he believed that they shared most of his intellectual values, that they preferred the "rational" to the irrational, candor to hypocrisy, truth to convenient fictions, and a guarded skepticism to blustering dogmatism. And the frequent occurrence of such words as "humanity," "rational," "reason," "justice," "candid," "sceptical," "truth," and "social" suggests that Gibbon was trying to remind his readers of the secular as well as the religious ideals they professed to accept. These reminders are useful to him because he constantly attempts to make his readers aware of the inconsistencies or contradictions among their beliefs.

[4] Gibbon was fully aware of the consequences of his depiction of the primitive Church: "The government of the church has often been the subject, as well as the prize, of religious contention. The hostile disputants of Rome, of Paris, of Oxford, and of Geneva, have alike struggled to reduce the primitive and apostolic model to the respective standards of their own policy." *The Decline and Fall of the Roman Empire,* ed. Oliphant Smeaton, introd. Christopher Dawson, 6 vols. (London, 1910, 1960), I, 470. All references to *The Decline and Fall* included in the text of this paper are to this Everyman Library edition.

But not only Gibbon's concern for his audience influenced his strategies in Chapter XV. He showed no particular reluctance to annoy or enrage the devout, and he responded with surprise, amusement, and equanimity to the first tirades against his personal morality and his scholarship.[5] His conception of historical truth was more akin to that of Richard Bentley than to that of Sir William Temple and Swift, but he was akin to them in prizing gentlemanly ease and in despising arrogant assertiveness. His own moral and intellectual values prevented him from writing a spiteful, dogmatic, or direct attack on either the tenets or institutions of Christianity; he had too much self-irony, was far too skeptical about the certainty of human knowledge, to be capable of exhibiting in his own work the positiveness which he found in the writings of the early churchmen—and which he would find in the attacks on his *Decline and Fall.* Yet if his history was to be effective he could not merely imply a set of values in his attitudes toward his subject. He had to reveal clearly what his values were, to establish the norms against which he measured the actions, opinions, and beliefs of the early Christians, just as Pope and Swift usually provide in their satires the norms by which the dunces, knaves, and fools they attack are to be measured. And like the satirists, Gibbon, too, had to play on his readers' values so as to direct their interpretations of the historical materials he presented. The arrangement of his materials contributed greatly to these ends.

II

The basic organization Gibbon uses in Chapter XV is very simple, and he has ensured that it will be clear even to a rather careless reader. The chapter, whose main contents he outlines in its title, is in two large parts, preceded by a two-paragraph introduction. The first, and by far the longer part, outlines the five "secondary causes of the rapid growth of the Christian church," which Gibbon summarizes in his second introductory paragraph:

[5] Edward Gibbon, "Memoirs," in *Miscellaneous Work of Edward Gibbon,* ed. John, Lord Sheffield, 3 vols. (London, 1796–1815), I, 153. For a full summary of contemporary attacks on Gibbon see Shelby T. McCloy, *Gibbon's Antagonism to Christianity* (Chapel Hill, N.C., 1933), pp. 49–228.

> I. The inflexible, and, if we may use the expression, the intolerant zeal of the Christians, derived, it is true, from the Jewish religion, but purified from the narrow and unsocial spirit which, instead of inviting, had deterred the Gentiles from embracing the law of Moses. II. The doctrine of a future life, improved by every additional circumstance which could give weight and efficacy to that important truth. III. The miraculous powers ascribed to the primitive church. IV. The pure and austere morals of the Christians. V. The union and discipline of the Christian republic, which gradually formed an independent and increasing state in the heart of the Roman empire. (431.)

The ironies in this apparently detached summary cannot be appreciated until one has read Gibbon's account of the "causes." The second part, which follows an ample summarizing paragraph for the first (483–85), traces the growth of church membership within and without the Roman Empire during the first centuries of the Church's history. In it Gibbon discusses the geographical distribution of the early Christians, their numbers, and their social levels and intellectual accomplishments. But such an outline reveals little about the disposition of parts in the chapter—just their content. To perceive the strategies Gibbon used in ordering them, and the materials in them, requires a closer examination.

Gibbon's strategy in ordering his five "secondary causes" can best be seen, not by starting at their beginning, but rather with a paragraph that will serve as an example of his ability to play on his readers' beliefs, expectations, and assumptions, the first paragraph in his discussion of this third "cause," miracles (458–59). His treatment of miracles is a good place to start for another reason: it is central to his attack, in this chapter, on Christianity. He introduces the subject early in discussing the origins of the Christians' zeal, and he concludes the chapter with it. And he could expect his readers to grasp its importance, for the historical fact of the Church's miracles had been frequently cited in the eighteenth century as proof—persuasive even to the skeptical—of the truth of Christianity.[6]

[6] In his next chapter, XVI, Gibbon considers another historical fact thought to be good evidence for the truth of Christianity—the believers who willingly died as martyrs for their faith.

In the main clause of the second sentence of this paragraph Gibbon enumerates the specific miracles he will enlarge upon in the remainder of it: ". . . the Christian church, from the time of the apostles and their first disciples, has claimed an uninterrupted succession of miraculous powers, the gifts of tongues, of vision, and of prophecy, the power of expelling dæmons, of healing the sick, and of raising the dead." To a devout believer these topics would appear to be set up in an order that runs from those topics conceivably capable of commonplace explanation to those capable only of supernatural explanation, that is, from those providing the least obvious proof for the intervention of Providence on the behalf of the Church, to those providing the most obvious, and therefore most persuasive, evidence for it.

The amount of space Gibbon devotes to each topic, and therefore the comparative fullness of the development of each, also suggests that he proceeds from the least to the most important and persuasive. He treats the gift of tongues and of vision in one sentence each (sentences 3 and 4), the gift of prophecy and the "expulsion of dæmons" in two sentences each (sentences 5 and 6, 7 and 8), the "healing of the sick" in just one clause (the first clause of sentence 9), and the "raising of the dead" finally in four sentences (9 through 12). Discussing the healing of the sick in a single clause would have seemed to subordinate it to the other miracles if Gibbon had not emphasized its importance by comparing it to the most convincing proof of all for divine intervention: "But the miraculous cure of diseases . . . can no longer occasion any surprise, when we recollect that in the days of Irenæus . . . the resurrection of the dead was very far from being esteemed an uncommon event." The increasing emphasis on each successive miracle thus *seems* to answer a devout reader's expectations of a climactic order, one comfortably reassuring to his confidence in the divine origins of his faith, just as the *literal* sense of Gibbon's comparison of healing the sick and raising the dead suggests that he shares his reader's faith and expectations.

But here, as throughout Chapter XV, Gibbon selects and arranges his materials as much to baffle as to satisfy expectations. His examples of miracles imply that he is playing off against the expected order, flattering to the orthodox, one that reveals an unflattering estimate of the primitive Christian's credulity and of the modern Christian's uncritical willingness to believe in miraculous gifts. He states that the "knowledge of foreign languages was frequently communicated to the contemporaries of Irenæus," but adds in a subordinate clause, "though Irenæus himself was left to struggle with the difficulties of a barbarous dialect whilst he preached the Gospel to the natives of Gaul." He thus raises by implication the question of whether it is likely that any primitive Christians actually possessed a gift which St. Irenæus himself was denied. Next, he grants that "divine inspiration . . . *is described* as a favour very liberally bestowed on all ranks of the faithful, on *women* as on *elders*, on *b*oys as well as upon *b*ishops" [italics mine]. But again the evidence for the miracles is rendered suspect because Gibbon leaves the authority for the gifts of vision purposely vague; the gift itself is made to seem slightly funny as he emphasizes a presumably appealing Christian doctrine with eccentric parallels, reinforced with undignified alliteration. The surrender of the intellect is made to appear even more complete in those who prepared themselves for the gift of prophecy "by a course of prayer, of fasting, and of vigils," after which they became "mere organs of the Holy Spirit, just as a pipe or flute is of him who blows into it"—almost an echo of Swift's "mechanical operation of the spirit." The "awful ceremony" of expelling demons he treats with apparent solemnity, only to add some nearly incredible details gathered from Tertullian: "the patient was relieved by the power or skill of the exorcist, and the vanquished dæmon was heard to confess that he was one of the fabled gods of antiquity, who had impiously usurped the adoration of mankind." Finally at the conclusion of the paragraph, where Gibbon has led his readers to expect the most convincing example of divine assistance, he turns from the Christian's miraculous gifts to the hesitations of their skeptical contemporaries:

> At such a period, when faith could boast of so many wonderful victories over death, it seems difficult to account for the scepticism of those philosophers who still rejected and derided the doctrine of the resurrection. A noble Grecian had rested on this important ground the whole controversy, and promised Theophilus, bishop of Antioch, that, if he could be gratified with the sight of a single person who had been actually raised from the dead, he would immediately embrace the Christian religion. It

is somewhat remarkable that the prelate of the first eastern church, however anxious for the conversion of his friend, thought proper to decline this fair and reasonable challenge.

Here as elsewhere in the *Decline and Fall,* Gibbon uses an ambiguous impersonal construction, "It is somewhat remarkable . . . ," to call his reader's attention both to the implications of his anecdote and to the ethical and intellectual standards by which it may be judged. It makes a reader pause and recognize at once what his faith demands that he believe and what his "reason" will allow him to accept. Gibbon may not demand that his reader choose between reason and faith, but he ensures that his reader cannot ignore the obvious disparity.

Gibbon has ordered his examples in this paragraph in what for him is a climactic order, but on a principle that undermines rather than satisfies the expectations of a devout reader. Instead of giving increasingly persuasive evidence for the Deity's intervention, he provides examples, and hints at estimates of them, that make the claims of the primitive Christians appear increasingly suspect or ridiculous. His appeal is to his readers' secular values, not their religious ones, and he emphasizes this preference not by ending with a most sublime mystery but rather with an anecdote of high comedy.

Clearly, no order can be *a priori* climactic or anti-climactic. It is said to be one or the other only as perceived by the writer who uses a particular order or by the audience that responds to it. A writer's perception of a climactic or an anti-climactic order, like a reader's, will be determined by his assumptions, and hence his expectations. A reader has little control over his response to what he reads; but a writer has considerable control over his materials, and he presumably will select some order appropriate to his purpose. He can arouse a reader's expectations and then satisfy or frustrate them as he chooses. A reader whose expectations are satisfied will probably grant that a writer's order is a "climactic" one, for the rhetorical concept implies a value judgment. But whether he sees a particular order as climactic or anti-climactic, he is essentially at the mercy of a writer's competence—or incompetence. A skillful, witty writer such as Gibbon can lead his reader to expect a climactic order based on one principle (here confidence in Christian mysteries) and then order his materials not only in an "anti-climactic" order (one failing to satisfy expectations), but in one that forces the reader to reconsider his expectations and the assumptions they are based on. That is, I believe, what Gibbon has done in this paragraph, and in his organization of the rest of the chapter as well. What is climactic order for Gibbon (one based on the supremacy of common sense and an unwillingness to believe anything without proof) would be anti-climactic to a reader who accepted the primacy of Christian faith. But since most of Gibbon's readers did not, and do not, have the single-minded zeal that would make them simply dismiss his examples, they can appreciate his play on both their knowledge of Christian doctrine and their skeptical habits of mind.

Besides illustrating Gibbon's ordering of his materials so as to disappoint purposely his readers' expectations, this paragraph also shows his habit of moving into the end position whatever he wants to emphasize. Here the concluding anecdote serves both the purpose of discrediting the primitive Christians' pretensions and of offering a model of the kind of conduct Gibbon venerates. It is, first, the inability of Theophilus to show his friend a single person actually raised from the dead that makes Gibbon's readers most suspicious about stories of saints performing resurrections. In direct contrast, and entirely consistent with Gibbon's moral and intellectual ideal, is the noble Grecian's vowing to embrace Christianity if shown a man raised from the dead. His conduct implies an honest skepticism that Gibbon holds up again and again as a contrast to Christian credulity, usually in positions which ensure that no one misunderstand the difference between unjustified belief and reasonable doubt. Such examples serve repeatedly to clarify the norms Gibbon has in mind. But whatever his immediate purpose, he can be counted on consistently to *end* his discussion of any topic with an extremely memorable, and often subversive, example.

This exemplary paragraph thus suggests what I believe are three of Gibbon's most effective means for manipulating his readers' responses: (1) he orders his materials in what appears from one point of view to be a climactic order, only to subvert his readers' expectations; (2) he puts into end position whatever he particularly wants to emphasize, often examples that give the lie to his readers' religious beliefs; (3) he introduces examples and anecdotes that clearly imply the criticisms he cannot make directly and the norms he cannot affirm vigorously if he is to maintain his affected detachment.

The ordering principle of Gibbon's five "secondary causes" is the same as that in our exemplary paragraph: Gibbon leads his readers to expect a climactic order that will reflect increasing credit on the progress of the primitive Church, but he plays off against this his own perceptions of the facts of history which repeatedly undercut the traditional veneration for the Church, and render even the faith itself somewhat suspect. What first appears a climactic order proves to be an anti-climactic one.

In his introduction to the chapter Gibbon disclaims any intention of discussing the "first" cause for Christianity's gaining "so remarkable a victory over the established religions of the earth," although he asserts that "it was owing to the convincing evidence of the doctrine itself, and to the ruling providence of its great Author" (431). Thus even while announcing his intention of limiting himself to the attitudes, beliefs, motives, and institutions capable of investigation, he reminds his readers of the more common explanations for the success of Christianity: the absolute truths it proclaims and the divine assistance rendered to it. To one accepting this implicit flattery of Christianity the order Gibbon uses in discussing his five causes would seem to reflect increasing honor on the religion, the Church, and its members. He begins with the "zeal" of the primitive Christians, which he characterizes as being both "inflexible" and "intolerant"—attributes hardly consistent with either the secular or religious ideals of most of his eighteenth-century readers. The next cause, the attractiveness of the "doctrine of eternal life," is far less discomforting to his readers, although it could be conceived of as reflecting the Christians' self-interest as much as their piety. The third, miracles, presumably gives clear proof of God's concern for his chosen people, and hence of their moral and spiritual worth. The "austere morals of the Christians," his fourth cause, would hardly seem to admit any qualifications of one's respect for the Christians. And finally, "the union and discipline of the Christian republic" could well seem to celebrate the triumphant Church, reflecting favorably on the faith, spiritual fervor, innocence, and selflessness of its members.

One does not have to read far before he realizes that Gibbon is not going to heap increasing glory on the Church, that he has arranged his materials in an order that would be anti-climactic to one expecting high praise for Christianity. Each step forward reveals not prospects of more and more glory, but rather scenes of more and more worldliness. Gibbon increasingly emphasizes the primitive Christians' very human fears and desires, their anti-intellectualism and propensity for self-deception. Instead of showing the expression of Christian ideals in the Church's institutions, he records the pride, ambition, and love for power among those responsible for them, and of their framing the organization of the Church, not on an analogy to the Kingdom of Heaven, but to the Empire of Rome. Stubborn zeal becomes, by the standards of orthodox Christianity, the most "admirable" of the causes. Gibbon's revelations would be shocking only to those who idealize an historical period and assume that men living in it were capable of unusual spiritual ecstasy and of unrealistically altruistic actions.

Contributing much to his readers' response to the order of his causes is Gibbon's arrangement of his materials within the discussion of each one. He regularly subordinates the evidence which allows the Christians the most credit, and emphasizes instead that which tends to discredit them. Gibbon mentions the best consequences of the five causes somewhere near the middle of the discussion of each (e.g. for the first cause in the fifth of fourteen paragraphs, for the second and fourth causes in the fourth of eight paragraphs); even then he usually does not develop these at all fully, and at that only with general rather than specific examples. Their worst consequences, on the other hand, he places in the end position of his discussion of each of the causes, where he develops them much more fully and with much more specific detail. This tactic also encourages Gibbon's readers to confound criticisms of "secondary causes" with errors about the "first" ones, and weaknesses in professing Christians with defects in the religion itself.

From a review of the organization of Chapter XV it is clear

that Gibbon has consistently selected his materials and arranged them so as to emphasize his own ideals and to discredit the legends about the virtue and spirituality of the primitive Church. He has framed the chapter at the beginning with a statement of his duties as a disinterested historian (and the necessary limitation, therefore, of his subject to "secondary" causes), at the conclusion with examples of literary evidence for and against miracles (and thereby dramatizes the habits of mind both in the classical and modern worlds that he most venerates). He has arranged his five causes in what turns out to be, from the point of view of his pious readers, an anti-climatic order, showing the primitive Christians and their institutions to reflect increasingly worldly motives. He regularly arranges his materials within the discussions of each cause so as to subordinate in a central position whatever examples cast most credit on the faithful; he reserves the end position of each for sketches or examples that imply questions about the efficacy of Christian doctrine itself: (1) the enervating credulity of the "trembling Christians"; (2) the savage vindictiveness of Tertullian; (3) the Christians' anti-intellectualism, or even near mindlessness; (4) their smug disregard for the social and political well-being of the Roman Empire; (5) Cyprian's preoccupation with the political power and organization of the Church, and his confusion of the religion itself with the institution formed to perpetuate it. In the last part, while tracing the growth of the Church, he dwells first on the exaggerations of the numbers of proselytes and then on their social ranks and dubious intellectual capabilities. What he specifically excludes are discussions of the *truth* of Christian doctrine, although he makes enough ambiguous references to the "first cause" to keep his readers alert to the question and therefore ready to draw the inferences about "first causes" from the evidence he provides for his avowed purpose of supporting his arguments about "secondary causes."

The most important effect of Gibbon's arrangement is to prepare his readers to draw the inferences that subvert Christianity. As Sir Leslie Stephen remarks, Gibbon "struck by far the heaviest blow which it had yet received from any single hand."[7] Yet he struck the blow by remaining consistent throughout the chapter

[7] Stephen, I, 449.

to his announced intention of discussing only what is explicable, or at least partly intelligible (e.g. men's instincts, passions, and desires). His method is especially effective for readers who, in spite of any pious professions, prefer the practical to the idealistic or the theoretical. He arouses their expectations of an order complimentary to the Christian religion, to its doctrines, and to its first proponents. He then provides examples that force his readers to recognize the disparity between their expectations and historical facts. The next question is the readers' not Gibbon's, although he has guided them to ask it: if Christianity, instead of making men humble, charitable, magnanimous, socially responsible, and tolerant, either makes or leaves them intolerant, zealous, self-righteous, vindictive, smugly ignorant, socially irresponsible, and ambitious for power, what must one conclude about this religion? It is a part of a simple test of utility that readers schooled on Bacon and Locke could be expected to make. The conduct of the Christians cannot help but reflect on their faith, no matter what Gibbon affects to profess. What he could and did control was what he included and in what order. And this ensures that readers will be left mainly with the most baffling, unexpected memories of the history of the primitive Church.

AUDIENCE

Antony in Behalf of the Play

KENNETH BURKE

[WHENEVER THE SO-CALLED "new rhetoric" is discussed, Kenneth Burke (1897–) is invariably mentioned. Although throughout his career he has operated impressively as a poet, a novelist, and a literary critic, he is fundamentally a rhetorician. In all of his major critical works—*Counter-Statement* (1931; revised 1953), *The Philosophy of Literary Form* (1941; revised 1957), *A Grammar of Motives* (1945), *A Rhetoric of Motives* (1950), *The Rhetoric of Religion* (1961)—he has consistently viewed literary discourse, whether spoken or written, as a means of influencing the attitudes and actions of an audience, as a "manipulation of men's beliefs for political ends." As early as 1931, in *Counter-Statement,* he was contending that "effective literature could be nothing else but rhetoric." It is this concern with the interrelationships of writer, work, and audience that mainly distinguishes rhetorical criticism from other modes of criticism. In his article "Kenneth Burke, Aristotle, and the Future of Rhetoric," *College Composition and Communication,* XVII (December, 1966), 210–16, Joseph Schwartz pointed out the remarkable similarities in the rhetorical systems of Aristotle and Burke; the differences in the two systems are the result either of shifts in emphasis, terminology, and epistemology or of the refinements that Burke brought to bear on rhetorical analysis from such disciplines as ethics, anthropology, and psychology.

In this article, Burke presents a clever analysis of the "Friends, Romans, countrymen" speech from the third act of Shakespeare's *Julius Caesar*. Antony delivers a monologue, not to the mob audience, as he did in the play, but to the theatre audience, in which he self-consciously analyzes how he is using language, in Burke's words, "as a symbolic means of inducing cooperation in beings that by nature respond to symbols."]

From *Philosophy of Literary Form,* revised edition (Vintage Books, 1957), pp. 279–90. Reprinted by permission of Kenneth Burke.

A READER-WRITER relationship is emphasized in the following article, which is an imaginary speech by Antony. Instead of addressing the mob, as he is pictured in the third act of *Julius Caesar*, he turns to the audience. And instead of being a dramatic character *within* the play, he is here made to speak as a critical commentator *upon* the play, explaining its mechanism and its virtues. Thus we have a tale from Shakespeare, retold, not as a plot but from the standpoint of the rhetorician, who is concerned with a work's processes of appeal.

Act III, Scene ii, *Antony has entered with the body of Caesar. Brutus has made his defense before the people, has won their sympathies to the cause of the conspirators, and has departed.*

Antony: Friends, Romans, countrymen . . . one—two—three syllables: hence, in this progression, a magic formula. "Romans" to fit the conditions of the play; "countrymen" the better to identify the play-mob with the mob in the pit—for we are in the Renaissance, at that point when Europe's vast national integers are taking shape, and all the wisdom that comes of the body is to be obscured by our putting in place of the body the political corpus, while we try to run this bigger hulk with the instincts for the little one—the Hobbesian metaphor—and the gloomy error has exalted us, so that no word handles as much, and as quickly, and as inexpressibly, as this word "countrymen," which must really mean, if pragmatic results are the test, that there is glory solely in being outdone by those within our own borders. Anyway, consider how much better my one-two-three arrangement is than was the opening salutation in Brutus' speech: "Romans, countrymen, lovers." He is an orator—but because you of England have thought the untrustworthy Latins eloquent, and because you don't think you are nearly so clever as you'd like to be, I shall seem closer to you if I apologize for bluntness. Yet how much more competent my opening syllables are: how much *truer,* since true to the processes of a spell, stressing a charm's *threeness.*

My Elizabethan audience, under the guise of facing a Roman mob I confront you at a most complicated moment. As a matter of fact, up to this point in our play you have been treated most outrageously. It can honestly be said that, in no major particular, have you been granted those clear and simple responses to which, as customers, you might feel yourselves entitled. Instead, your author has kept you in as vacillating a condition as this very Roman mob you have been watching with so little respect. I doubt if he distinguishes between the two of you. All that I as Antony do to this play-mob, as a character-recipe I do to you. Our author would play upon you; he would seem to know your stops; he would sound you from your lowest note to the top of your compass. He thinks you as easy to be played upon as a pipe.

Oh, there have been signs you recognize quickly, signs that serve to make you feel familiar with the road upon which you have been stumbling. The conspirators have met during storms and in the "vile contagion of the night." They have pulled caps over their eyes. One plucked at another's sleeve. Such labels are easily read by anyone. The streets of Rome have bristled with bad omens. Caesar's wife has cried in sleep that they are murdering Caesar. Outlandish astronomical and biologic marvels have occurred—to point the direction of our plot and give it weight by implicating the very heavens. And finally, Caesar was struck with daggers. Yet these standard things have lured you into a region where you are not competent at all.

Consider the burden you now carry, as I step before the play-mob with the fresh-murdered body of Caesar. We have established a Caesar-principle and a Brutus-principle, though I blush to consider some of the devices whereby the two principles have been set into your minds. Realize for what slight reasons you have been willing to let Caesar die. (The conspirators would not so much as touch him until you also had been brought into their band. And when Casca shouted, "Speak, hands, for me!" stabbing great Caesar, those homicidal hands spoke for you also.) First, we had the portents, beginning with the soothsayer's admonition that Caesar beware the Ides of March. In showing how things were going, these signs prepared you somewhat to go in the same direction.

But in addition, *your sympathies have been poisoned.* Caesar a conqueror, a monarch by reason of his attainments? Yet he was deaf in one ear. He had the falling-sickness, and "swounded" from the intense strain of refusing a crown he coveted. "He had a fever when he was in Spain," cried out "like a sick girl," his feebleness amazing Cassius. Cassius was a better swimmer than Caesar—and when the two of them had leaped into the Tiber on a dare, Cassius had to pull out Caesar, to whom he must "bend his body if Caesar carelessly but nod on him." His wife is barren. For all this determination to be bold, there is a timid and superstitious trait in him. And worst, for an emperor, on a night of storm and portents he appeared on the stage in his nightgown—so let him die. For such reasons as these you are willing to put a knife through the ribs of Caesar.

Still, you are sorry for Caesar. We cannot profitably build a play around the horror of a murder if you do not care whether the murdered man lives or dies. So we had to do something for Caesar—and you would be ashamed if you stopped to consider what we did. I believe we made Caesar appealing by proxy. That is: I, Antony, am a loyal follower of Caesar; you love me for a good fellow, since I am expansive, hearty, much as you would be after not too heavy a meal; and as one given to pleasure, I am not likely to lie awake at night plotting you injury. If such a man loves Caesar, his love lifts up Caesar in your eyes.

I serve a double purpose. Not only do I let Caesar shine a bit warmly by his reflection of my glow, but when the actual *persona* of the Caesar-principle is dispatched by daggers, the principle lives on in me, who continue the function of Caesar in the play. In the next act, the fourth, the *persona* itself will reappear momentarily as a ghost in Brutus' tent—but on the whole, after Caesar's death, I am the plot-substitute for Caesar. No wonder Brutus, in his address to the play-mob but a short time ago, told them that only Caesar's vices had been slain, while his virtues lived on, still active. So they do, in me, whom you like because I am marked by so serviceable a trait as loyalty. And when this play is over, Antony alone of the major characters will live; for you like to have about you such a man as might keep guard at the door while you sleep. Given certain conceptions of danger, I become the sign of safety. A little sunshine-thought, to take home with you after these many slaughterings. Only as much of the Caesar-principle as will let you relax, is left to bid you goodnight—and the Brutus-principle will have died to purchase you this handsome privilege.

I grant that on this last score I am not the perfect recipe. My author has provided purer comfort-recipes for you elsewhere. I show a little too much aptitude at deception, but you should not hold that against me. This trait was merely a by-product of my place in the story: it arose from the fact that upon me fell the burden of keeping things going, and the plottiness of our drama makes naturally for plotting. Besides, recall that I was wholly the reveler as long as Caesar lived. Once he is dead, it is no longer so necessary that I be likable in Caesar's behalf and warm him by my warmth. Henceforth I am no mere Caesar-adjunct, but the very vessel of the Caesar-principle. So, in expanding to my expanded rôle, I must break the former mold somewhat. Let *savants* explain the change by saying that carefree Antony was made a soberer man, and a bitter one, by the death of Caesar. But it is an obvious fact that if an important cog in the plot vanishes in the very middle of our drama, something has to take its place. In deputizing for Caesar, I found it impossible to remain completely Antony. Let *savants* explain my altered psychology as they will—I know it was a playwright's necessity.

You have been made conspirators in a murder. For this transgression, there must be some expiative beast brought up for sacrifice. Such requirements guided us in the mixing of the Brutus-recipe, for it is Brutus that must die to absolve you of your stabbing an emperor who was deaf in one ear and whose wife was sterile. But let us be fair. There is also the fact that you wrested certain political prerogatives from King John, and have been taught to cherish them. Here also was a source of conviction to be tapped as an ingredient in our formula. We discredited Caesar from the very opening of the play, even before he had appeared (significant timing), by letting you see the tribunes angry with certain commoners who were too cordial in their preparations for the return of Caesar after victory. Caesar, it seems, would try to retract your *Magna Carta* from the Romans. Conversely, it is the Brutus-recipe that would prevent this threatened undoing of English political emancipation. So we make Brutus honorable in your eyes by starting his conduct primarily from this fear, which is always your fear as regards conditions in the contemporary state. He is virtuous because he does for Romans what you want your popular leaders to do for you. He takes on the nobility that comes of being good for private enterprise.

On the other hand, he is a conspirator; hence from the general censure takes corruption. For tough Casca is a Brutus-adjunct; and lean, envious Cassius; and Decius the flatterer. Here are qualities which, if lodged in any but yourselves, are not comforting to contemplate—hence are "vices." Brutus' acts, though done in a good cause, have shadiness. One cannot be stealthy as a thief without partially earning the kind of judgments that are laid against thieves. Nobleness, yes, but dirty business. And if his wife, Portia, speaks for him by her deep affection (as I obediently did for Caesar), note that she is allowed to show this affection only at those moments when he is sinisterly engaged, and answers her evasively. That is: her *love* is conveyed by her *misgivings*, as she worries because her once regular husband roams about at night, in "rheumy and unpurged air" sucking up "the humours of the dank morning," so that even the quality of swamps is drawn upon to discredit Brutus a little, right when Portia is loving him. All told: a fit expiative offering for our offense of murder: worthy, since he was noble and aroused affection, yet yieldable on good legalistic grounds, since he was a conspirator, like a bog. In weeping for his death, you will be sweetly absolved.

At this particular point in the play, however, as I rise to address you, accompanied by Caesar's corpse, Brutus has just confronted the play-mob, stated before them the case of the conspirators, and been exonerated. They have clamored their approval. They are convinced that Caesar would have been a tyrant. And they have shouted to the Brutus-principle, who must die for you, "Live, Brutus! live! live!" It is my task, as I stand before the play-mob, to contrive a *peripety* for my audience, reversing the arrows of your expectations. When my speech is finished, we must have set you to making the preparations for Brutus' death.

Well, a dramatist is a *professional* gambler. He prefers playing with loaded dice. And don't think that we should try to bring about this reversal without first making sure that we had furtively dealt ourselves some trumps. We have stacked the cards a little—not so shamelessly as some of our rival Shake-scenes might have done, but enough. Here, I believe, we have drawn from the well of magic. As follows:

Recall how, in the early rites of communion, whereby one man's interests were made identical with another's, the risks of competitive harms were eliminated by a partnership, a partnership established by three distinct symbolic acts: the sharing of one's wife, the exchanging of blood, the sitting down together at table. Of these, the sharing of the wife is dead, buried beneath notions of virtue that go with later concepts of ownership. Yet we give you something similar, in Caesar's dying words, *"Et tu, Brute?* Then fall, Caesar!" which suggests that in Caesar's pain there is more than the pain of knives, there is the pain of wrenched intimacy, eliciting a rebuke almost Christlike in its replacing of vengefulness with sorrow, as the victim saw that "Caesar's angel" was among his slayers. At this moment Caesar becomes great—for he must die well, at the expense of Brutus. They had shared affection; hence a promise contracted within the deep-lying terms of magic had been violated.

As for the rites at table: When the conspirators had come, to make sure that Caesar would be on hand at the Senate to be murdered, Caesar welcomed them heartily: "Good friends, go in, and taste some wine with me." And lastly, as for the blood-communion, how grimly it is vivified and mocked (in pious profanation) when the conspirators, at Brutus' word, bathe in the blood of Caesar's wounds. Three magic formulae, outraged—thus Shakespeare speaks to you in accents you had heard while not listening.

I now stand before you, assigned to the definite task of contriving our peripety, turning the arrows of your future while apparently engaged only in turning those of this unruly play-mob. I shall, by what immediately follows, proclaim myself in all thoroughness the Caesar-principle perpetuated. Here I fulfill the pledge I gave when first I came upon the stage after Caesar's murder. I came ostensibly to reassure the conspirators that I was ready to make peace with them, now that the offense was definitely beyond reparation. I shook hands with them, one after the other—but in the very act of doing so, I forgot them, and fell to musing aloud upon the destroyed magnificence of Caesar. In this way I signaled you to the effect that I was not turning against Caesar, even while "shaking the bloody fingers of his foes." (You wanted me to remain with Caesar, since that has been established as my part in this play. I have been given my label—and like children, you insist that a thing's *true* name is the name you first heard it called by. In your insistence that I remain allied with Caesar, repeating my number, you are grateful for the little cue I give you by my absent-minded musings over Caesar's body. In your satisfaction at receiving from me this sign, to restate my identity even as I make peace with the conspirators, you do not stop to ask why the conspirators should not interpret this sign precisely as you do. Your concern with your own aesthetic problem leads you to overlook this straining of verisimilitude, as we thought you would. We judged that, in your eagerness to receive the clue, you would not be overexacting as regards our manner of conveying it.)

Brutus, you will remember, had asked the mob to weigh what he said, and to judge his statements as critics. But, as a matter of fact, he gave them no opportunity to follow his advice. He told them to choose, then stated the issue in such a way that there was no choice. Those that love Rome, he said, must agree that Caesar should have been killed. Those that do not love Rome, should object. If there are any that do not love Rome, let them step forward in protest. No move—hence, the killing is endorsed.

And now, my countrymen, hear me ask the play-mob to lend me their ears, as I proceed to lay before you a plot in miniature. It will not be a very difficult pattern that I ask you to appreciate: a rudimentary piece of translation, by which I awaken in you the satisfactions of authorship, as you hear me say one thing and know that I mean another. "I come to bury Caesar, not to praise him"—whereat I praise him so roundly that all the vigor of the Caesar-principle is brought to life again.

> . . . if I were dispos'd to stir
> Your heart and minds to mutiny and rage,
> I should do Brutus wrong, and Cassius wrong, . . .

Whereat I stir hearts and minds to mutiny and rage. And as the pattern grows clear, I can subtilize it, making Brutus and his band dishonorable by calling them all, all honorable men. And by the time I mention Caesar's will, saying that I would not read it because it would inflame the people, in accordance with the pattern you wait to hear me read the will. You hear them entreat me, you hear me refuse. Then you observe me stepping down, to be among them, that I may better "realize" Caesar's death for them, and make them tearful coroners while I appraise the wounds:

If you have tears, prepare to shed them now.
You all do know this mantle: I remember
The first time ever Caesar put it on;
'Twas on a summer's evening in his tent,
That day he overcame the Nervii.
Look! in this place ran Cassius' dagger through:
See what a rent the envious Casca made:
Through this the well-beloved Brutus stabb'd;
And, as he pluck'd his cursed steel away,
Mark how the blood of Caesar follow'd it,
As rushing out of doors, to be resolv'd
If Brutus so unkindly knock'd or no;
For Brutus, as you know, was Caesar's angel:
Judge, O you gods! how dearly Caesar lov'd him.
This was the most unkindest cut of all;
For when the noble Caesar saw him stab,
Ingratitude, more strong than traitor's arms,
Quite vanquish'd him: then burst his mighty heart;
And, in his mantle muffling up his face,
Even at the base of Pompey's statue,
Which all the while ran blood, great Caesar fell.
O! what a fall was there, my countrymen;
Then I, and you, and all of us fell down,
Whilst bloody treason flourish'd over us.
O! now you weep, and I perceive you feel
The dint of pity; these are gracious drops.
Kind souls, what! weep you when you but behold
Our Caesar's vesture wounded? Look you here,
Here is himself, marr'd as you see, with traitors.

You see my "transference," as I turn from the mantle to the dead man that had worn the mantle. You see the play-mob grow *inflamed* under my talk of *pity* (remember our pattern). There is loud talk of mutiny; the people are about to rush away in anger—but we would "consolidate" our position. And now, rounding out the pattern, I return to the matter of the will, which I had refused to read:

Why, friends, you go to do you know not what.
Wherein hath Caesar thus deserv'd your loves?
Alas! you know not: I must tell you then.
You have forgot the will I told you of.

Whereupon I read them the will of a rich philanthropist—and their vindictiveness against the conspirators is complete. You have been engrossed—faugh! you demons, how you do love plottings, for all your censure of plotters. Or is it machinery that delights you—and are you pleased with joining me to make a smoothly running engine of fatality?

Cassius was right in proposing that they slay me, along with Caesar. But Brutus held it was enough to slay the *persona* of the Caesar-principle, on the ground that the *adjunct* would subside through want of its source:

> Our course will seem too bloody, Caius Cassius,
> To cut the head off and then hack the limbs, . . .
> For Antony is but a limb of Caesar.
>
> . . . .
>
> And, for Mark Antony, think not of him;
> For he can do no more than Caesar's arm
> When Caesar's head is off.

So the Brutus-principle slays half the Caesar-principle, and spares the other half that will in turn destroy it.

Recall these steps: How first, after the murder, I had sent word by a servant offering to join the cause of the conspirators, if they would guarantee me safety. How I fell to musing over the body of Caesar. How, after *exeunt all but Antony*, I had let loose my full-throated venom:

> O! pardon me, thou bleeding piece of earth,
> That I am meek and gentle with these butchers;
> Thou art the ruins of the noblest man
> That ever lived in the tide of times.
> Woe to the hand that shed this costly blood!
> Over thy wounds now do I prophesy,
> Which like dumb mouths do ope their ruby lips,
> To beg the voice and utterance of my tongue,
> A curse shall light upon the limbs of men;
> Domestic fury and fierce civil strife
> Shall cumber all the parts of Italy;
> Blood and destruction shall be so in use,
> And dreadful objects so familiar,
> That mothers shall but smile when they behold

Their infants quarter'd with the hands of war;
All pity chok'd with custom of fell deeds:
And Caesar's spirit, ranging for revenge,
With Ate by his side come hot from hell,
Shall in these confines with a monarch's voice
Cry "Havoc!" and let slip the dogs of war;
That this foul deed shall smell above the earth
With carrion men, groaning for burial.

Then, in my speech before the Romans, I fulfilled my promises, starting those processes by which the Brutus-principle, which killed the Caesar-*persona,* is driven to his death by the Caesar-adjunct.

Thank us for this growing thing by growing with it—and in the following scene we shall allow you to squeeze the last available sum of emotion from the mounting sequence, causing it to drip, not by still hotter pressure, but by a sudden cooling. Prominent among the conspirators, there was a certain Cinna. Now another Cinna comes upon the stage, Cinna the poet, ludicrous, the cartoon of a poet, the aesthete, such as you have long before now been taught to laugh at (our author is treading on safe ground here). He is an earnest but ineffectual wretch, who probably knows a good line when he sees it, and would doubtless have been entranced to write just such verses as Shakespeare wrote; and perhaps he might even have written them had he known, like Shakespeare, how to draw finenesses from toughnesses. Yet our dramatist betrays him for the delectation of you, my stinking audience, makes him your laughing stock, ridicules one of his own Guild for your benefit, though you have no desire whatever to write like Shakespeare, would much rather eat beef than hear a play, but cannot go on eating beef forever, and so come here occasionally, demanding firm, beefy diction. The mob stumbles upon this Cinna, overwhelming him. First Citizen, Second Citizen, Third Citizen, and Fourth Citizen, each ask him a different question, all at the same time, insisting imperiously that he answer without delay. It is all quite hilarious, as Cinna is in a daze, comically. And when they ask him his name, and he says with assurance, "Cinna," they start pawing at him in earnest—and when he begs them for a little accuracy, insisting that he is not Cinna the conspirator but Cinna the poet, they unanswerably answer that they abominate the name, and so will pummel him for his verses, and the act ends with the brawling group moving from the stage. You somehow know that the poetic Cinna will suffer no fundamental harm. He will merely be slain-notslain, like a clown hit by cannon balls—yet by this let-down we have reaffirmed in another way the grim intentions of the mob. We have clinched the arrows of your expectancy, incidentally easing our obligations as regards the opening of Act IV.

You will be still more wisely handled by what follows, as our Great Demagogue continues to manipulate your minds. I think particularly of the second scene of the next act, weighted by the steadily organized pressure of events. You will witness a startling quarrel between Brutus and Cassius. After this violence and the sad reconciliation (these men are disintegrating), there will be a contrasted descent to soft tearfulness, as Brutus' drowsy servant plays him a disconsolate little tune in the dead of night (Portia is dead)—and the servant is drowsy, that he may fall asleep as Varro and Claudius have done; then with three men sleeping (and you drooping in sympathy) and Brutus alone awake, there will be, all about, a sleepiness, and a Brutus-loneliness—whereat the Caesar-*persona,* now as a ghost, may return to indicate, by a vague prophecy, that all will be ended for Brutus at Philippi.

Control of Distance in Jane Austen's *Emma*

WAYNE C. BOOTH

[WAYNE BOOTH'S *The Rhetoric of Fiction* is generally regarded, along with Northrup Frye's *Anatomy of Criticism* and M. H. Abrams's *The Mirror and the Lamp*, as one of the best books of criticism published in the last ten years. He once remarked that "whatever the faults or merits of *The Rhetoric of Fiction*, it has profited factitiously from my having used a fad term, quite unwittingly, in the title" (see "The Revival of Rhetoric," *PMLA*, LXXX (May, 1965), 8–12). But there is more to the book's success than just the presence in its title of the vogue word *rhetoric*. Anyone who has read the book knows that in addition to the astonishing range and depth of Booth's reading in fiction the author has added greatly to our understanding of fictional techniques by his examination of "the rhetorical resources available to the writer of epic, novel, or short story as he tries, consciously or unconsciously, to impose his fictional world upon the reader." In the first part of the book, Booth attacks some of the shibboleths about fictional technique that Henry James and his disciples had helped to give currency to—"True Novels Must Be Realistic," "All Authors Should Be Objective," "True Art Ignores the Audience." In the next two parts of the book, he goes on to show us the difference in effect between personal and impersonal narration.

This selection is from Part II, "The Author's Voice in Fiction." Booth shows us how Jane Austen secured and maintained the sympathy of her audience for a heroine who had some seriously alienating flaws in her character. "Jane Austen, in developing the sustained use of a sympathetic inside view," he says, "has mastered one of the most successful of all devices for inducing a parallel emotional response between the deficient heroine and the reader." Here then, without any of the jargon of classical rhetoric, is a classic study of the rhetoric of manipulating an audience's response to a fictional world.]

Sympathy and Judgment in "Emma"

Henry James once described Jane Austen as an instinctive novelist whose effects, some of which are admittedly fine, can best be explained as "part of her unconsciousness." It is as if she "fell-a-musing" over her work-basket, he said, lapsed into "wool-gathering," and afterward picked up "her dropped stitches" as "little master-strokes of imagination."[1] The amiable accusation has been repeated in various forms, most recently as a claim that Jane Austen creates characters toward whom we cannot react as she consciously intends.[2]

Although we cannot hope to decide whether Jane Austen was entirely conscious of her own artistry, a careful look at the technique of any of her novels reveals a rather different picture from that of the unconscious spinster with her knitting needles. In *Emma* especially, where the chances for technical failure are great indeed, we find at work one of the unquestionable masters of the rhetoric of narration.

At the beginning of *Emma,* the young heroine has every requirement for deserved happiness but one. She has intelligence, wit, beauty, wealth, and position, and she has the love of those around her. Indeed, she thinks herself completely happy. The only threat to her happiness, a threat of which she is unaware, is herself: charming as she is, she can neither see her own excessive pride honestly nor resist imposing herself on the lives of others. She is deficient both in generosity and in self-knowledge. She discovers and corrects her faults only after she has almost ruined herself and her closest friends. But with the reform in her character, she is ready for marriage with the man she loves, the man who throughout the book has stood in the reader's mind for what she lacks.

[1] "The Lesson of Balzac," *The Question of Our Speech* (Cambridge, 1905), p. 63. A fuller quotation can be found in R. W. Chapman's indispensable *Jane Austen: A Critical Bibliography* (Oxford, 1955). Some important Austen items published too late to be included by Chapman are: (1) Ian Watt, *The Rise of the Novel* (Berkeley, Calif., 1957); (2) Stuart M. Tave, review of Marvin Mudrick's *Jane Austen: Irony as Defense and Discovery* (Princeton, N.J., 1952) in *Philological Quarterly,* XXXII (July 1953), 256–57; (3) Andrew H. Wright, *Jane Austen's Novels: A Study in Structure* (London, 1953), pp. 36–82; (4) Christopher Gillie, "*Sense and Sensibility:* An Assessment," *Essays in Criticism,* IX (January 1959), 1–9, esp. 5–6; (5) Edgar F. Shannon, Jr., "*Emma:* Character and Construction," *PMLA,* LXXI (September 1956), 637–50.

[2] See, for example, Mudrick, *op. cit.,* pp. 91, 165; Frank O'Connor, *The Mirror in the Roadway* (London, 1957), p. 30.

It is clear that with a general plot of this kind Jane Austen gave herself difficulties of a high order. Though Emma's faults are comic, they constantly threaten to produce serious harm. Yet she must remain sympathetic or the reader will not wish for and delight sufficiently in her reform.

Obviously, the problem with a plot like this is to find some way to allow the reader to laugh at the mistakes committed by the heroine and at her punishment, without reducing the desire to see her reform and thus earn happiness. In *Tom Jones* this double attitude is achieved, as we have seen, partly through the invention of episodes producing sympathy and relieving any serious anxiety we might have, and partly through the direct and sympathetic commentary. In *Emma,* since most of the episodes must illustrate the heroine's faults and thus increase either our emotional distance or our anxiety, a different method is required. If we fail to see Emma's faults as revealed in the ironic texture from line to line, we cannot savor to the full the comedy as it is prepared for us. On the other hand, if we fail to love her, as Jane Austen herself predicted we would [3]—if we fail to love her more and more as the book progresses—we can neither hope for the conclusion, a happy and deserved marriage with Knightley following upon her reform, nor accept it as an honest one when it comes.[4] Any attempt to solve the problem by reducing either the love or the clear view of her faults would have been fatal.

Sympathy through Control of Inside Views

The solution to the problem of maintaining sympathy despite almost crippling faults was primarily to use the heroine herself as a kind of narrator, though in third person, reporting on her own experience. So far as we know, Jane Austen never formulated any

[3] "A heroine whom no one but myself will much like" (James Edward Austen-Leigh, *Memoir of His Aunt* [London, 1870; Oxford, 1926], p. 157).

[4] The best discussion of this problem is Reginald Farrer's "Jane Austen," *Quarterly Review,* CCXXVIII (July 1917), 1–30; reprinted in William Heath's *Discussions of Jane Austen* (Boston, 1961). For one critic the book fails because the problem was never recognized by Jane Austen herself: Mr. E. N. Hayes, in what may well be the least sympathetic discussion of *Emma* yet written, explains the whole book as the *author's* failure to see Emma's faults. "Evidently Jane Austen wished to protect Emma. . . . The author is therefore in the ambiguous position of both loving and scorning the heroine" ("'Emma': A Dissenting Opinion," *Nineteenth-Century Fiction,* IV [June 1949], 18, 19).

theory to cover her own practice; she invented no term like James's "central intelligence" or "lucid reflector" to describe her method of viewing the world of the book primarily through Emma's own eyes. We can thus never know for sure to what extent James's accusation of "unconsciousness" was right. But whether she was inclined to speculate about her method scarcely matters; her solution was clearly a brilliant one. By showing most of the story through Emma's eyes, the author insures that we shall travel with Emma rather than stand against her. It is not simply that Emma provides, in the unimpeachable evidence of her own conscience, proof that she has many redeeming qualities that do not appear on the surface; such evidence could be given with authorial commentary, though perhaps not with such force and conviction. Much more important, the sustained inside view leads the reader to hope for good fortune for the character with whom he travels, quite independently of the qualities revealed.

Seen from the outside, Emma would be an unpleasant person, unless, like Mr. Woodhouse and Knightley, we knew her well enough to infer her true worth. Though we might easily be led to laugh at her, we could never be made to laugh sympathetically. While the final unmasking of her faults and her humiliation would make artistic sense to an unsympathetic reader, her marriage with Knightley would become irrelevant if not meaningless. Unless we desire Emma's happiness and her reform which alone can make that happiness possible, a good third of this book will seem irredeemably dull.

Yet sympathetic laughter is never easily achieved. It is much easier to set up a separate fool for comic effects and to preserve your heroine for finer things. Sympathetic laughter is especially difficult with characters whose faults do not spring from sympathetic virtues. The grasping but witty Volpone can keep us on his side so long as his victims are more grasping and less witty than he, but as soon as the innocent victims, Celia and Bonario, come on stage, the quality of the humor changes; we no longer delight unambiguously in his triumphs. In contrast to this, the great sympathetic comic heroes often are comic largely because their faults, like Uncle Toby's sentimentality, spring from an excess of some virtue. Don Quixote's madness is partly caused by an excess of idealism, an excess of loving concern for the unfortunate.

Every crazy gesture he makes gives further reason for loving the well-meaning old fool, and we can thus laugh at him in somewhat the same spirit in which we laugh at our own faults—in a benign, forgiving spirit. We may be contemptible for doing so; to persons without a sense of humor such laughter often seems a wicked escape. But self-love being what it is, we laugh at ourselves in a thoroughly forgiving way, and we laugh in the same way at Don Quixote: we are convinced that his heart, like ours, is in the right place.

Nothing in Emma's comic misunderstandings can serve for the same effect. Her faults are not excesses of virtue. She attempts to manipulate Harriet not from an excess of kindness but from a desire for power and admiration. She flirts with Frank Churchill out of vanity and irresponsiblity. She mistreats Jane Fairfax because of Jane's *good* qualities. She abuses Miss Bates because of her own essential lack of "tenderness" and "good will."

We have only to think of what Emma's story would be if seen through Jane Fairfax' or Mrs. Elton's or Robert Martin's eyes to recognize how little our sympathy springs from any natural view, and to see how inescapable is the decision to use Emma's mind as a reflector of events—however beclouded her vision must be. To Jane Fairfax, who embodies throughout the book most of the values which Emma discovers only at the end, the early Emma is intolerable.

But Jane Austen never lets us forget that Emma is not what she might appear to be. For every section devoted to her misdeeds—and even they are seen for the most part through her own eyes—there is a section devoted to her self-reproach. We see her rudeness to poor foolish Miss Bates, and we see it vividly. But her remorse and act of penance in visiting Miss Bates after Knightley's rebuke are experienced even more vividly. We see her successive attempts to mislead Harriet, but we see at great length and in high color her self-castigation (chaps. xvi, xvii, xlviii). We see her boasting proudly that she does not need marriage, boasting almost as blatantly of her "resources" as does Mrs. Elton (chap. x). But we know her too intimately to take her conscious thoughts at face value. And we see her, thirty-eight chapters later, chastened to an admission of what we have known all along to be her true human need for love. "If all took place that might take place among the circle of her friends, Hartfield must be comparatively deserted; and she left to cheer her father with the spirits only of ruined happiness. The child to be born at Randalls must be a tie there even dearer than herself; and Mrs. Weston's heart and time would be occupied by it. . . . All that were good would be withdrawn" (chap. xlviii).

Perhaps the most delightful effects from our sustained inside view of a very confused and very charming young woman come from her frequent thoughts about Knightley. She is basically right all along about his pre-eminent wisdom and virtue, and she is our chief authority for taking *his* authority so seriously. And yet in every thought about him she is misled. Knightley rebukes her; the reader knows that Knightley is in the right. But Emma?

> Emma made no answer, and tried to look cheerfully unconcerned, but was really feeling uncomfortable, and wanting him very much to be gone. She did not repent what she had done; she still thought herself a better judge of such a point of female right and refinement than he could be; but yet she had a sort of habitual respect for his judgment in general, which made her dislike having it so loudly against her; and to have him sitting just opposite to her in angry state, was very disagreeable [chap. viii].

Even more striking is the lack of self-knowledge shown when Mrs. Weston suggests that Knightley might marry Jane Fairfax.

> Her objections to Mr. Knightley's marrying did not in the least subside. She could see nothing but evil in it. It would be a great disappointment to Mr. John Knightley [Knightley's brother]; consequently to Isabella. A real injury to the children—a most mortifying change, and material loss to them all;—a very great deduction from her father's daily comfort—and, as to herself, she could not at all endure the idea of Jane Fairfax at Donwell Abbey. A Mrs. Knightley for them all to give way to!—No, Mr. Knightley must never marry. Little Henry must remain the heir of Donwell [chap. xxvi].

Self-deception could hardly be carried further, at least in a person of high intelligence and sensitivity.

Yet the effect of all this is what our tolerance for our own faults produces in our own lives. While only immature readers ever really identify with any character, losing all sense of distance and hence all chance of an artistic experience, our emotional reaction to every event concerning Emma tends to become like her own. When she feels anxiety or shame, we feel analogous emotions. Our modern awareness that such "feelings" are not identical with those we feel in our own lives in similar circumstances has tended to blind us to the fact that aesthetic form can be built out of patterned emotions as well as out of other materials. It is absurd to pretend that because our emotions and desires in responding to fiction are in a very real sense disinterested, they do not or should not exist. Jane Austen, in developing the sustained use of a sympathetic inside view, has mastered one of the most successful of all devices for inducing a parallel emotional response between the deficient heroine and the reader.

Sympathy for Emma can be heightened by withholding inside views of others as well as by granting them of her. The author knew, for example, that it would be fatal to grant any extended inside view of Jane Fairfax. The inadequacies of impressionistic criticism are nowhere revealed more clearly than in the suggestion often made about such minor characters that their authors would have liked to make them vivid but didn't know how.[5] Jane Austen knew perfectly well how to make such a character vivid; Anne in *Persuasion* is a kind of Jane Fairfax turned into heroine. But in *Emma,* Emma must shine supreme. It is not only that the slightest glance inside Jane's mind would be fatal to all of the author's plans for mystification about Frank Churchill, though this is important. The major problem is that any extended view of her would reveal her as a more sympathetic person than Emma herself. Jane is superior to Emma in most respects except the stroke of good fortune that made Emma the heroine of the book. In matters of taste and ability, of head and of heart, she is Emma's superior, and Jane Austen, always in danger of losing our sympathy for Emma, cannot risk any degree of distraction. Jane could, it is true, be granted fewer virtues, and *then* made more

[5] A. C. Bradley, for example, once argued that Jane Austen intended Jane Fairfax to be as interesting throughout as she becomes at the end, but "the moralist in Jane Austen stood for once in her way. The secret engagement is, for her, so serious an offence, that she is afraid to win our hearts for Jane until it has led to great unhappiness" ("Jane Austen," in *Essays and Studies, by Members of the English Association,* II [Oxford, 1911], 23).

vivid. But to do so would greatly weaken the force of Emma's mistakes of heart and head in her treatment of the almost faultless Jane.

Control of Judgment

But the very effectiveness of the rhetoric designed to produce sympathy might in itself lead to a serious misreading of the book. In reducing the emotional distance, the natural tendency is to reduce—willy-nilly—moral and intellectual distance as well. In reacting to Emma's faults from the inside out, as if they were our own, we may very well not only forgive them but overlook them.[6]

There is, of course, no danger that readers who persist to the end will overlook Emma's serious mistakes; since she sees and reports those mistakes herself, everything becomes crystal clear at the end. The real danger inherent in the experiment is that readers will overlook the mistakes as they are committed and thus miss much of the comedy that depends on Emma's distorted view from page to page. If readers who dislike Emma cannot enjoy the preparation for the marriage to Knightley, readers who do not recognize her faults with absolute precision cannot enjoy the details of the preparation for the comic abasement which must precede that marriage.

It might be argued that there is no real problem, since the conventions of her time allowed for reliable commentary when-

[6] I know of only one full-scale attempt to deal with the "tension between sympathy and judgment" in modern literature, Robert Langbaum's *The Poetry of Experience* (London, 1957). Langbaum argues that in the dramatic monologue, with which he is primarily concerned, the sympathy engendered by the direct portrayal of internal experience leads the reader to suspend his moral judgment. Thus, in reading Browning's portraits of moral degeneration—e.g., the duke in "My Last Duchess" or the monk in "Soliloquy of a Spanish Cloister"—our moral judgment is overwhelmed "because we prefer to participate in the duke's power and freedom, in his hard core of character fiercely loyal to itself. Moral judgment is in fact important as the thing to be suspended, as a measure of the price we pay for the privilege of appreciating to the full this extraordinary man" (p. 83). While I think that Langbaum seriously underplays the extent to which moral judgment remains even after psychological vividness has done its work, and while he perhaps defines "morality" too narrowly when he excludes from it such things as power and freedom and fierce loyalty to one's own character, his book is a stimulating introduction to the problems raised by internal portraiture of flawed characters.

ever it was needed to place Emma's faults precisely. But Jane Austen is not operating according to the conventions, most of which she had long since parodied and outgrown; her technique is determined by the needs of the novel she is writing. We can see this clearly by contrasting the manner of *Emma* with that of *Persuasion,* the next, and last-completed, work. In *Emma* there are many breaks in the point of view, because Emma's beclouded mind cannot do the whole job. In *Persuasion,* where the heroine's viewpoint is faulty only in her ignorance of Captain Wentworth's love, there are very few. Anne Elliot's consciousness is sufficient, as Emma's is not, for most of the needs of the novel which she dominates. Once the ethical and intellectual framework has been established by the narrator's introduction, we enter Anne's consciousness and remain bound to it much more rigorously than we are bound to Emma's. It is still true that whenever something must be shown that Anne's consciousness cannot show, we move to another center; but since her consciousness can do much more for us than Emma's, there need be few departures from it.

The most notable shift for rhetorical purposes in *Persuasion* comes fairly early. When Anne first meets Captain Wentworth after their years of separation that follow her refusal to marry him, she is convinced that he is indifferent. The major movement of *Persuasion* is toward her final discovery that he still loves her; *her* suspense is thus strong and inevitable from the beginning. The reader, however, is likely to believe that Wentworth is still interested. All the conventions of art favor such a belief: the emphasis is clearly on Anne and her unhappiness; the lover has returned; we have only to wait, perhaps with some tedium, for the inevitable outcome. Anne learns (chap. vii) that he has spoken of her as so altered "he should not have known her again!" "These were words which could not but dwell with her. Yet she soon began to rejoice that she had heard them. They were of sobering tendency; they allayed agitation; they composed, and consequently must make her happier." And suddenly we enter Wentworth's mind for one time only: "Frederick Wentworth had used such words, or something like them, but without an idea that they would be carried round to her. He had thought her wretchedly altered, and, in the first moment of appeal, had spoken as he felt. He had not forgiven Anne Elliot. She had used him ill"—and so he goes on, for five more paragraphs. The necessary point, the fact that Frederick believes himself to be indifferent, has been made, and it could not have been made without some kind of shift from Anne's consciousness.

At the end of the novel, we learn that Wentworth was himself deceived in this momentary inside view: "He had meant to forget her, and believed it to be done. He had imagined himself indifferent, when he had only been angry." We may want to protest against the earlier suppression as unfair, but we can hardly believe it to be what Miss Lascelles calls "an oversight." [7] It is deliberate manipulation of inside views in order to destroy our conventional security. We are thus made ready to go along with Anne in her long and painful road to the discovery that Frederick loves her after all.

The only other important breaks in the angle of vision of *Persuasion* come at the beginning and at the end. Chapter one is an excellent example of how a skilful novelist can, by the use of his own direct voice, accomplish in a few pages what even the best novelist must take chapters to do if he uses nothing but dramatized action. Again at the conclusion the author enters with a resounding reaffirmation that the Wentworth-Elliot marriage is as good a thing as we have felt it to be from the beginning.

> Who can be in doubt of what followed? When any two young people take it into their heads to marry, they are pretty sure by perseverance to carry their point, be they ever so poor, or ever so imprudent, or ever so little likely to be necessary to each other's ultimate comfort. This may be bad morality to conclude with, but I believe it to be truth; and if such parties succeed, how should a Captain Wentworth and an Anne Elliot, with the advantage of maturity of mind, consciousness of right, and one independent fortune between them, fail of bearing down every opposition? [8]

[7] *Jane Austen and Her Art* (Oxford, 1939), p. 204.

[8] It seems to be difficult for some modern critics, accustomed to ferreting values out from an impersonal or ironic context without the aid of the author's voice, to make use of reliable commentary like this when it is provided. Even a highly perceptive reader like Mark Schorer, for example, finds himself doing unnecessary acrobatics with the question of style, and particularly metaphor, as clues to the norms against which the author judges her characters. In reading *Persuasion,* he finds these clues among the metaphors "from commerce and property, the counting house and the inherited estate" with which it abounds ("Fiction and the Matrix of Analogy," *Kenyon Review* [Autumn, 1949], p. 540). No one would deny

Except for these few intrusions and one in chapter xix, Anne's own mind is sufficient in *Persuasion,* but we can never rely completely on Emma. It is hardly surprising that Jane Austen has provided many correctives to insure our placing her errors with precision.

The chief corrective is Knightley. His commentary on Emma's errors is a natural expression of his love; he can tell the reader and Emma at the same time precisely how she is mistaken. Thus, nothing Knightley says can be beside the point. Each affirmation of a value, each accusation of error is in itself an action in the plot. When he rebukes Emma for manipulating Harriet, when he attacks her for superficiality and false pride, when he condemns her for gossiping and flirting with Frank Churchill, and finally when he attacks her for being "insolent" and "unfeeling" in her treatment of Miss Bates, we have Jane Austen's judgment on Emma, rendered dramatically. But it has come from someone who is essentially sympathetic toward Emma, so that his judgments against her are presumed to be temporary. His sympathy reinforces ours even as he criticizes, and her respect for his opinion, shown in her self-abasement after he has criticized, is one of our main reasons for expecting her to reform.

If Henry James had tried to write a novel about Emma, and had cogitated at length on the problem of getting her story told dramatically, he could not have done better than this. It is possible, of course, to think of *Emma* without Knightley as *raison-*

that the novel is packed with such metaphors, although Schorer is somewhat over-ingenious in marshaling to his cause certain dead metaphors that Austen could not have avoided without awkward circumlocution (esp. p. 542). But the crucial question surely is: What precisely are these metaphors of the countinghouse doing in the novel? *Whose* values are they supposed to reveal? Accustomed to reading modern fiction in which the novelist very likely provides no direct assistance in answering this question, Schorer leaves it really unanswered; at times he seems almost to imply that Jane Austen is unconsciously giving herself away in her use of them (e.g., p. 543).

But the novel is really very clear about it all. The introduction, coming directly from the wholly reliable narrator, establishes unequivocally and without "analogy" the conflict between the world of the Elliots, depending for its values on selfishness, stupidity, and pride—and the world of Anne, a world where "elegance of mind and sweetness of character" are the supreme values. The commercial values stressed by Schorer are only a selection from what is actually a rich group of evils. And Anne's own expressed views again and again provide direct guidance to the reader.

neur, just as it is possible to think of *The Golden Bowl,* say, without the Assinghams as *ficelles* to reflect something not seen by the Prince or Princess. But Knightley, though he receives less independent space than the Assinghams and is almost never seen in an inside view, is clearly more useful for Jane Austen's purposes than any realistically limited *ficelle* could possibly be. By combining the role of commentator with the role of hero, Jane Austen has worked more economically than James, and though economy is as dangerous as any other criterion when applied universally, even James might have profited from a closer study of the economies that a character like Knightley can be made to achieve. It is as if James had dared to make one of the four main characters, say the Prince, into a thoroughly good, wise, perceptive man, a thoroughly clear rather than a partly confused "reflector."

Since Knightley is established early as completely reliable, we need no views of his secret thoughts. He has no secret thoughts, except for the unacknowledged depths of his love for Emma and his jealousy of Frank Churchill. The other main characters have more to hide, and Jane Austen moves in and out of minds with great freedom, choosing for her own purposes what to reveal and what to withhold. Always the seeming violation of consistency is in the consistent service of the particular needs of Emma's story. Sometimes a shift is made simply to direct our suspense, as when Mrs. Weston suggests a possible union of Emma and Frank Churchill, at the end of her conversation with Knightley about the harmful effects of Emma's friendship with Harriet (chap. v). "Part of her meaning was to conceal some favourite thoughts of her own and Mr. Weston's on the subject, as much as possible. There were wishes at Randalls respecting Emma's destiny, but it was not desirable to have them suspected."

One objection to this selective dipping into whatever mind best serves our immediate purposes is that it suggests mere trickery and inevitably spoils the illusion of reality. If Jane Austen can tell us what Mrs. Weston is thinking, why not what Frank Churchill and Jane Fairfax are thinking? Obviously, because she chooses to build a mystery, and to do so she must refuse, arbitrarily and obtrusively, to grant the privilege of an inside view to characters whose minds would reveal too much. But is not the mystery purchased at the price of shaking the reader's faith in Jane Austen's integrity? If she simply withholds until later what she might as well relate now—if her procedure is not dictated by the very nature of her materials—why should we take her seriously?

If a natural surface were required in all fiction, then this objection would hold. But if we want to read *Emma* in its own terms, the real question about these shifts cannot be answered by an easy appeal to general principles. Every author withholds until later what he "might as well" relate now. The question is always one of desired effects, and the choice of any one effect always bans innumerable other effects. There is, indeed, a question to be raised about the use of mystery in *Emma,* but the conflict is not between an abstract end that Jane Austen never worried about and a shoddy mystification that she allowed to betray her. The conflict is between two effects both of which she cares about a good deal. On the one hand she cares about maintaining some sense of mystery as long as she can. On the other, she works at all points to heighten the reader's sense of dramatic irony, usually in the form of a contrast between what Emma knows and what the reader knows.

As in most novels, whatever steps are taken to mystify inevitably decrease the dramatic irony, and, whenever dramatic irony is increased by telling the reader secrets the characters have not yet suspected, mystery is inevitably destroyed. The longer we are in doubt about Frank Churchill, the weaker our sense of ironic contrast between Emma's views and the truth. The sooner we see through Frank Churchill's secret plot, the greater our pleasure in observing Emma's innumerable misreadings of his behavior and the less interest we have in the mere mystery of the situation. And we all find that on second reading we discover new intensities of dramatic irony resulting from the complete loss of mystery; knowing what abysses of error Emma is preparing for herself, even those of us who may on first reading have deciphered nearly all the details of the Churchill mystery find additional ironies.

But it is obvious that these ironies could have been offered even on a first reading, if Jane Austen had been willing to sacrifice her mystery. A single phrase in her own name—"his secret engagement to Jane Fairfax"—or a short inside view of either of the lovers could have made us aware of every ironic touch.

The author must, then, choose whether to purchase mystery at the expense of irony. For many of us Jane Austen's choice here is perhaps the weakest aspect of this novel. It is a commonplace of our criticism that significant literature arouses suspense not about the "what" but about the "how." Mere mystification has been mastered by so many second-rate writers that her efforts at mystification seem second-rate.

But again we must ask whether criticism can be conducted effectively by balancing one abstract quality against another. Is there a norm of dramatic irony for all works, or even for all works of a given kind? Has anyone ever formulated a "law of first and second readings" that will tell us just how many of our pleasures on page one should depend on our knowledge of what happens on page the last? We quite properly ask that the books we call great be able to stand up under repeated reading, but we need not ask that they yield identical pleasures on each reading. The modern works whose authors pride themselves on the fact that they can never be read but only re-read may be very good indeed, but they are not *made* good by the fact that their secret pleasures can only be wrested from them by repeated readings.

In any case, even if one accepted the criticism of Jane Austen's efforts at mystification, the larger service of the inside views is clear: the crosslights thrown by other minds prevent our being blinded by Emma's radiance.

The Reliable Narrator and the Norms of "Emma"

If mere intellectual clarity about Emma were the goal in this work, we should be forced to say that the manipulation of inside views and the extensive commentary of the reliable Knightley are more than is necessary. But for maximum intensity of the comedy and romance, even these are not enough. The "author herself"—not necessarily the real Jane Austen but an implied author, represented in this book by a reliable narrator—heightens the effects by directing our intellectual, moral, and emotional progress. She performs, of course, most of the functions described in chapter

vii. But her most important role is to reinforce both aspects of the double vision that operates throughout the book: our inside view of Emma's worth and our objective view of her great faults.

The narrator opens *Emma* with a masterful simultaneous presentation of Emma and of the values against which she must be judged: "Emma Woodhouse, handsome, clever, and rich, with a comfortable home and happy disposition, seemed to unite some of the best blessings of existence; and had lived nearly twenty-one years in the world with very little to distress or vex her." This "seemed" is immediately reinforced by more directly stated reservations. "The real evils of Emma's situation were the power of having rather too much her own way, and a disposition to think a little too well of herself; these were the disadvantages which threatened alloy to her many enjoyments. The danger, however, was at present so unperceived, that they did not by any means rank as misfortunes with her."

None of this could have been said by Emma, and if shown through her consciousness, it could not be accepted, as it must be, without question. Like most of the first three chapters, it is non-dramatic summary, building up, through the ostensible business of getting the characters introduced, to Emma's initial blunder with Harriet and Mr. Elton. Throughout these chapters, we learn much of what we must know from the narrator, but she turns over more and more of the job of summary to Emma as she feels more and more sure of our seeing precisely to what degree Emma is to be trusted. Whenever we leave the "real evils" we have been warned against in Emma, the narrator's and Emma's views coincide: we cannot tell which of them, for example, offers the judgment on Mr. Woodhouse that "his talents could not have recommended him at any time," or the judgment on Mr. Knightley that he is "a sensible man," "always welcome" at Hartfield, or even that "Mr. Knightley, in fact, was one of the few people who could see faults in Emma Woodhouse, and the only one who ever told her of them."

But there are times when Emma and her author are far apart, and the author's direct guidance aids the reader in his own break with Emma. The beautiful irony of the first description of Harriet, given through Emma's eyes (chap. iii) could no doubt be grasped intellectually by many readers without all of the preliminary commentary. But even for the most perceptive its effect is heightened, surely, by the sense of standing with the author and observing with her precisely how Emma's judgment is going astray. Perhaps more important, we ordinary, less perceptive readers have by now been raised to a level suited to grasp the ironies. Certainly, most readers would overlook some of the barbs directed against Emma if the novel began, as a serious modern novelist might well begin it, with this description:

> [Emma] was not struck by any thing remarkably clever in Miss Smith's conversation, but she found her altogether very engaging—not inconveniently shy, not unwilling to talk—and yet so far from pushing, shewing so proper and becoming a deference, seeming so pleasantly grateful for being admitted to Hartfield, and so artlessly impressed by the appearance of every thing in so superior a style to what she had been used to, that she must have good sense and deserve encouragement. Encouragement should be given. Those soft blue eyes . . . should not be wasted on the inferior society of Highbury. . . .

And so Emma goes on, giving herself away with every word, pouring out her sense of her own beneficence and general value. Harriet's past friends, "though very good sort of people, must be doing her harm." Without knowing them, Emma knows that they "must be coarse and unpolished, and very unfit to be the intimates of a girl who wanted only a little more knowledge and elegance to be quite perfect." And she concludes with a beautiful burst of egotism: "*She* would notice her; she would improve her; she would detach her from her bad acquaintance, and introduce her into good society; she would form her opinions and her manners. It would be an interesting, and certainly a very kind undertaking; highly becoming her own situation in life, her leisure, and powers." Even the most skilful reader might not easily plot an absolutely true course through these ironies without the prior direct assistance we have been given. Emma's views are not so outlandish that they could never have been held by a female novelist writing in her time. They cannot serve effectively as signs of *her* character unless they are clearly disavowed as signs of Jane Austen's views. Emma's unconscious catalogue of her egotistical uses for Harriet, given under the pretense of listing the services *she* will perform, is thus given its full force by being framed explicitly in a world of values which Emma herself cannot discover until the conclusion of the book.

The full importance of the author's direct imposition of an elaborate scale of norms can be seen by considering that conclusion. The sequence of events is a simple one: Emma's faults and mistakes are brought home to her in a rapid and humiliating chain of rebukes from Knightley and blows from hard fact. These blows to her self-esteem produce at last a genuine reform (for example, she brings herself to apologize to Miss Bates, something she could never have done earlier in the novel). The change in her character removes the only obstacle in the way of Knightley's proposal, and the marriage follows. "The wishes, the hopes, the confidence, the predictions of the small band of true friends who witnessed the ceremony, were fully answered in the perfect happiness of the union."

It may be that if we look at Emma and Knightley as real people, this ending will seem false. G. B. Stern laments, in *Speaking of Jane Austen,* "Oh, Miss Austen, it was *not* a good solution; it was a bad solution, an unhappy ending, could we see beyond the last pages of the book." Edmund Wilson predicts that Emma will find a new protégée like Harriet, since she has not been cured of her inclination to "infatuations with women." Marvin Mudrick even more emphatically rejects Jane Austen's explicit rhetoric; he believes that Emma is still a "confirmed exploiter," and for him the ending must be read as ironic.[9]

But it is precisely because this ending is neither life itself nor a simple bit of literary irony that it can serve so well to heighten our sense of a complete and indeed perfect resolution to all that has gone before. If we look at the values that have been realized in this marriage and compare them with those realized in conventional marriage plots, we see that Jane Austen means what she says: this will be a happy marriage because there is simply nothing left to make it anything less than perfectly happy. It fulfils every value embodied in the world of the book—with the possible exception that Emma may never learn to apply herself as she ought to her reading and her piano! It is a union of intelligence:

[9] The first two quotations are from Wilson's "A Long Talk about Jane Austen," *A Literary Chronicle: 1920–1950* (New York, 1952). The third is from *Jane Austen,* p. 206.

of "reason," of "sense," of "judgment." It is a union of virtue: of "good will," of generosity, of unselfishness. It is a union of feeling: of "taste," "tenderness," "love," "beauty,"[10]

In a general way, then, this plot offers us an experience superficially like that offered by most tragicomedy as well as by much of the cheapest popular art: we are made to desire certain good things for certain good characters, and then our desires are gratified. If we depended on general criteria derived from our justified boredom with such works, we should reject this one. But the critical difference lies in the precise quality of the values appealed to and the precise quality of the characters who violate or realize them. All of the cheap marriage plots in the world should not lead us to be embarrassed about our pleasure in Emma and Knightley's marriage. It is more than just the marriage: it is the *rightness* of *this* marriage, as a conclusion to all of the comic wrongness that has gone before. The good for Emma includes both her necessary reform and the resulting marriage. Marriage to an intelligent, amiable, good, and attractive man is the best thing that can happen to this heroine, and the readers who do not experience it as such are, I am convinced, far from knowing what Jane Austen is about—whatever they may say about the "bitter spinster's" attitude toward marriage.

Our modern sensibilities are likely to be rasped by any such formulation. We do not ordinarily like to encounter perfect endings in our novels—even in the sense of "perfectedness" or completion, the sense obviously intended by Jane Austen. We refuse to accept it when we see it: witness the many attempts to deny Dostoevski's success with Alyosha and Father Zossima in *The Brothers Karamazov*. Many of us find it embarrassing to talk of emotions based on moral judgment at all, particularly when the emotions have any kind of affirmative cast. Emma herself is some-

[10] It has lately been fashionable to underplay the value of tenderness and good will in Jane Austen, in reaction to an earlier generation that overdid the picture of "gentle Jane." The trend seems to have begun in earnest with D. W. Harding's "Regulated Hatred: An Aspect of the Work of Jane Austen," *Scrutiny*, VIII (March 1940), 346–62. While I do not feel as strongly aroused against this school of readers as does R. W. Chapman (see his *A Critical Bibliography*, p. 52, and his review of Mudrick's work in the *T.L.S.* [September 19, 1952]), it seems to me that another swing of the pendulum is called for: when Jane Austen praises the "relenting heart," she means that praise, though she is the same author who can lash the unrelenting heart with "regulated hatred."

thing of a "modern" in this regard throughout most of the book. Her self-deception about marriage is as great as about most other important matters. Emma boasts to Harriet of her indifference to marriage, at the same time unconsciously betraying her totally inadequate view of the sources of human happiness.

> If I know myself, Harriet, mine is an active, busy mind, with a great many independent resources; and I do not perceive why I should be more in want of employment at forty or fifty than one-and-twenty. Woman's usual occupations of eye and hand and mind will be as open to me then, as they are now; or with no important variation. If I draw less, I shall read more; if I give up music, I shall take to carpet-work.

Emma at carpet-work! If she knows herself indeed.

> And as for objects of interest, objects for the affections, which is, in truth, the great point of inferiority, the want of which is really the great evil to be avoided in *not* marrying [a magnificent concession, this] I shall be very well off, with all the children of a sister I love so much, to care about. There will be enough of them, in all probability, to supply every sort of sensation that declining life can need. There will be enough for every hope and every fear; and though my attachment to none can equal that of a parent, it suits my ideas of comfort better than what is warmer and blinder. My nephews and nieces!—I shall often have a niece with me [chap. x].

Without growing solemn about it—it is wonderfully comic—we can recognize that the humor springs here from very deep sources indeed. It can be fully enjoyed, in fact, only by the reader who has attained to a vision of human felicity far more profound than Emma's "comfort" and "want" and "need." It is a vision that includes not simply marriage, but a kind of loving converse not based, as is Emma's here, on whether the "loved" person will serve one's irreducible needs.

The comic effect of this repudiation of marriage is considerably increased by the fact that Emma always thinks of marriage for others as *their* highest good, and in fact unconsciously encourages her friend Harriet to fall in love with the very man she herself loves without knowing it. The delightful denouement is thus what we want not only because it is a supremely good thing for Emma, but because it is a supremely comic outcome of Emma's profound misunderstanding of herself and of the human condition. In the schematic language of chapter v, it satisfies both our practical desire for Emma's well-being and our appetite for the qualities proper to these artistic materials. It is thus a more resounding resolution than either of these elements separately could provide. The other major resolution of the work—Harriet's marriage with her farmer—reinforces this interpretation. Emma's sin against Harriet has been something far worse than the mere meddling of a busybody. To destroy Harriet's chances for happiness—chances that depend entirely on her marriage—is as close to viciousness as any author could dare to take a heroine designed to be loved. We can laugh with Emma at this mistake (chap. liv) only because Harriet's chance for happiness is restored.

Other values, like money, blood, and "consequence," are real enough in *Emma,* but only as they contribute to or are mastered by good taste, good judgment, and good morality. Money alone can make a Mrs. Churchill, but a man or woman "is silly to marry without it." Consequence untouched by sense can make a very inconsequential Mr. Woodhouse; untouched by sense or virtue it can make the much more contemptible Mr. and Miss Elliot of *Persuasion.* But it is a pleasant thing to have, and it does no harm unless, like the early Emma, one takes it too seriously. Charm and elegance without sufficient moral force can make a Frank Churchill; unschooled by morality it can lead to the baseness of Henry Crawford in *Mansfield Park* or of Wickham in *Pride and Prejudice.* Even the supreme virtues are inadequate in isolation: good will alone will make a comic Miss Bates or a Mr. Weston, judgment with insufficient good will a comic Mr. John Knightley, and so on.

I am willing to risk the commonplace in such a listing because it is only thus that the full force of Jane Austen's comprehensive view can be seen. There is clearly at work here a much more detailed ordering of values than any conventional public philosophy of her time could provide. Obviously, few readers in her own time, and far fewer in our own, have ever approached this novel in full and detailed agreement with the author's norms. But they were led to join her as they read, and so are we.

Explicit Judgments on Emma Woodhouse

We have said in passing almost enough of the other side of the coin—the judgment of particular actions as they relate to the general norms. But something must be said of the detailed "placing" of Emma, by direct commentary, in the hierarchy of values established by the novel. I must be convinced, for example, not only that tenderness for other people's feelings is an important trait but also that Emma's particular behavior violates the true standards of tenderness, if I am to savor to the full the episode of Emma's insult to Miss Bates and Knightley's reproach which follows. If I refuse to blame Emma, I may discover a kind of intellectual enjoyment in the episode, and I will probably think that any critic who talks of "belief" in tenderness as operating in such a context is taking things too seriously. But I can never enjoy the episode in its full intensity or grasp its formal coherence. Similarly, I must agree not only that to be dreadfully boring is a minor fault compared with the major virtue of "good will," but also that Miss Bates's exemplification of this fault and of this virtue entitle her to the respect which Emma denies. If I do not—while yet being able to laugh at Miss Bates—I can hardly understand, let alone enjoy, Emma's mistreatment of her.

But these negative judgments must be counteracted by a larger approval, and, as we would expect, the novel is full of direct apologies for Emma. Her chief fault, lack of good will or tenderness, must be read not only in relationship to the code of values provided by the book as a whole—a code which judges her as seriously deficient; it must also be judged in relationship to the harsh facts of the world around her, a world made up of human beings ranging in degree of selfishness and egotism from Knightley, who lapses from perfection when he tries to judge Frank Churchill, his rival, down to Mrs. Elton, who has most of Emma's faults and none of her virtues. In such a setting, Emma is easily forgiven. When she insults Miss Bates, for example, we remember that Miss Bates lives in a world where many others are insensitive and cruel. "Miss Bates, neither young, handsome, rich, nor married, stood in the very worst predicament in the world for having much of the public favour; and she had no intellectual superiority to make atonement to herself, or frighten those who might hate her, into outward respect." While it would be a mistake to see only this "regulated hatred" in Jane Austen's world, overlooking the tenderness and generosity, the hatred of viciousness is there, and there is enough vice in evidence to make Emma almost shine by comparison.

Often, Jane Austen makes this apology-by-comparison explicit. When Emma lies to Knightley about Harriet, very close to the end of the book, she is excused with a generalization about human nature: "Seldom, very seldom, does complete truth belong to any human disclosure; seldom can it happen that something is not a little disguised, or a little mistaken; but where, as in this case, though the conduct is mistaken, the feelings are not, it may not be very material.—Mr. Knightley could not impute to Emma a more relenting heart than she possessed, or a heart more disposed to accept of his."

The Implied Author as Friend and Guide

With all of this said about the masterful use of the narrator in *Emma,* there remain some "intrusions" unaccounted for by strict service to the story itself. "What did she say?" the narrator asks, at the crucial moment in the major love scene. "Just what she ought, of course. A lady always does.—She said enough to show there need not be despair—and to invite him to say more himself." To some readers this has seemed to demonstrate the author's inability to write a love scene, since it sacrifices "the illusion of reality." [11] But who has ever read this far in *Emma* under the delusion that he is reading a realistic portrayal which is suddenly shattered by the unnatural appearance of the narrator? If the narrator's superabundant wit is destructive of the kind of illusion proper to this work, the novel has been ruined long before.

But we should now be in a position to see precisely why the narrator's wit is not in the least out of place at the emotional climax of the novel. We have seen how the inside views of the characters and the author's commentary have been used from the

[11] Edd Winfield Parks, "Exegesis in Austen's Novels," *The South Atlantic Quarterly,* LI (January, 1952), 117.

beginning to get the values straight and to keep them straight and to help direct our reactions to Emma. But we also see here a beautiful case of the dramatized author as friend and guide. "Jane Austen," like "Henry Fielding," is a paragon of wit, wisdom, and virtue. She does not talk about her qualities; unlike Fielding she does not in *Emma* call direct attention to her artistic skill. But we are seldom allowed to forget about her for all that. When we read this novel we accept her as representing everything we admire most. She is as generous and wise as Knightley; in fact, she is a shade more penetrating in her judgment. She is as subtle and witty as Emma would like to think herself. Without being sentimental she is in favor of tenderness. She is able to put an adequate but not excessive value on wealth and rank. She recognizes a fool when she sees one, but unlike Emma she knows that it is both immoral and foolish to be rude to fools. She is, in short, a perfect human being, within the concept of perfection established by the book she writes; she even recognizes that human perfection of the kind *she* exemplifies is not quite attainable in real life. The process of her domination is of course circular; her character establishes the values for us according to which her character is then found to be perfect. But this circularity does not affect the success of her endeavor; in fact it insures it.

Her "omniscience" is thus a much more remarkable thing than is ordinarily implied by the term. All good novelists know all about their characters—all that they need to know. And the question of how their narrators are to find out all that *they* need to know, the question of "authority," is a relatively simple one. The real choice is much more profound than this would imply. It is a choice of the moral, not merely the technical, angle of vision from which the story is to be told.

Unlike the central intelligences of James and his successors, "Jane Austen" has learned nothing at the end of the novel that she did not know at the beginning. She needed to learn nothing. She knew everything of importance already. We have been privileged to watch with her as she observes her favorite character climb from a considerably lower platform to join the exalted company of Knightley, "Jane Austen," and those of us readers who are wise enough, good enough, and perceptive enough to belong up there too. As Katherine Mansfield says, "the truth is that every true admirer of the novels cherishes the happy thought that he alone —reading between the lines—has become the secret friend of their author." [12] Those who love "gentle Jane" as a secret friend may undervalue the irony and wit; those who see her in effect as the greatest of Shaw's heroines, flashing about her with the weapons of irony, may undervalue the emphasis on tenderness and good will. But only a very few can resist her.

The dramatic illusion of her presence as a character is thus fully as important as any other element in the story. When she intrudes, the illusion is not shattered. The only illusion we care about, the illusion of traveling intimately with a hardy little band of readers whose heads are screwed on tight and whose hearts are in the right place, is actually strengthened when we are refused the romantic love scene. Like the author herself, we don't care about the love scene. We can find love scenes in almost any novelist's works, but only here can we find a mind and heart that can give us clarity without oversimplification, sympathy and romance without sentimentality, and biting irony without cynicism.

[12] *Novels and Novelists,* ed. J. Middleton Murry (London, 1930), p. 304.

Robert Browning's *My Last Duchess*

ROBERT LANGBAUM

[THE TERM *dramatic monologue* accurately describes the genre of poetry exemplified by *My Last Duchess*. The poem is "dramatic" in the sense that a little scene is acted out before us, without any narrative or commentary by the author. But this kind of poetry differs from drama in that instead of dialogue we get a monologue—a single person speaking from beginning to end of the poem. There are other "actors" in the poem, listening and reacting to the speaker, but we never hear their voices. Sometimes we can infer what the audience in the poem must have said or done in response to the speaker, but we can only deduce that interaction because we do not actually hear what the other actors say and we do not actually see what they do. When well managed, this kind of poem can be immensely satisfying, not only because of the story that has been told dramatically and economically but because of the deep insights we get into the character of the speaker.

One of the classic examples of the dramatic monologue is Robert Browning's *My Last Duchess*. This poem is a perfectly executed instance of the genre, and it presents us with one of the most fascinating characters in English literature—the proud, arrogant, self-satisfied duke, who while displaying and commenting on the portrait of his deceased wife, whose death he probably caused, is trying to impress an envoy from his prospective bride. In this rhetorical analysis, Robert Langbaum shows us how Browning managed to create and reconcile the tension between our fascination with the duke and our moral judgment on his past and present actions. Everything we know about the story and about the characters involved we have learned through the speech of a single man; nevertheless, through skillful selection and disposition of details, Browning is manipulating our emotional and moral response to what we hear. We respond in the way that Browning intended us to respond.]

When we have said all the objective things about Browning's *My Last Duchess,* we will not have arrived at the meaning until we point out what can only be substantiated by an appeal to effect—that moral judgment does not figure importantly in our response to the duke, that we even identify ourselves with him. But how is such an effect produced in a poem about a cruel Italian duke of the Renaissance who out of unreasonable jealousy has had his last duchess put to death, and is now about to contract a second marriage for the sake of dowry? Certainly, no summary or paraphrase would indicate that condemnation is not our principal response. The difference must be laid to form, to that extra quantity which makes the difference in artistic discourse between content and meaning.

The objective fact that the poem is made up entirely of the duke's utterance has of course much to do with the final meaning, and it is important to say that the poem is in form a monologue. But much more remains to be said about the way in which the content is laid out, before we can come near accounting for the whole meaning. It is important that the duke tells the story of his kind and generous last duchess to, of all people, the envoy from his prospective duchess. It is important that he tells his story while showing off to the envoy the artistic merits of a portrait of the last duchess. It is above all important that the duke carries off his outrageous indiscretion, proceeding triumphantly in the end downstairs to conclude arrangements for the dowry. All this is important not only as content but also as form, because it establishes a relation between the duke on the one hand, and the portrait and the envoy on the other, which determines the reader's relation to the duke and therefore to the poem—which determines, in other words, the poem's meaning.

The utter outrageousness of the duke's behaviour makes condemnation the least interesting response, certainly not the response that can account for the poem's success. What interests us more than the duke's wickedness is his immense attractiveness. His conviction of matchless superiority, his intelligence and bland amorality, his poise, his taste for art, his manners—high-handed aristocratic manners that break the ordinary rules and assert the duke's superiority when he is being most solicitous of the envoy, waiving their difference of rank ("Nay, we'll go / Together down, sir"); these qualities overwhelm the envoy, causing him apparently to suspend judgment of the duke, for he raises no demur. The reader is no less overwhelmed. We suspend moral judgment because we prefer to participate in the duke's power and freedom, in his hard core of character fiercely loyal to itself. Moral judgment is in fact important as the thing to be suspended, as a measure of the price we pay for the privilege of appreciating to the full this extraordinary man.

It is because the duke determines the arrangement and relative subordination of the parts that the poem means what it does. The duchess's goodness shines through the duke's utterance; he makes no attempt to conceal it, so preoccupied is he with his own standard of judgment and so oblivious of the world's. Thus the duchess's case is subordinated to the duke's, the novelty and complexity of which engages our attention. We are busy trying to understand the man who can combine the connoisseur's pride in the lady's beauty with a pride that caused him to murder the lady rather than tell her in what way she displeased him, for in that

> would be some stooping; and I choose
> Never to stoop.

The duke's paradoxical nature is fully revealed when, having boasted how at his command the duchess's life was extinguished, he turns back to the portrait to admire of all things its lifelikeness:

> There she stands
> As if alive.

This occurs ten lines from the end, and we might suppose we have by now taken the duke's measure. But the next ten lines produce a series of shocks that outstrip each time our understanding of the duke, and keep us panting after revelation with no opportunity to consolidate our impression of him for moral judgment. For it is at this point that we learn to whom he has been talking; and he goes on to talk about dowry, even allowing himself to murmur the hypocritical assurance that the new bride's self and not the dowry is of course his object. It seems to me that one side of the duke's nature is here stretched as far as it will go; the dazzling figure threatens to decline into paltriness admitting moral judgment, when Browning retrieves it with two brilliant strokes. First, there is the lordly waiving of rank's privilege as the duke and the envoy are about to proceed downstairs, and then there is the perfect all-revealing gesture of the last two and a half lines when the duke stops to show off yet another object in his collection:

> Notice Neptune, though,
> Taming a sea-horse, thought a rarity,
> Which Claus of Innsbruck cast in bronze for me!

The lines bring all the parts of the poem into final combination, with just the relative values that constitute the poem's meaning. The nobleman does not hurry on his way to business, the connoisseur cannot resist showing off yet another precious object, the possessive egotist counts up his possessions even as he moves toward the acquirement of a new possession, a well-dowered bride; and most important, the last duchess is seen in final perspective. She takes her place as one of a line of objects in an art collection; her sad story becomes the *cicerone's* anecdote lending piquancy to the portrait. The duke has taken from her what he wants, her beauty, and thrown the life away; and we watch with awe as he proceeds to take what he wants from the envoy and by implication from the new duchess. He carries all before him by sheer force of will so undeflected by ordinary compunctions as even, I think, to call into question—the question rushes into place behind the startling illumination of the last lines, and lingers as the poem's haunting afternote—the duke's sanity.

The duke reveals all this about himself, grows to his full stature, because we allow him to have his way with us; we subordinate all other considerations to the business of understanding him. If we allowed indignation, or pity for the duchess, to take over when the duke moves from his account of the murder to admire the life-likeness of the portrait, the poem could hold no further surprises for us; it could not even go on to reinforce our judgment as to the duke's wickedness, since the duke does not grow in wickedness after the account of the murder. He grows in strength of character, and in the arrogance and poise which enable him to continue command of the situation after his confession of murder has threatened to turn it against him. To take the full measure of the duke's distinction we must be less concerned to condemn than to appreciate the triumphant transition by which he ignores clean out of existence any judgment of his story that the envoy might have presumed to invent. We must be concerned to appreciate the exquisite timing of the duke's delay over Neptune, to appreciate its fidelity to the duke's own inner rhythm as he tries once more the envoy's already sorely tried patience, and as he teases the reader too by delaying for a lordly whim the poem's conclusion. This willingness of the reader to understand the duke, even to sympathize with him as a necessary condition of reading the poem, is the key to the poem's form. It alone is responsible for a meaning not inherent in the content itself but determined peculiarly by the treatment.

I have chosen *My Last Duchess* to illustrate the working of sympathy, just because the duke's egregious villainy makes especially apparent the split between moral judgment and our actual feeling for him. The poem carries to the limit an effect peculiarly the genius of the dramatic monologue—I mean the effect created by the tension between sympathy and moral judgment. Although we seldom meet again such an unmitigated villain as the duke, it is safe to say that most successful dramatic monologues deal with speakers who are in some way reprehensible.

STYLE

The Figures of Rhetoric in Spenser's *Colin Clout*

SAM MEYER

[STUDIES LIKE William G. Crane's *Wit and Rhetoric in the Renaissance* (1937), Sister Miriam Joseph's *Shakespeare's Use of the Arts of Language* (1947), and Rosemond Tuve's *Elizabethan and Metaphysical Imagery* (1947) have revealed the great amount of attention that was devoted in Renaissance schools to the study of style in general and to the figures of speech in particular. And Herbert David Rix's *Rhetoric in Spenser's Poetry* (1940) gave ample evidence that Edmund Spenser (c. 1552–1599) was thoroughly schooled in and consciously practiced the figurist tradition of Renaissance rhetoric. In the following article, Sam Meyer not only catalogues the thirty-six figures he found in the last hundred lines of *Colin Clout's Come Home Again* (1595) but, more importantly, demonstrates "the efficacy of figures in providing both the form of the material and the material itself." Without denying the aesthetic and decorative value of the figures, Mr. Meyer shows that these figures perform three distinct functions: "(1) to constitute the framework and the substance of blocks of verse, (2) to control the stylistic level, and (3) to provide emotional fervor."

Although contemporary writers still use, perhaps unconsciously for the most part, the 200 or more schemes and tropes that Renaissance schoolboys were required to learn, our schools generally have neglected a formal study of the figures. While I. A. Richards, one of the new rhetoricians, takes a rather dim view of the Renaissance preoccupation with the figures, he did admit in his *Speculative Instruments* (1955), "Some sort of systematic study of some at least of the devices of language so painstakingly labelled and arranged by these [Renaissance] logicians, rhetoricians, and figurists may still be what education chiefly lacks."]

From *Publications of the Modern Language Association,* LXXIX (June 1964), 206–18. Reprinted by permission of the Modern Language Association and the author. This essay, in a slightly altered form, will appear as Chapter 2 in Mr. Meyer's *An Interpretation of Edmund Spenser's Colin Clout* (Cork University Press, and Notre Dame University Press, 1969).

MODERN CRITICISM has given increasing recognition to the functional, as distinguished from the decorative, aspect of rhetorical figures in the poetry of the English Renaissance.[1] The continuance of this emphasis is particularly appropriate to Spenser's pastoral, *Colin Clouts Come Home Againe* (1595), where the relevance of the figures to the larger considerations of style—indeed, to the total discourse—is so cardinal. The importance of the figures is enhanced by the natural use of rhetorical arts by characters, set in a kind of *mise en scène,* whose suasory speeches largely comprise the poem. Stress of the functional side of the rhetorical elements in the poem need not deny or denigrate the role of the figures in conferring upon the verse an aura of conspicuous beauty. The office of the figures in this respect is simply another manifestation of the same taste for elegance which reflected itself in Renaissance dress, manners, ceremonial processions, and décor. The beautifying characteristics of the numerous word orders, comprised of tropes and schemes, were recognized and frankly accepted by literati of the Tudor period. In their eyes, figures possessed value as ornament by reason of their constituting departures from everyday speech patterns. The idea is conventionally phrased by Abraham Fraunce, whom many believe to be the Corydon praised in lines 383–384 of the poem: [2] "A figure is a certeine decking of speach, whereby the vsual and simple fashion therof is altered and changed to that which is more elegant and conceipted." [3]

To belletrists of the Renaissance most assuredly—and it requires some effort for us to accept this—there was no discrepancy between the functional and embellishing aspects of figures. In that favored pamphlet of the era, the *Ars Poetica* of Horace, the aims of poetry are enunciated as being to teach (*prodesse*) or to

[1] Rosemond Tuve, *Elizabethan and Metaphysical Imagery: Renaissance Poetic and Twentieth-Century Critics* (Chicago, 1947), maintains that all elements in figures of comparison assist in conveying meaning; and that classification of figures of any time would be clearer if similarities in logical nature (e.g., images of "quality" or "manner of doing") were observed. Herbert David Rix, *Rhetoric in Spenser's Poetry,* Penn. State Coll. Studies, No. 7 (State College, 1940), applies the teleological concept of the figures and other rhetorical formulae to the poetry of Spenser.

[2] *Daphnaïda and Other Poems,* ed. W. L. Renwick, An Elizabethan Gallery, No. 4 (London, 1929), p. 186; Kathrine Koller, "Abraham Fraunce and Edmund Spenser," *ELH,* VII (1940), 108.

[3] *The Arcadian Rhetorike,* ed. Ethel Seaton, Luttrell Society Reprints, No. 9 (Oxford, 1950), p. 26.

delight (*delectare*), or to do both at once. To this dictum, which is rhetorical in its conception of the poetic art, the Renaissance conjoined Cicero's third aim of oratory—to persuade or sway—and applied it to the poet. To this humanistic formulation of moving as an object of eloquence in all forms, it required, in a Christian era, little extension on the part of critics and poets to make the direction of movement specifically ethical and moral.[4] Applied to poetry, the threefold aim of oratory meant that poetry teaches through its appeal to the intellect of the reader or listener by means of its content or *doctrina;* pleases through its appeal to the aesthetic sense by means of its style, elaborated largely through figures of speech; and moves to virtuous action by means of its appeal to emotion, acting through message and mode together. Thus, delight in poetry, whether achieved by means of pleasing fables or of patterned language, was not considered by discerning men of the period to exist for its own sake; and we may be reasonably certain that to mature critics like Sidney and George Puttenham, who were also practicing poets, and to poetic craftsmen like Spenser, who was also a critic,[5] rhetorical figures would hardly be thought of as elements super-added to poetry even though they were often referred to as ornament.[6]

Of course, where taste is deficient and conception weak,

[4] See Bernard Weinberg, *A History of Literary Criticism in the Italian Renaissance* (Chicago, 1961), II, 721–724, for Daniello's view of the similarity between oratory and poetry in having for their object pleasurable teaching of exemplary morality; also pp. 737, 748, for emphasis on the same point by Minturno and Scalinger, whose *De Poeta* (1559) and *Poetices Libri Septem* (1561) respectively were prime sources for Sir Philip Sidney's *Apologie for Poetrie* (c. 1583, printed in 1595). G. Gregory Smith's notes to the *Apologie* in *Elizabethan Critical Essays* (Oxford, 1904), I, 382–403, reveal how closely Sidney, in numerous passages, echoes his Italian models.

[5] The writer of the Argument to the *October* eclogue of *The Shepheardes Calender* refers to a book of the author's called the *English Poete,* which had just recently come into his hands. In *A Discourse of English Poetrie* (1586), William Webbe expresses the wish that he might see the *English Poet,* which E. K., the author's friend, had promised to publish (*Eliz. Critical Essays,* I, 232).

[6] Father Ong's reminder that the first meaning of *ornamentum* in Latin rhetorical terminology is "equipment or accoutrements, which the 'naked causes' of dialectic, like naked persons, would need rather more than pretty clothing to get along in this world," is pertinent here. He recalls that Miss Tuve (in Ch. iv of *Elizabethan and Metaphysical Imagery*) and others have shown that the Renaissance notion of ornament "does not necessarily mean appliqué work in the way the English term ornament suggests today" (Rev. Walter J. Ong, S.J., *Ramus: Method, and the Decay of Dialogue,* Cambridge, Mass., 1958, p. 277).

abuses are inevitable. Renewed awareness of this gloomy truism doubtless prompted Henry Peacham to add a section entitled "Caution" to the discussion of each of his figures when he issued his revised edition of *The Garden of Eloquence* in 1593. Indeed, dutiful injunctions against abuse of the figures accompanied treatment of them in both ancient and Renaissance treatises. Classical authors of textbooks still used in the educational system of the sixteenth century warned, for instance, against inflated speech ("sufflata oratio"), outlandish metaphors ("verbis . . . duriter aliunde translatis") [7] and excessive reliance upon the colors of rhetoric ("magis infucata vitia").[8] That those vices of overabundant and tasteless rhetoric which the anonymous author of the *Ad Herennium* and Cicero had inveighed against were by no means absent from the Elizabethan literary scene is made evident by Sidney himself in the famous passage about Matron Eloquence being at times "with figures and flowers, extreamelie winter-starued." [9]

Sidney's strictures here allude, one must not forget, to the *improper* employment of "figures and flowers." In their proper employment, formal patterns of words, phrases, and larger elements of discourse, together with locutions accorded special meanings, could hardly exist as appliquéd ornament. On the contrary, the conception and deployment of these rhetorical devices are linked on a general plane through content and through emotional appeal with the exacting disciplines of logic and rhetoric respectively—the heart and core of formal education during the period in which Spenser lived.[10] Inasmuch as many of the fig-

[7] *Rhetorica ad Herennium* iv.10.15, Loeb Classical Library, trans. Harry Caplan (Cambridge, Mass., 1944), p. 264.

[8] Cicero, *De Oratore* iii.25.100, Loeb Classical Library, trans. H. Rackham (Cambridge, Mass., 1942), p. 80.

[9] *Apologie for Poetrie*, in *Eliz. Critical Essays*, I, 201–202. Another less famaliar but equally zestful contemporary diatribe against rhetorical affectation (which borrows its imagery directly from Cicero) is contained in a commencement oration delivered at Oxford University in 1572 by John Rainolds, a candidate for the M.A. (*Oratio in Laudem Artis Poeticae*, ed. William Ringler; trans. Walter Allen, Jr., Princeton Univ. Studies in English, No. 20, Princeton, 1940, p. 48).

[10] For a selective list of references detailing the teaching of composition through the media of the trivium in English educational institutions of the Renaissance, see Wilbur Samuel Howell, *Logic and Rhetoric in England, 1500–1700* (Princeton, 1956), n. 1, p. 64. To this list should be added Donald Lemen Clark, *John Milton at St. Paul's School: A Study of Ancient Rhetoric in English Renaissance Education* (New York, 1948).

ures, particularly those which lend themselves to amplification of matter, derive from, or are identical to, the places of rhetorical or dialectical investigation, their connection with the basic compositional arts becomes integral rather than incidental.[11] The precise way in which figures of rhetoric, especially those of comparison, are elaborated from the dialectical places is more than a matter of historical interest. This methodology and its relevance to meaning in *Colin Clout* is special and significant, but adequate treatment

[11] See William G. Crane, *Wit and Rhetoric in the Renaissance: The Formal Basis of Elizabethan Prose Style* (New York, 1937), p. 5, for a summary of the vital connection between the figures and the places. Also see p. 55 for a brief statement on the effects of the Ramist reorganization of logic and rhetoric in relation to figures. For an expanded account of the whole movement for the reform of the Aristotelian and Ciceronian system of logic and rhetoric, see Howell, *Logic and Rhetoric in England,* Ch. iv. According to Howell, by the fifteen-seventies the struggle to keep Aristotle and Cicero supreme in logic and rhetoric respectively was beginning to be lost (p. 178). The supremacy of Cicero was challenged at Cambridge University as early as 1574, the year Spenser received his B.A. degree from Pembroke College. In this year Spenser's best friend, Gabriel Harvey (Hobbinol in the poem), as praelector in rhetoric at Cambridge, began preparation of the lectures delivered in 1575–76 and published in 1577 (pp. 247–248).

Whether Spenser came to adopt the Ramist reorganization is not known, although his acquaintance with the Cambridge and Sidney circles which advocated it would make his familiarity with the reformed disciplines virtually certain. Some details concerning Spenser's place in these circles is given in Miss Koller's article on "Edmund Spenser and Abraham Fraunce." *The Lawiers Logicke* and *The Arcadian Rhetoricke,* which Fraunce, a confirmed Ramist, published at London in 1588, are liberally interspersed with illustrative passages of poetry, including some one hundred from Spenser in the former and three in the latter work. These works of Fraunce serve to demonstrate not only the extent to which Ramist books in England point up places and figures with quotations from poetry but also to show how closely proponents of the reformed program of liberal arts continue to associate rhetoric and poetry. (See also Father Ong, *Ramus,* pp. 282–283, on Ramist conceptions of the relationship between poetry and rhetoric.) If Spenser can be counted among those who embraced the new approaches, his adoption in whole or in part of the revised system would not have required any basic readjustment of ingrained habit patterns as regards composition through logical and rhetorical modes. In Ch. xii of *Elizabethan and Metaphysical Imagery,* Miss Tuve treats, under the title "Ramist Logic: Certain General Conceptions Affecting Imagery," the possible effects of the redirection of peripatetic logic on the creation of poetic images during the latter part of the sixteenth and early part of the seventeenth centuries in England. She holds the influence of Ramus to have been inescapable on the part of writers of this era (p. 339). (This conclusion is strongly fortified by Father Ong in his recent book on Ramus.) However, Miss Tuve believes this influence, whether direct or indirect, resulted, not in images with new qualities, but in images with old qualities highlighted (p. 351). The change of emphasis fostered by the Ramists would, in her view, operate to produce images more notable for logical toughness and intellectual fineness (p. 353).

of this aspect would carry us considerably beyond the bounds of the present inquiry.

The specific aim of this investigation is to exhibit and discuss the figures of rhetoric found in a single Renaissance poem. But figurative elements in an age which deferred so much to tradition can hardly be studied profitably, or even intelligibly, without reference to literary positions which supply a context for their employment. In touching on relevant aspects of these positions, I strive, for the sake of brevity, to stick to the critical high roads. What I have said thus far has been intended to provide, in highly synoptic form, a frame of reference compatible with the canons of the age in which to examine figures in *Colin Clout.* These canons suggest that the contribution of the figures to the whole poem can be approached from two separate but related points of view: that of rhetoric, the open hand, which views figures in their overt aspect as patterns of a given variety, with specific textbook names; and that of logic, the closed fist, which views figures, more limited in number and type, as elaboration of ways to discover places and follow a method of inquiry. I shall confine myself here to the first and more inclusive of these approaches, with the reservation, in Howell's words, that to Englishmen of the sixteenth and seventeenth centuries "poetry was considered to be the third great form of communication, open and popular but not fully explained by rhetoric, concise and lean but not fully explained by logic." [12]

The real ubiquity of tropes and schemes in *Colin Clout* may be unsuspected by the reader who has merely noted Rix's incidental reference to the "profusion of tropes and schemes" [13] or Miss Rubel's statement that, "as far as the rhetoric of *Colin Clout* is concerned, it is not so lavishly ornamental as that of the poetry which was intended to be more polite." [14] The Table shown below, identifying the figure for the last hundred lines, will give a more adequate idea of their almost unbelievable multiplicity. Selection of the closing lines for the purpose of exhibiting the figures is a purely arbitrary choice; almost any section would

[12] Howell, p. 4.

[13] Rix, *Rhetoric in Spenser's Poetry*, p. 62.

[14] Veré L. Rubel, *Poetic Diction in the English Renaissance from Skelton through Spenser* (New York, 1941), p. 258.

show about the same relative frequency of figures. Counting only once alliteration (*paroemion*), which is well-nigh omnipresent, and reversals of normal syntactical order (*hyperbaton*), which occurs on the average of once in every six lines, I have found thirty-five figures in the last one hundred lines. On the same basis, I have counted thirty-one figures in the first one hundred lines. The average throughout the poem is approximately one figure for every three lines. Besides indicating the number and variety of figures, the Table, by presenting a consecutive listing of the figures in context, permits the reader to observe the complexity of rhetorical patterning—that is, the way in which the figures are interwoven within a passage. This interlacing is a conventional as well as integral part of the lore.

THE FIGURES ILLUSTRATED FOR THE LAST ONE HUNDRED LINES OF *Colin Clout*[15]

Lines	*Quotation*	*Rhetorical Figure(s)*
851–854	So being former foes, they wexed friends,	compar
	And gan by litle learne to loue each other:	antithesis
	So being knit, they brought forth other kynds	
	Out of the fruitfull wombe of their great mother.	
855–860	Then first gan heauen out of darknesse dread	distributio
	For to appeare, and brought forth chearfull day:	auxesis

[15] All citations from Spenser follow the text of *The Works of Edmund Spenser: A Variorum Edition,* eds. Edwin Greenlaw et al., 10 vols. in 11 (Baltimore, 1932–57). Line citations only will be given for *Colin Clout,* which appears in *Minor Poems,* Vol. I (*Works,* VII), edited by C. G. Osgood and H. C. Lotspeich, assisted by D. E. Malone. Except that the editors have corrected misprints and made a few relatively minor emendations, the *Variorum* version reproduces the text of the poem as contained in the revised issue of the 1595 Quarto, a collection titled from the pastoral under consideration. For a detailed study of the genesis and transmission of the text, see my "*Colin Clout:* The Poem and the Book," *PBSA,* LVI (fourth quarter, 1962), 397–413.

THE FIGURES ILLUSTRATED FOR THE LAST ONE HUNDRED LINES OF *Colin Clout* (*continued*)

Lines	*Quotation*	*Rhetorical Figure(s)*
	Next gan the earth to shew her naked head,	prosopopoeia
	Out of deep waters which her drownd alway.	
	And shortly after euerie liuing wight,	
	Crept forth like wormes out of her slimie nature.	
863–864	Thenceforth they gan each one his like to loue,	ploce
	And like himselfe desire for to beget.	
865–866	The Lyon chose his mate, the Turtle Doue	zeugma
	Her deare, the Dolphin his own Dolphinet.	synonymia
871–874	For beautie is the bayt which with delight	sententia
	Doth man allure, for to enlarge his kynd,	ploce
	Beautie the burning lamp of heauens light,	metaphora
	Darting her beames into each feeble mynd.	
883–886	So loue is Lord of all the world by right,	sententia
	And rules the creatures by his powrfull saw:	acclamatio
	All being made the vassalls of his might,	
	Through secret sence which therto doth them draw.	
891–894	For their desire is base, and doth not merit,	aetiologia
	The name of loue, but of disloyall lust:	synonymia
	Ne mongst true louers they shall place inherit,	antithesis
	But as Exuls out of his court be thrust.	comparatio

Lines	*Quotation*	*Rhetorical Figure(s)*
896–898	*Colin,* thou now full deeply hast divynd: Of loue and beautie and with wondrous skill, Hast *Cupid* selfe depainted in his kynd.	transitio
911–914	But who can tell what cause had that faire Mayd To vse him so that vsed her so well: Or who with blame can iustly her vpbrayd, For louing not? for who can loue compell?	pysma antanaclasis sententia
919–924	And well I wote, that oft I heard it spoken, How one that fairest *Helene* did reuile, Through iudgement of the Gods to been ywroken Lost both his eyes and so remaynd long while, Till he recanted had his wicked rimes, And made amends to her with treble praise.	periphrasis [Rix, p. 71] prothesis
925–926	Beware therefore, ye groomes, I read betimes, How rashly blame of *Rosalind* ye raise.	apostrophe
935–938	Not then to her that scorned thing so base, But to my selfe the blame that lookt so hie: So hie her thoughts as she her selfe haue place, And loath each lowly thing with loftie eie.	anadiplosis antithesis
939–946	Yet so much grace let her vouchsafe to grant To simple swaine, sith her I may not loue:	ploce compar

THE FIGURES ILLUSTRATED FOR THE LAST ONE HUNDRED LINES OF *Colin Clout* (*continued*)

Lines	*Quotation*	*Rhetorical Figure(s)*
	Yet that I may her honour paravant,	anaphora
	And praise her worth, though far my wit aboue.	meiosis
	Such grace shall be some guerdon for the griefe,	paroemion
	And long affliction which I haue endured:	
	Such grace sometimes shall giue me some reliefe,	
	And ease of paine which cannot be recured.	
947–950	And ye my fellow shepheardes which do see	apostrophe
	And heare the languours of my too long dying,	polyptoton
	Vnto the world for euer witnesse bee,	
	That hers I die, nought to the world denying.	
952–955	So hauing ended, he from ground did rise,	hyperbaton
	And after him vprose eke all the rest:	
	All loth to part, but that the glooming skies	chronographia
	Warnd them to draw their bleating flocke to rest.	

Among the numerous tropes, schemes of words, and schemes of thought and amplification,[16] Spenser employs, under Greek and Latin appellations, many standard compositional devices found in current writing, but his use of the figures differs most significantly from that in vogue today because, following typical Renaissance practice, he employs them to a degree heightened

[16] I assume as standard for the Elizabethan period the meanings ascribed to the figures by Rix, pp. 22–61. These meanings are made clear by definitions and specimens. The definitions quoted by Rix in this section are nearly all from Joannes Susenbrotus, *Epitome Troporum ac Schematum* (1563). The English translations

beyond that of the moderns to accomplish one or more of three distinct functions: (1) to constitute the framework and the substance of blocks of verse; (2) to control the stylistic level; and (3) to provide emotional fervor. The first of these ends has to do mainly with development or amplification, which is subsumed within the two standard rhetorical divisions of *inventio* and *dispositio,* which are processes of discovering matter and arranging it. The latter two ends are aspects of tone and emotion.

With reference to the first end to which use of the figures is directed, the two famous passages evaluating contemporary poets and praising the ladies at court (ll. 377–449, 488–575) may serve to exemplify the efficacy of figures in providing both the form of the material and the material itself. These passages both employ *divisio* or *distributio,* by which figure, according to Peacham's rendering of Susenbrotus' Latin, "we dilate and spread abroade the generall kinde, by numbering and reckning vp the speciall kindes." [17] That is, the sections set forth concrete details to support a generality. They possess the character of a formal design, achieved to some extent in the section on the poets by the repetition of the transitional phrase "There is," and in the section on the ladies by the phrase "ne lesse praise worthie." That the second formula for transition was part of a common lore for the

of the Latin definitions are mostly from Henry Peacham, *The Garden of Eloquence* (1577). A great many of the specimens are from Alexander Gill, *Logonomia Anglica* (1619, rev. 1621). Gill devotes four chapters of his work to the various figures and illustrates many of them by quotations from *The Faerie Queene, The Ruines of Time,* and *The Shepheardes Calender.* On pp. 19–20 of *Rhetoric in Spenser's Poetry,* Rix explains his division of the figures into tropes (words employed in other than their literal meanings, as in metaphor and metonymy) and schemes (words or longer units arranged or repeated according to a definite pattern, as in alliteration and simile). Rix refines the category of schemes by subdividing them into schemes of words and schemes of thought and amplification. His system of classification is an adaptation of one of the commonly accepted groupings in Spenser's period, although no two Renaissance sources agree *in toto* on precise classifications of different figures. In the ensuing discussion of the wide variety of stylistic devices which appear in *Colin Clout* and which are encompassed by the term figures in its Renaissance acceptation, I have found no need to maintain these distinctions in categories. I have profited much from the way in which Rix treats Spenser's use of rhetorical figures. For *Colin Clout,* however, Rix's coverage is negligible, since he includes only ten illustrative figures from the poem in his Table of Figures (pp. 21–61) and mentions in passing another figure (p. 71).

[17] Rix, p. 48.

use of *distributio* or *merismus* is suggested by Puttenham's treatment and illustration in *The Arte of English Poesie* (1589), where he cites a passage in praise of the maiden Queen with the "*merismus* in the negatiue for the better grace." [18] *Distributio,* then, operates to create an orderly channel through which the poet can apply individualizing comments to persons in the two groups. The raw material, as it were, of the verse is constructed in the two passages largely out of another figure—*epitheton* or *appositum,* defined by Peacham as "when we ioyne adiectiues to those Substantiues, to whome they doe properly belong, and that eyther to prayse, disprayse, to amplify or extenuate." [19] With respect to *epitheton* or epithet, one might assume from the two illustrative lines cited by Rix out of *The Faerie Queene* that the figures might be limited, as in the modern conception, to adherent adjectives. The first of these illustrations, taken from the second edition of the elder Alexander Gill's *Logonomia Anglia* (1619), revised in 1621, is "But wise *Speranza* gave him comfort sweet." The second is "So false *Duessa,* but vile *Ate* thus." However, as King James VI of Scotland's *Ane Schort Treatise* (1584) and Puttenham's *Arte* clearly show,[20] the interchangeable terms *epitheton* or *appositum* could properly embrace not only prepositional adjectives but post-positional adjectives and substantive phrases as well. Thus, in the passage on the poets one finds "good *Harpalus* now woxen aged, / In faithfull seruice of faire *Cynthia*" (ll. 380–381); "*Corydon* though meanly waged, / Yet hablest wit of most I know this day" (ll. 382–383); "sad *Alcyon* bent to mourne" (l. 384), etc.; and in the passage on the ladies one finds "*Vrania* sister vnto *Astrofell*" (l. 487); "faire *Marian,* the *Muses* onely darling" (l. 505); "*Mansilia,* / Best knowne by bearing vp great *Cynthiaes* traine" (ll. 508–509), etc. In short, two important sections of the poem are organized by one figure—*distributio,* and their content is derived largely from another—*epitheton.*

[18] George Puttenham, *The Arte of English Poesie,* eds. Gladys Doidge Willcock and Alice Walker (Cambridge, Eng., 1938), p. 223.

[19] Rix, p. 31.

[20] King James VI of Scotland, in *Eliz. Critical Essays,* I, 219; Puttenham, pp. 176–177.

This use of figures to supply *copia* is so pervasive in *Colin Clout* that it will be profitable to observe the principle at work in more detail. For this purpose, we may select almost at random four additional examples. The first three show the process for separate figures. The fourth demonstrates the more complex technique of interweaving. The first example is the speech (ll. 22–31) of Hobbinol, in which all nature is represented as lamenting Colin's absence. Though this passage is in the main line of classical pastoral tradition by way of Ronsard's *Adonis,*[21] it is nevertheless built upon *prosopopoeia,* the personification of Nature in this case, which is the *raison d'être* of the unit. The second example is the *allegoria* of the ocean as Cynthia's pasture (ll. 240–251)—the "marine pastoral"[22] motif. The description is given a mythological coloring, but the chief element is the extended metaphor likening the sea to a meadow. Spenser's dispraise of the courtiers who pervert the sacred concept of love is the third example showing how he uses the figures to furnish the main substance of his units. The figure (ll. 786–792) through which Spenser has Colin ring the changes on the key words *serve* and *use* in their contrasting shades of meaning is *antanaclasis,* a play on words in their varying senses.

The final example of Spenser's use of figures to supply *copia* is Colin's blazon (ll. 464–479) in which he praises his mistress and protests devoted service and undying love. The passage is typical of the many in *Colin Clout* that employ an elaborate blending of figures to make up the block of verse, in this case, a lyric cry. It is one of two extended tributes by Colin to his mistress, Rosalind. The complaint opens with a mild *exclamatio,* followed by *aetiologia,* the reason that the speaker does not deserve ill of "gentle Mayds" (l. 465). The heart of the next six lines is *expolitio,* termed by Puttenham "the Gorgious," and said by him to be used to "polish our speech & as it were attire it with copious & pleasant amplifications and much varietie of sentences all running vpon one point & to one intēt" (p. 247). The entire speech is then

[21] Merritt Y. Hughes, "Spenser and the Greek Pastoral Triad," *SP,* xx (1929), 208–209, cited in *Works,* vii, 410.

[22] Elkin Calhoun Wilson, *England's Eliza,* Harvard Studies in English, xx (Cambridge, Mass., 1939), 302.

rounded off with two lines of *acclamatio,* the summing up, and two lines of complicated word play, combining with epigrammatic neatness *antimetabole* and *antistrophe.*

While figures in *Colin Clout* perform the basic functions of filling out details of a passage, they are also instrumental, along with diction generally, in achieving the second major objective of rhetorical patterning—that of adjusting the style to suit Renaissance notions of decorum respecting genre, subject, and persons, with genre being the most impelling determinant. The general relationship between the figures and the styles, as conceived by men of the period, is clear. Abundant use of figures is a distinguishing characteristic of the high style. The middle and low styles are marked by decreasing employment of the figures. The bald application of the principle governing decorum of the kinds would have resulted in *Colin Clout's* being written throughout in "the lawe kinde, when we vse no *Metaphores* nor translated words, nor yet vse any amplifications but goe plainly to worke, and speake altogether in common wordes." [23] No poet of consequence, however, applies the theory undiscriminatingly. To do so would be to forgo the rich possibilities for registering fine discriminations in value—and consequent aesthetic effects—when changing from one subject or one person to another subject or another person.

In the Dedicatory Letter to Sir Walter Raleigh, when Spenser refers to *Colin Clout* as a "simple pastorall" and apologizes for the "meanesse of the style," which is "vnworthie of your higher conceipt," he is using in the first two quoted phrases terms familiar to the critical discussions of the time. The conventional designation of pastoral was "simple" and, as Puttenham makes quite clear, the "low and base stile" was understood to be reserved for "all *Eglogues* and pastorall poemes" (p. 153). In view of the multiplicity of figures in *Colin Clout,* hardly compatible with conventions governing the low style, one may feel that Spenser's statement in the Dedication is inconsistent with his practice, or that he is simply throwing the standard theory overboard. Actually, neither alternative reflects the true situation. His statement, when taken in a larger context, does not identify the poem unreservedly

[23] Thomas Wilson, *Wilson's Arte of Rhetorique,* 1560, ed. George Herbert Mair (Oxford, 1909), p. 169.

as written in unadorned style, nor would Sir Walter, in all likelihood, have construed the deprecatory phrases so to identify it. Perhaps the reasons for discounting Spenser's statement as an indication of his intention to eschew elevation should be specified. First, one has to make ample allowances for the convention of humility and disparagement in dedications to one's patron in the 1590's. Part of this engaging air of self-disparagement reflects also the courtly fashion of *sprezzatura,* the word Castiglione first uses in his influential *Il Libro del Cortegiano* (1528) to characterize the temper by which a gentleman conceals a purpose of high seriousness with a show of studied negligence.[24] Had not Spenser in his Dedicatory Sonnets disparaged even the high style of *The Faerie Queene* itself in such lines as the following to "The Right Honourable the Earle of Ormund and Ossory":

> Receiue most noble Lord a simple taste
> Of the wilde fruit, which saluage soyle hath bred,
> Which being through long wars left almost waste,
> With Brutish barbarisme is ouerspredd;
> (*Works,* III, 193)

Or in such lines as the following to "The Most renowned and valiant Lord, the Lord Grey of Wilton, knight of the Noble order of the Garter, & Cn"?—

> Rude rymes, the which a rustick Muse did weaue
> In sauadge soyle, far from Parnasso mount.
> (*Works,* III, 194)

In alluding to the poem as "simple," Spenser was in little danger of creating for his immediate readers a misleading supposition as to its actual quality.

Second, Spenser may well have been using the word "meanesse" to accord with the conventional classification of style into three levels, "mean" being the term commonly employed to designate the intermediate level. Finally, even if, as is conceivable, Spenser meant "meanesse" to suggest a degree of baseness, the convention implied that *all* poetry was raised above common discourse (Puttenham, pp. 8–9) and that the lower

[24] *Il Libro del Cortegiano de Conte Baldesar Castiglione* (Venice, 1528), sig. biiii^r.

flight merely restricted the kinds of figures and modes of using them, not the figures themselves. The copiousness of figures in an out-and-out pastoral like Spenser's *The Shepheardes Calender* indicates convincingly that the low style, at least in poetry, did not outlaw the figures. *Colin Clout,* moreover, being far from "pure pastoral" in genre, by reason of its containing matters "that concerne the Gods and diuine things" and the "noble gests and great fortunes of Princes" (Puttenham, p. 152), would be pushed upward under the principle of decorum toward conventions of middle and high style.

Though all the figures inasmuch as they "passe the ordinary limits of common vtterance" (Puttenham, p. 154) serve to raise the style, certain figures are more efficacious to this end than others. I shall confine myself to those figures in the poem which best exemplify this function: *comparatio* and *allegoria; antonomasia* and *epitheton; periphrasis, sententia;* and *acclamatio.* The first of these is quite common. The main way in which *comparatio,* defined as "a comparing of thinges, persons, deedes, examples, contrairies, lyke, or vnlyke" (Rix, p. 55), imparts elevation of style is in the drawing of its subject matter from Biblical or mythological sources, with their rich store of associations for Christian humanists of the time. Cases involving the use of *comparatio* to call up Biblical associations for the reader are the praise of Urania

> In whose braue mynd as in a golden cofer,
> All heauenly gifts and riches locked are:
> More rich than pearles of *Ynde* or gold of *Opher;*
> (ll. 488–490)

And the figurative deification of Cynthia, whose

> thoughts are like the fume of Franckincence,
> Which from a golden Censer forth doth rise.
>
> . . . .
>
> Emongst the seats of Angels heauenly wrought,
> Much like an Angell in all forme and fashion.
> (ll. 608–609; 614–615)

An example of a comparison depending upon mythological lore for its effectiveness is the injunction by Colin to Daniel bidding that poet to "rouze thy feathers quickly" (l. 424) and "to what course thou please thy selfe aduance" (l. 425).[25] Thus the author of the sonnet-sequence *Delia* (which Spenser probably saw in manuscript)[26] is equated with, or considered to be under the inspiration of, the Muse of Poetry by way of Pegasus, the winged horse on which the Muses sometimes traveled. Similarly, the one clear example of *allegoria*—in Peacham's phrase, "a contynued Metaphor" (Rix, p. 24)—derives its tone from the classical tradition. This is the ocean-meadow fancy (ll. 240–251) contained in "the shepheards" description of Cynthia's "Regiment" at sea. The marine divinities Triton and Proteus figure prominently in this description.

From one point of view, of course, *Colin Clout* is in its entirety an extended metaphor—an *allegoria,* in which a thin veil is thrown over all by the poet's casting the poem in the pastoral mode. Colin's life is placed in an atmosphere of shepherds and shepherdesses, bearing names appearing in prestigious classical works—the idylls of Theocritus and the eclogues of Virgil, for the most part. All locutions which arise from the pastoral mode were well understood by the convention to designate an order of things and beings different from such empirical things and beings as Ireland, Kilcolman, England, the English Court, Queen Elizabeth, Raleigh, Spenser, Harvey, Bryskett.

With reference to *epitheton* and *antonomasia,* the two succeeding figures in the above list of those serving to raise the style, both represent adaptations of utterances to reflect real or attributed differences in rank or dignity between the speaker, the shepherd Colin, and the person spoken about. *Epitheton* and *antonomasia,* distinguished by Puttenham as "the Qualifier" and "the figure of attribution" (pp. 176–177), serve to register the speaker's awareness of special difference owing to the subject persons. They create a kind of aesthetic distance between him and them. As pointed out in the discussion of the passages on poets and ladies as set pieces of conventional formalism, these two long passages (ll. 377–449, 485–575) are interpenetrated with epi-

[25] The comparison would now be called a metaphor, but Renaissance criticism normally has *metaphora* denote a single word "translated from the proper and natural signification, to another not proper, yet nie and/likely" (Peacham, in Rix, p. 22).

[26] *Daphnaïda and Other Poems,* ed. Renwick, p. 187.

thets, each person, in fact, being honored by one or more appropriate "qualifiers." Among the poets, for instance, there is "*Alabaster* throughly taught, / In all this skill, though knowen yet to few" (ll. 400–401); among the maids of honor, there are "Faire *Galathea* with bright shining beames" (l. 518), and Neaera, "the blosome of grace and curtesie" (l. 528). Interestingly enough, of the ten ladies lauded, only Stella has no epithet bestowed upon her. The reason for this, given by Colin himself, is that Sidney has already "prais'd [her] and rais'd [her] aboue each other starre" (l. 535).

There can be little question as to the efficacy of these qualifiers to enhance the dignity of the person to whom a description or qualifying word or phrase is attached and at the same time to indicate the speaker's awareness of his comparative unworthiness. The value of *antonomasia* in creating a sense of aesthetic distance between speaker and subject is even greater than that of the epithet. Puttenham terms *antonomasia* "the surnamer" and defines it as "the manner of naming of persons or things . . . by a conuenient difference, and such as is true or esteemed and likely to be true." His illustrations of the figure include reference to "the Westerne king" (King Philip II of Spain) and to "*The maiden Queene*, for that is her hiest peculiar among all the Queenes of the World" (p. 181). In *Colin Clout,* too, *antonomasia* is used to register the speaker's humble position in relation to persons of high estate: the speaker's refusal to mention Queen Elizabeth's name outright, referring to her instead as "*Cynthia* the Ladie of the sea" (l. 166), "that Goddesse grace" (l. 359), "dreaded Dread" (l. 406); and Colin's reference to Sir Walter Raleigh as "a straunge shepheard" (l. 60) and "the shepheard of the Ocean" (l. 358).

Of other figures calculated to raise the style, *periphrasis,* or circumlocution, is exceedingly rare in *Colin Clout,* being employed in only two instances. The first is the phraseology chosen by the speaker, Colin, to indicate that he had actually been in Elizabeth's presence: "since I saw that Angels blessed eie" (l. 40). In this case, the circumlocution permits Colin to avoid direct reference to a person greatly above him in rank and dignity. Thus, *periphrasis,* like *antonomasia,* is used to create aesthetic distance. The second instance is the *periphrasis* for Stesichorus:

And well I wote, that oft I heard it spoken,
How one that fairest *Helene* did reuile,
Through iudgement of the Gods to been ywroken
Lost both his eyes and so remaynd long while.
(ll. 919–922)

Here *periphrasis* acts to ennoble the language by bringing in an implied comparison between the shepherd Colin and Stesichorus, a character connected with epic matter *par excellence*—that of Helen and of Troy.

Sententia, or the apothegmatic statement, is somewhat more common than *periphrasis,* though it must be conceded that the modern reader can easily overlook some aphorisms that Elizabethan readers recognized at once.[27] The gnomic figure is also more adaptable than *periphrasis* for varying the stylistic level because it may be either learned or folkish in origin. Whatever the origin, however, *sententia* may be regarded as operating to elevate the tone. Something of this idea is contained in Erasmus' Preface to his *Apophthegmata* (1531), where he says that "all these uniuersalle sorte of writyinges, as doe comprehende prouerbes, sage sentencies, and notable saiynges or actes, is moste fitte for Princes and noble menne." [28] The vogue of the commonplace books, which many compiled for themselves or had convenient access to in printed works like Erasmus' *Apophthegmata* or his earlier *Adagia,* testify to the value placed by men of Spenser's era on sententious materials as aids to wit.[29] Moreover, the tragedies of Seneca the Younger, abounding in quotable declarations, gave impressive classical sanction to the use of *sententiae* as an elevating device. In the *Apologie,* Sidney indirectly specifies the peculiar value Seneca possessed in the eyes of literary Londoners when he praises the English blood-and-thunder play *Gorboduc* for its "stately speeches and well sounding Phrases, clyming to the height of *Seneca* his stile, and as full of notable moralitie." [30]

[27] See Morris Palmer Tilley, *A Dictionary of the Proverbs in England in the Sixteenth and Seventeenth Centuries* (Ann Arbor, Mich., 1940), p. v.

[28] *The Apophthegmes of Erasmus,* trans. Nicolas Udall, from the edition of 1564, ed. Robert Roberts (Boston, 1877), p. xxii.

[29] See Crane, *Wit and Rhetoric in the Renaissance,* Chs. ii and iii, for a discussion of commonplace books and the way in which they were utilized by men of the Renaissance as helps to composition.

[30] In *Eliz. Critical Essays,* I, 196–197.

William Cornwallis' *Discourse upon Seneca the Tragedian* (1601) also reflects the strong interest of Elizabethan writers in the Stoic playwright's sententious line, which often took precedence over their interest in the tragedies themselves.[31]

In *Colin Clout*, gnomes with a vaguely bookish cast sometimes appear in the dialogue, as when Colin defends his reason for leaving the court to return "back to my sheep to tourne" (l. 672) rather than, "hauing learned repentance late, to mourne / Emongst those wretches which I there descryde" (ll. 674–675). The repentance reference is a slight turn of the proverb cited as "Repentance never comes too late" by Morris Palmer Tilley in *A Dictionary of the Proverbs in the Sixteenth and Seventeenth Centuries* (p. 569, R80). Another example of proverbs appearing in the dialogue is the question by which Lucida seeks to excuse Rosalind's lack of reciprocity in love: "for who can loue compell?" (l. 914). This truism receives more formal expression in the river myth passage earlier in the poem when Colin explains why Mulla refused to follow her father Mole's wish for her union with Allo: "For loue will not be drawne, but must be ledde" (l. 129). Tilley's entry for a series of quotations current in Spenser's time expressing the same idea is "Love cannot be compelled (forced)" (p. 395, l. 499).

The foregoing examples of *sententiae* in the poem illustrate their customary office of raising the style. Because of their currency in untutored language, proverbs were also available for the purpose of lowering the level of utterance. King James VI of Scotland, writing in *Ane Schort Treatise,* obviously has in mind the adaptability of proverbs for varying the style when, in a short section on "thrie speciall ornamentis to verse," he warns: "As for the *Prouerbis,* they man be proper for the subiect." They must, he adds, be chosen on the same basis as comparisons. Of the latter, he had just specified that they ought to be "sa proper for the subiect that nather they be ouer bas, gif your subiect be heich, for then sould your subiect disgrace your *Comparisoun,* nather your *Comparisoun* be heich quhen your subiect is basse, for then

[31] *Discourses upon Seneca the Tragedian,* ed. Robert Hood Bowers (Gainesville, Fla., 1952), pp. iv–ix. For a full account of Seneca's influence on English letters, which, in opposition to Ciceronianism, was on the rise during the latter part of the sixteenth century, see George Williamson, *The Senecan Amble* (Chicago, 1951).

sall your *Comparisoun* disgrace your subiect." [32] An outstanding example of the use of a proverb to deliberately debase the style occurs in the satirical passage in *Colin Clout* containing the most bitter denunciation of bad courtiers to be found in Spenser's poetry outside of *Mother Hubberds Tale* (1591):

> For each mans worth is measured by his weed,
> As harts by hornes, or asses by their eares.
> (ll. 711–712)

The proverbial nature of the "tailor-made man" concept is established by Tilley's numerous citations under the entry, "Apparel makes (Clothes make) the man" p. 16, A283). While Tilley gives no proverb referring directly to horns as a distinguishing mark of the hart, he does cite the comparable byword of the Devil's being known by his horns (p. 152, D252). There is no dearth of variations by sixteenth- and seventeenth-century writers on the theme that "An Ass is known by his ears" (p. 20, A355).

It remains true, nevertheless, that the customary effect of the *sententia* in *Colin Clout* is to confer dignity upon the places where it is used. Its contribution to this end is nowhere more clearly marked than in the miniature "Hymne in Honour of Love" near the end of the poem. Here the two lofty utterances of general truth combine *sententia* and another figure, *acclamatio,* the pithy restatement or summing up of preceding matter, to give added grandeur to the whole discourse:

> For beautie is the bayt which with delight
> Doth man allure,[33] for to enlarge his kynd.
>
> . . . .
>
> So loue is Lord of all the world by right
> And rules the creatures by his powrfull saw.[34]
> (ll. 871–872, 883–884)

[32] Quotations from *Ane Schort Treatise* in *Eliz. Critical Essays,* I, 219.

[33] Cf. Tilley, p. 28, B50, citations from Pettie, *A Petite Pallace of Pettie His Pleasure* (1576): "he bit so greedily at the bait of her beauty, that he swallowed down the hook of hateful hurt"; also from Lyly, *Euphues, The Anatomy of Wit* (1578): "Beautie . . . was a deceiptfull bayte with a deadly hooke."

[34] Cf. *ibid.,* p. 398, L527, citations from Wilmot et al., *Gismond* (1566–68): "Loue rules the world, Loue onely is the Lorde"; and from Wilmot, *Tancred and Gismond* (1591–92): "I . . . am that great God of loue, who with high might Ruleth the wast wide world, and liuing things."

Acclamatio, without *sententia* but in combination with other figures, appears at intervals and elevates the style because of the stately and considered calm which it engenders. Note, for example, the following epitomizing declaration which Spenser has Colin make—a declaration of importance, moreover, since it helps clear away the apparent paradox in Colin's position: Why does a vicious element continue to exist in English court and society which otherwise are of such surpassing virtue and refinement? The answer is contained in the *acclamatio:*

For end, all good, all grace there freely growes,
Had people grace it gratefully to vse:
For God his gifts there plenteously bestowes,
But gracelesse men them greatly do abuse.
(ll. 324–327)

The fact that Spenser's use of rhetorical figures in *Colin Clout* reflects a conscious and deliberate control for clearly envisaged ends now seems evident. His use of the figures to build up blocks of verse is not thereby necessarily mechanical or "unpoetic." Indeed, to let one example stand for many, one of the most admired passages of the entire poem, the charming river myth concerning the love of Mulla and Bregog (ll. 103–153) is a set piece embodying in the figure *topographia* the poet's imaginative conception. Spenser could have found numerous models in Boccaccio and in later Renaissance poets of Florence and Naples for the myth of locality.[35] Yet on this conventional pattern he has superimposed a story in which the actual physical environs of his Kilcolman estate, with meticulous accuracy of detail, are interwoven. This employment of the figures to fill out the matter of the poem is the first main use to which Spenser put rhetoric in *Colin Clout.* The second main use—to vary the style—has just been discussed. In general, Spenser applies the elevating power of rhetoric to maintain that studied level of tone and style which would not ascend too high for pastoral nor yet fall too low for the praise of noble persons and causes with which the poem is chiefly concerned.

[35] Rudolph B. Gottfried, "Spenser and the Italian Myth of Locality," *SP,* XXXIV (1937), 111–114, 117–124.

I should like now to consider the most powerful of Spenser's three main overt uses of the figures—that of moving the affections or passions. The standard doctrine of the three styles is particularly relevant to a consideration of Spenser's reliance upon figures to "inueigle and appassionate the mind." [36] It is true that the doctrine of the styles was originally a concept applicable to oratory, but in an age like the Renaissance, when men like Richard Stanyhurst could praise Virgil indifferently as a poet, an orator, or a philosopher,[37] the influence of rhetorical precept on poetic practice was bound to be immense. In the *Orator,* Cicero has a section describing the perfect orator and the highest eloquence. In it he comments that a poet deserves credit for seeking the virtues of the orator and that, despite the differences between the two arts of poetry and oratory, they are identical in the fact that both require discrimination in selection of subject matter and in choice of words. A large part of that discrimination, Cicero's subsequent discussion makes clear, lies in the ability of the man of eloquence to choose, control, and combine the three different styles, each of which has its particular forte. For each of the three aims—to prove, to please, and to sway—one style is most effective. The plain style is for proof, the middle style for pleasure, and the high style for persuasion. And of the three purposes, the last is the most important since, in the final analysis, the judge or deliberative body must be moved before it will accede to the pleasure of the speaker.[38] Elsewhere in the same work Cicero relates the figures to stylistic levels by telling us that figures are used sparingly in the plain style, moderately in the middle style, and lavishly in the grand style.[39] Quintilian stresses, in the *Institutio Oratoria,* the efficacy of the intermediate and high styles for emotional persuasion. He distinguishes these styles from the low by their comparatively high proportion of ornamental devices. The pleader who uses the high style will,

[36] Puttenham, p. 154. See Tuve, Ch. ix, for a valuable discussion concerning the way in which Renaissance notions of decorum and the styles affected the fashioning of figurative devices in poetic writing.

[37] Dedication to *Thee First Foure Bookes of Virgil his Aeneis,* in *Eliz. Critical Essays,* I, 137.

[38] Cicero, *Orator,* 67–70, Loeb Classical Library, trans. H. M. Hubbell (Cambridge, Mass., 1939), pp. 354, 356.

[39] *Ibid.,* 20–22, pp. 318, 320; 79–82, pp. 364, 366.

according to him, be able to call the dead to life, inspire anger or pity, and cause the listening judges to be swept impetuously from one emotion to another, as they weep and call upon the gods.[40]

The relevance of this kind of rhetorical teaching to which the Tudor scholar was almost continuously exposed in its application to poetry need hardly be labored. In connection with the three aims of eloquence, one should note in passing that they are considered conplementary, not mutually exclusive. The Renaissance followed the classical writers in making no hard and fast distinction between feeling and intellect. Puttenham, for instance, emphasizes the inseparable nature of emotion and thought, in contradistinction to our modern dichotomy, in these words: "For to say truely, what els is man but his minde? . . . He therefore that hath vanquished the minde of man, hath made the greatest and most glorious conquest. But the minde is not assailable vnlesse it be by sensible approches." [41] "Sensible," it need hardly be added, is employed in its usual sixteenth-century denotation of affecting the senses or passions.

As one might anticipate, the figures of principal import in helping achieve the aim of moving the passions are in the category of schemes of thought and amplification rather than of tropes—turns of a single word—or schemes of words only. Unlike similes, definitions, metaphors, and the like, these figures tend not to be definable by reference to common places or standard positions of argument. In Ramist manuals, therefore, most of them appear in the rhetorics rather than in the logics. This class of figures, which includes exclamations, moderations, or revocations of exclamations (*epanorthosis*), apostrophe, and other fashionings largely in imitation of the spoken word, is called "figures of sentences" in *The Arcadian Rhetorike* of Abraham Fraunce. Fraunce recognizes the emotional force of this group in the paragraph introducing them: "now folow the figures in Sentences, which in the whole sentēce expres some motion of the minde. These are more forcible & apt to perswade, than those of words,

[40] *Institutio Oratoria* xii.10.58–65, IV. 482, 484, 486.

[41] P. 197. See Tuve, pp. 166–175, 396–402, for a succinct discussion of Renaissance psychological theories, with particular reference to tropical language in poetry. Her note on p. 396 lists a few selected references on the mental operations as conceived by learned Elizabethans and Jacobeans.

which be rather pleasant and fit to delight. Generallie, as in tropes there is a certaine grace, in figures of words a kind of delicacie, so in these of sentences appeareth force and maiestie" (p. 63). The schemes of thought and amplification that contribute so much to the emotive and dramatic effect of the poem are *exclamatio* or exclamation; *interrogatio* or rhetorical question; *pysma,* the extended form of *interrogatio; apostrophe* or direct address; and *synathroismus* or a "heaping up of many different things" (Rix, p. 42 n.). In stressing the emotive force of such figures as these, the Ramist rhetoricians were simply confirming what the older ones, following Cicero and Quintilian, had been saying all along. It is significant, for example, that the definitions of these figures from Susenbrotus, translated by Peacham, reflect the critics' awareness of the exclamatory quality of the particular figures, e.g., "Apostrophe, when we sodeinly forsake the former frame of our speach and goe to another" (Rix, p. 41); "Pysma, when we aske often times together, and vse many questions in one place, wherby we do make the oration sharp and vehement" (p. 39). Collectively, these figures account in no small measure for the generally spirited tone of the entire poem, and, as a result of their very frequent occurrence, constitute the leading means by which the emotions of friendship, love, and indignation are strongly imitated.

Though it is necessary to isolate the figures for the purpose of detailing their special office, it is not necessarily helpful to do so when one is attempting to show their cumulative force. Indeed, as the Table presented earlier shows, the figures seldom occur alone in Spenser; rather they frequently reinforce one another; and for key passages are often massed to make a triple assault, as it were, upon the reader or listener. This triple assault combines the possible effects envisaged by Puttenham in grouping all the figures into the three categories of auricular, "sensible," and sententious, that is, affecting the ear, mind, and all faculties respectively (pp. 159–160). This massing is sometimes used to heighten the emotional quality even in passages of lesser importance. In the lines giving recognition to Alabaster, for instance, Spenser employs a combination of *exclamatio, interrogatio,* and *apostrophe:*

Yet were he knowne to *Cynthia* as he ought,
His Eliseïs would be redde anew.
Who liues that can match that heroick song,
Which he hath of that mightie Princesse made?
O dreaded Dread, do not thy selfe that wrong,
To let thy fame lie so in hidden shade:
But call it forth, O call him forth to thee,
To end thy glorie which he hath begun.
(ll. 402–409)

There are three other cases of *apostrophe* in the same section on the poets. The figure, by reason of its purposeful abruptness, injects life into a passage which might otherwise lull the reader to sleep. Two of these invocations—those to Alcyon (ll. 388–391) and to Daniel (ll. 424–425)—are of lesser intensity. The third to Amyntas gains strength through being reinforced by *anaphora*, initial repetition, sometimes used, according to John Hoskins, to beat "upon one thing to cause the quicker feeling in the audience." [42]

Helpe, O ye shepheards helpe ye all in this.
Help *Amaryllis* this her losse to mourne.
(ll. 436–437)

The poem closes, except for the completion of the narrative frame in the form of *chronographia* or description of the time of day, on the forceful and eloquent plea by Colin to his fellow-shepherds to witness his undying devotion to Rosalind:

And ye my fellow sheepheardes which do see
And heare the languours of my too long dying,
Vnto the world for euer witnesse bee,
That hers I die, nought to the world denying,
This simple trophe of her great conquest.
(ll. 947–951)

Interrogatio in the form of the rhetorical question is relatively abundant. At the conclusion of the first panegyric to Queen Elizabeth, Spenser has Colin exclaim:

[42] *Directions for Speech and Style*, ed. Hoyt H. Hudson, Princeton Studies in English, No. 12 (Princeton, 1935), p. 13.

Why then do I base shepheard bold and blind,
Presume the things so sacred to prophane?
(ll. 348–349)

This figure has particularly incisive force in Colin's encomium to Love, where he poses the great crux: What is the secret force that attracts unlike elements to each other, causing them to unite and eventually to culminate in the creation of man?

For how should else things so far from attone
And so great enemies as of them bee,
Be euer drawne together into one,
And taught in such accordance to agree?
(ll. 843–846)

With reference to the expanded form of *interrogatio,* there is only one passage employing *pysma,* a series of rhetorical questions. It is the comment by Lucida, one of the interlocutors, in response to Hobbinol's snide remark about how poorly women have requited Colin for stating the cause of love so well:

But who can tell what cause had that faire Mayd
To vse him so that vsed her so well:
Or who with blame iustly her vpbrayd,
For louing not? for who can loue compell?
(ll. 911–914)

The employment by Spenser of *synathroismus,* or congeries, aptly called the "heaping figure" by Puttenham (p. 236), to stimulate emotion can be well illustrated by the passage in which Colin characterizes England by contrasting it with Ireland. In England

No wayling there nor wretchednesse is heard,
No bloodie issues nor no leprosies,
No griesly famine, nor no raging sweard,
No nightly bodrags, nor no hue and cries;
The shepheards there abroad may safely lie,
On hills and downes, withouten dread or daunger:
No rauenous wolues the good mans hope destroy,
No outlawes fell affray the forest raunger.
(ll. 312–319)

While some of the sense of excitement in this passage derives from the verbs, particularly the active participles, the repetitive insistence that in England no factors exist which are disruptive of peace and harmony compels attention and conviction. *Anaphora,* iteration of the same sound at the beginning of successive lines, and *paroemion,* consonantal alliteration, help reinforce the sense. *Synathroismus* is also one important element of the rhetorically-rich passage in which Colin ecstatically expresses his chivalric devotion to his mistress:

> To her my thoughts I daily dedicate,
> To her my heart I nightly martyrize;
> To her my loue I lowly do prostrate,
> To her my life I wholly sacrifice:
> My thought, my heart, my loue, my life is shee.
> (ll. 472–476)

Here again, the insistent repetition, underscored by *anaphora* and alliteration and climaxed by *acclamatio,* takes on extraordinary passional force.

The foregoing account of the figures considers them as comprising all the linguistic patterns to which names are assigned in rhetorical manuals of the Renaissance. At the same time it takes cognizance of the fact that these patterns are by no means formulations distinctive to that period. The discussion attempts to set forth the main ways in which the figures are consciously used in one important poem of the high Renaissance in England for what we can be almost certain were ends predetermined by the poet. To recapitulate, the three main groupings of figures, conceived in terms of their special functions in *Colin Clout,* are: to furnish details of the matter, to give variety and elevation to the style, and to generate affective power at important junctures. To particularize the functional efficacy of the figures of rhetoric is not, again, to denigrate their aesthetic contribution. Poets of the Renaissance found it exhilarating to experiment with fashioning in the vernacular figurative formations which they had been taught to admire in Isocrates, Cicero, Virgil, Ovid, and Seneca. Readers of the time took frank delight in the figures as leading resources in providing the formal beauty of design which they deemed essential to a good poem. That delight was enhanced for those readers when the poet displayed logical aptness in turning up places and figures which in many cases amounted to the same thing. This study reveals something of the part that internal pressure played in shaping outward expression—in producing a style nicely toned and modulated to changes in subject, person, and circumstances by the studied application of figures. It conveys how important the figures are to the texture and the architecture of *Colin Clout.* In this sense, they tend to exemplify the aesthetic principle enunciated elsewhere by Spenser in these lines:

> That Beautie is not, as fond men misdeeme,
> An outward shewe of things, that onely seeme;
>
> For of the soule the bodie forme doth take.[43]

[43] *An Hymne in Honour of Beautie,* ll. 90–91, *Works,* VII, 206, and l. 132, p. 207.

A Technique of Irony in *A Tale of a Tub*

WINSTON WEATHERS

[IRONY HAS long been associated with rhetoric, both as a trope and as a general rhetorical strategy for effecting persuasion. Whether it is used as a trope (literally, a *turning* of the meaning of a word) or as a general strategy, irony is the device whereby an author says one thing but means something else, usually the exact opposite. It was one of the favorite devices of the great English satirist Jonathan Swift. Irony presents a special problem, however, not only for Swift but for any writer who resorts to it: how to convey one's true meaning to the audience. Anyone who has ever taught Defoe's "The Shortest Way with the Dissenters" or Swift's "A Modest Proposal" in an English class knows that even sophisticated students are as likely to misunderstand the intended meaning of these pieces as did contemporary readers. The danger of a misreading is compounded when an author uses the device of a persona. How can we determine whether or not the persona speaks for the author? And even in cases where we have determined that the persona does *not* speak for the author, how can we determine whether the persona is speaking literally or ironically?

In the following sentence-by-sentence analysis of the first paragraph of Section V, "A Digression in the Modern Kind," from *A Tale of a Tub,* Winston Weathers sets forth some criteria that will help us discriminate Swift's ironic voice. Although he analyzes only one paragraph from one of Swift's works, Professor Weathers claims that we can use these same criteria for detecting Swift's irony in most of his works. The analysis reveals all the subtleties of a master satirist's manipulation of his persona and ultimately of his audience.]

From *Jonathan Swift: Tercentenary Essays.* The University of Tulsa Department of English Monograph Series, No. 3 (1967), pp. 53–60. Reprinted by permission of The University of Tulsa and Winston Weathers.

IN *A Tale of a Tub,* Swift is faced with an age-old rhetorical problem: how to communicate meaning to readers clearly and unambiguously when the ideas to be communicated would be most effectively or judiciously presented in fictive, symbolic, or ironic modes. To solve this rather complex problem, Swift developed a number of stylistic techniques that would permit him the delights of irony at the very time he was achieving precise and definite meaning. It is one of these rhetorical techniques that I wish to discuss in this paper. Boldly, I might suggest that this one technique gives insight into the entire rationale of Swift's irony in all his work. Modestly, I might suggest that this one technique, even though limited to *A Tale of a Tub,* should be added to the catalogue of Swift's rhetorical devices and included in our subsequent discussions of his style.

The technique of irony that I wish to identify is based actually upon three Swiftian assumptions concerning language, audience, and rhetorical effect. First, Swift believed in a normal language, the proper use of which would contribute a great deal of clarity to his meaning; he believed that his meaning depended upon a conventional use of words that were well established in the social order and that could be defined adequately and publicly to everyone's agreement. Second, Swift believed in a normal audience, an audience of readers who were like unto himself; he assumed that the audience who would understand him would be the "right people," those who had "the harmony of human understanding." Third, Swift believed in a normal level of denotative meaning, a level against which he could set certain manipulations of language to bring forth his own special meaning; in fact, at times he seems to play a little game—what with persona and all—which he expected his audience to comprehend if they were to understand what he had to say.

II

Upon these assumptions, Swift developed the various techniques of his irony, including the one I wish to discuss in particular and which is adequately demonstrated in a paragraph taken from the opening of Section V, "A Digression in the Modern

Kind." [1] This one paragraph will suffice for an initial identification of the technique, and a sentence-by-sentence analysis of the paragraph will reveal, as well as analysis of a more extended passage would, the basic principle of "norm and deviation" that Swift employs so decisively in this particular work.

> [1] We whom the World is pleased to honor with the title of *Modern Authors,* should never have been able to compass our great Design of an everlasting Remembrance, and never-dying Fame, if our Endeavours had not been so highly serviceable to the general Good of Mankind. [p. 123]

First of all, Swift names a persona, "modern authors," which is to condition all subsequent statements: The persona becomes something of a context that qualifies all following statements. By using the persona, Swift (a) gains control over irony and satire, but (b) complicates the transmission of his intended meaning. For the reader, when aware of the double authorship, is constrained to ask in regard to any particular statement: Shall I read this as seriously meant by the persona; or by both Swift and the persona; by Swift alone and only ironically by the persona; or ironically by both Swift and persona?

Swift obviously has a problem if he wishes to dismiss the persona and speak directly. He must either speak through the persona and agree with him, or he must transform the persona in some way.

We begin to see Swift's solution in his use of adjectives of exaggeration. We read his first sentence literally and straightforwardly until we come to the word "great," which faintly suggests irony. We must ask, of course, is the persona being ironic or is Swift? But the answer is: Swift always expects his reader to start with the assumption that the persona is serious and non-ironic; that the persona believes what he says.

Yet the problem is not entirely solved—for how is Swift to let us know that he does not agree with the persona, that what the persona says seriously is actually an ironic comment from Swift? Swift counts, no doubt, on a certain norm of agreement in his audience that will enable them to recognize the irony. If a reader

[1] Jonathan Swift, *A Tale of a Tub,* ed. A. C. Guthkelch and D. Nichol Smith (2nd ed.; Oxford, 1958). Subsequent page references are to this edition.

feels as Swift does about modern authors, then he will recognize irony. But if this norm is not present, Swift feels that perhaps the ironic exaggeration in the adjectives will save the reader from literal and thus incorrect readings; and Swift, in this sentence, uses the adjectives "great," "everlasting," "never-dying," and "so highly serviceable."

In this first sentence then, Swift relies on the "norm of agreement" and adjectival exaggeration to call attention to the possibility of irony. Actually, he does more than that by his use of adjectives that are ameliorative—but we shall see how that aspect of the technique is employed when, farther on, we encounter the opposite device of pejoration.

> [2] This, *O Universe,* is the Adventurous Attempt of me thy Secretary;—
>
> *Quemvis perferre laborem*
> *Suadet, & Inducit noctes vigilare serenas.* [p. 123]

In this sentence, the apostrophe "O Universe" and the accompanying Miltonic diction is also a stylistic key to meaning since, even though the persona may be pretentious, he would not be expected to rise to this poetic height. This shift in tone is Swift's device (comparable to the adjectival exaggeration in the first sentence) to indicate his own involvement in the meaning. By introducing the unexpected apostrophe and Miltonic diction, Swift startles his readers to a keener observation of what is going on. In case a reader missed the possibility of irony in the first sentence, Swift makes another rhetorical disturbance in the second, to shock the reader into realization that meaning is not on the normal persona level at this particular point in the passage.

Likewise, Swift's main purpose in the Latin quotation is to confirm the idea of deviation away from the persona norm. By deviation, Swift hopes the reader will be less inclined to accept the statement as merely that of the persona. That is, Swift hopes the reader will realize that (1) the persona speaks at a normal denotative level, with normal meaning occurring at that denotative level; and (2) any deviation from that norm creates a disturbance in meaning, indicating that Swift is beginning to speak *instead of* or *through* the persona.

> [3] To this End I have some Time since, with a World of Pains and Art, dissected the Carcass of *Humane Nature,* and read many useful Lectures upon the several Parts, both *Containing* and *Contained;* till at last it *smelt* so strong, I could preserve it no longer. [p. 123]

This sentence is regular in meaning until the reader comes to the metaphor which, by nature, lifts meaning from a denotative to a figurative level. Swift does more than shift to metaphorical meaning, however. His use of the connotative word "carcass" indicates a pejorative attitude in the metaphor, an attitude confirmed in the last phrase of the sentence—all of which, of course, is a metaphorical trick: Swift establishes the vehicle "carcass" for the tenor "human nature," but ends the sentence as though the vehicle were really the tenor with some reality of its own. A version of the extended metaphor, this device enables the persona to say something about human nature in an oblique fashion.

In using the metaphor, Swift is assuming that readers (1) will recognize a figurative construction, (2) will respond to the pejorative connotation of "carcass," and (3) will see an implied criticism of human nature in the persona's statement.

But how has Swift shown that he agrees or disagrees with the persona? Our hypothesis remains: Swift keeps persona meaning on a normal denotative level, and variations from that level indicate Swift's involvement in meaning. In this sentence then, Swift shifts to metaphor to indicate his involvement; *he,* along with the persona, is speaking about human nature.

But Swift not only shifts from normal denotative level to metaphor, he also shifts in the direction of pejoration. And thus an interesting dimension is added to Swift's meaning: Swift's movement from the ameliorative apostrophe in the previous sentence to the pejorative metaphor in this third sentence reveals to the reader the two basic forms of variation from the denotative or persona norm that Swift is using.

What Swift seems to be doing with amelioration and pejoration is to indicate *what sort* of involvement he is making. If, as in the first and second sentences, the deviations from the persona norm are essentially ameliorative, Swift seems to be saying, "No, this is not so," or "No, this should not be so." With an ameliorative swing, Swift is actually making ironic criticism. If, however, the swing is to the pejorative side, as in the third sentence, then Swift, becoming involved in the meaning, seems to say "Yes, this is unfortunately so," or "Yes, this is the way things are."

In general then, Swift uses deviation (exaggeration, high diction, metaphor) to indicate his own involvement. Having established that involvement, he uses amelioration to indicate his disagreement with the persona, pejoration to indicate his agreement.

> [4] Upon which, I have been at great Expence to fit up all the Bones with exact Contexture, and in due Symmetry; so that I am ready to show a very compleat Anatomy thereof to all curious *Gentlemen and others.* [p. 123]

Because the metaphorical trick is continued in this sentence (vehicle transformed to reality), the meaning, we assume, is Swift's own, in that the metaphor is a rhetorical deviation from the persona norm. But now, instead of a pejorative tone, we have an ameliorative one, with some exaggeration, and we recognize that Swift is not speaking seriously in agreement with the persona, but ironically in disagreement. Whereas in the previous sentence Swift meant "Yes, human nature as such is a stinking carcass," in this sentence he is saying, "No, this is meaningless, we cannot recreate what we have destructively analyzed."

> [5] But not to Digress farther in the midst of a Digression, as I have known some Authors inclose Digressions in one another, like a Nest of Boxes; I do affirm, that having carefully cut up *Humane Nature,* I have found a very strange, new, and important Discovery; that the Publick Good of Mankind is performed by two Ways, *Instruction,* and *Diversion.* [pp. 123–24]

In the first long period of this sentence we find regular denotation, at least until we come to the simile. Generally, in this first period, Swift and the persona are saying the same thing—or at least Swift is not disagreeing with the persona's statement. Some authors do digress! In the second long period, however, Swift shows his involvement by way of the metaphor and by way of the exaggerated words "strange, new, and important." And since the tone is generally ameliorative, Swift would seem to be saying something contrary to the persona's literal statement: "No, it is not a strange, new, or important discovery." And we do know, by extra-textual information, that this is so; our knowledge of Horace makes us consider this an ironic statement, even if Swift's rhetoric did not.

> [6] And I have farther proved in my said several Readings, (which, perhaps, the World may one day see, if I can prevail on my Friend to steal a Copy, or on certain Gentlemen of my Admirers, to be very Importunate) that, as Mankind is now disposed, he receives much greater Advantage by being *Diverted* than *Instructed;* His Epidemical Disease being *Fastidiosity, Amorphy,* and *Oscitation;* whereas in the present universal Empire of Wit and Learning, there seems but little Matter left for *Instruction.* [p. 124]

The first period of this sentence, through the phrase "as mankind is now disposed," is fairly level, with no rhetorical disturbances, and we assume Swift fairly well agrees with it or is not concerned with it. It's simply the persona talking. With the word "greater," we have the key exaggeration, and with "epidemical," "fastidiosity," "amorphy," and "oscitation," the key learned words lift us to the ironic level where we know Swift is saying, "No!" In the second period, beginning "whereas," the exaggeration of "universal empire" indicates that the ironic meaning on Swift's part is continued—he is still disagreeing.

> [7] However, in Compliance with a lesson of Great age and Authority, I have attempted carrying the Point in all its Heights; and accordingly throughout this Divine Treatise, have skilfully kneaded up both together with a (Layer) of *Utile,* and a *Layer of Dulce.* [p. 124]

Up to the baking metaphor, this sentence is simply exaggerated language—"of great age and authority," "in all its heights," and "divine"; we therefore assume that Swift is still being ironic in regard to the persona and his statement, or at least Swift is humorously protesting against it. When we come to the metaphor, however, only the word "skilfully" lifts the keyed statement onto the side of irony; and since metaphor in itself is a key only to movement from normal meaning to an involvement on Swift's part, we have some ambiguity here: on the ironic level, Swift is criticizing the persona for his "kneading," but on the remaining serious level, he is, by not disagreeing, affirming his own attempts in the *Tale* to do just this sort of intermingling of both *dulce* and *utile*.

III

This paragraph is slight evidence, of course, from *A Tale of a Tub*, but it does reveal, I believe, an essential technique that Swift uses throughout the entire work.

In summary, the technique works this way: Swift lets the persona (non-Swift) talk in regular denotative language (the norm), but to indicate the distinction between the persona (non-Swift) and the persona-through-which-Swift-is-talking, Swift uses various rhetorical keys: (1) *words of exaggeration, learned language, ameliorative connotations* move the persona's statement onto a level where Swift is speaking mockingly of the persona or is speaking ironically through the persona, saying, "No, this is not so; this should not be so"; (2) *words of exaggeration, learned language, pejorative connotations,* and *general negation* move the persona's statement onto a level where Swift is speaking rather seriously in agreement with what the persona has inadvertently said: "Yes, this is unfortunately so; this is the way things are." Swift uses the metaphor to move onto either level—if the metaphor is essentially ameliorative or pleasant, Swift is emphasizing the irony; if the metaphor is essentially pejorative, Swift is emphasizing a serious direct criticism.

This entire technique rests, of course, upon Swift's belief in some sort of standard in language, taste, and style. Without a standard or norm, his technique will not work. Whether or not he was justified in his belief in the norm is debatable. Even if a norm can be identified at any given moment, the extent to which one can count on the norm as a basis for literary meaning is questionable. The norm is going to change, from decade to decade, generation to generation. Swift perhaps counted on the norm too much, with the consequence that his meaning today is frequently obscure and ambiguous. Yet by taking into consideration the norm which Swift had in mind, we can begin to glimpse more clearly what he had to say. By taking into consideration the standard upon which he based his deviations, we begin to see pattern and sense in his literary statement rather than a chaos of contradiction and inconsistency.

The First Paragraph of *The Ambassadors*: An Explication

IAN WATT

[THE FIRST TEN PARAGRAPHS of this critique, which was originally delivered to a conference of teachers of English at Oxford University on April 5, 1959, are omitted here. In those paragraphs, Ian Watt pointed out the virtues and limitations of such methods of exegesis as the French *explication de texte*, the New Criticism, the German philological approach, historical criticism, and the linguistic approach. Because of the limitations of these methods, Mr. Watt felt that he had to strike out on his own to devise a method for explicating a piece of literary prose, making use, however, of those other critical approaches wherever they seemed likely to aid in unfolding the text.

Ian Watt has produced here a multidimensional stylistic analysis of the initial paragraph of Henry James's novel *The Ambassadors*. Working from the objectively observable idiosyncrasies of James's diction and syntax, he relates these to their functions in the paragraph, to their effects on the reader, to the character traits of Strether and the narrator, and ultimately to the philosophical qualities of James's mind. After reading everything he can from these six sentences, Mr. Watt ranges outside the paragraph to compare it to the novel as a whole, to James's other novels, and to other novels of the period, in order to convince us that the stylistic features of this single paragraph are not only characteristic of James's later prose but also indicative of his complex vision of life and his general conception of the novel as an art form. This remarkably perceptive rhetorical analysis can serve as a model of a method for explicating prose comparable to the methods many of us have learned for explicating poetry.]

From *Essays in Criticism,* X (July 1960), 250–74. Reprinted by permission of *Essays in Criticism* and Ian Watt.

I

Strether's first question, when he reached the hotel, was about his friend; yet on his learning that Waymarsh was apparently not to arrive till evening he was not wholly disconcerted. A telegram from him bespeaking a room "only
5 if not noisy," reply paid, was produced for the inquirer at the office, so that the understanding they should meet at Chester rather than at Liverpool remained to that extent sound. The same secret principle, however, that had prompted Strether not absolutely to desire Waymarsh's
10 presence at the dock, that had led him thus to postpone for a few hours his enjoyment of it, now operated to make him feel he could still wait without disappointment. They would dine together at the worst, and, with all respect to dear old Waymarsh—if not even, for that matter, to him-
15 self—there was little fear that in the sequel they shouldn't see enough of each other. The principle I have just mentioned as operating had been, with the most newly disembarked of the two men, wholly instinctive—the fruit of a sharp sense that, delightful as it would be to find him-
20 self looking, after so much separation, into his comrade's face, his business would be a trifle bungled should he simply arrange for this countenance to present itself to the nearing steamer as the first "note" of Europe. Mixed with everything was the apprehension, already, on Strether's
25 part, that it would, at best, throughout, prove the note of Europe in quite a sufficient degree.[1]

It seems a fairly ordinary sort of prose, but for its faint air of elaborate portent; and on second reading its general quality reminds one of what Strether is later to observe—approvingly—in Maria Gostrey: an effect of "expensive, subdued suitability." There's certainly nothing particularly striking in the diction or

[1] Henry James, *The Ambassadors* (Revised Collected Edition, Macmillan: London, 1923). Since there are a few variants that have a bearing on the argument, it seems desirable to give a collation of the main editions; P is the periodical publication (*The North American Review,* clxxvi, 1903); 1A the first American edition (Harper and Brothers, New York, 1903); 1E the first English edition (Methuen and Co., London, 1903); N.Y., the "New York Edition," New York and London, 1907–9 (the London Macmillan edition used the sheets of the American edition); CR the "Collected Revised Edition," London and New York, 1921–31 (which uses the text of the New York Edition). It should perhaps be explained that the most widely used editions in England and America make misleading

syntax; none of the immediate drama or rich description that we often get at the beginning of novels; and certainly none of the sensuous concreteness that, until recently, was regarded as a chief criterion of good prose in our long post-imagistic phase: if anything, the passage is conspicuously unsensuous and un-concrete, a little dull perhaps, and certainly not easy reading.

The difficulty isn't one of particularly long or complicated sentences: actually they're of fairly usual length: I make it an average of 41 words; a little, but not very much, longer than James's average of 35 (in Book 2, ch. 2. of *The Ambassadors,* according to R. W. Short's count, in his very useful article "The Sentence Structure of Henry James" (*American Literature,* XVIII [March 1946], 71–88.[2] The main cause of difficulty seems rather to come from what may be called the delayed specification of referents: "Strether" and "the hotel" and "his friend" are mentioned before we are told who or where they are. But this difficulty is so intimately connected with James's general narrative technique that it may be better to begin with purely verbal idiosyncrasies, which are more easily isolated. The most distinctive ones in the passage seem to be these: a preference for non-transitive verbs; many abstract nouns; much use of "that"; a certain amount of elegant variation to avoid piling up personal pronouns and adjectives such as "he," "his" and "him"; and the presence of a great many negatives and near-negatives.

By the preference for non-transitive verbs I mean three re-

claims about their text: the "Everyman" edition claims to use the text "of the revised Collected Edition," but actually follows the 1st English edition in the last variant; while the "Anchor" edition, claiming to be "a faithful copy of the text of the Methuen first edition," actually follows the first American edition, including the famous misplaced chapters.

ll.4–5 *reply paid* NY, CR; *with the answer paid* P, 1A, 1E.
l.5. *inquirer* P, 1A, 1E, CR; *enquirer* NY.
l.6. *Understanding they* NY, CR; *understanding that they* P, 1A, 1E.
l.11. *feel he* NY, CR; *feel that he* P, 1A, IE.
l.15. *Shouldn't* CR; *shouldn't* NY; *should not* P, 1A, 1E.
l.16. *Newly disembarked,* all eds. except P: *Newly-disembarked.*
l.20. *arrange that this countenance to present* NY, CR; *arrange that this countenance should present* P, 1A, 1E.
l.22. *"note" of Europe* CR; *"note," for him, of Europe,* P, 1A, 1E; *"note", of Europe,* NY.
l.23. *that it would* P, 1A, NY, CR; *that he would,* 1E.

[2] I am also indebted to the same author's "Henry James's World of Images," *PMLA* LXVIII (Dec., 1953), 943–960.

lated habits: a great reliance on copulatives—"Strether's first question *was* about his friend"; "*was* apparently not to arrive": a frequent use of the passive voice—"*was* not wholly *disconcerted*"; "a telegram . . . *was produced*"; "his business *would be* a trifle *bungled*": and the employment of many intransitive verbs—"the understanding . . . remained . . . sound"; "the . . . principle . . . operated to." My count of all the verbs in the indicative would give a total of 14 passive, copulative or intransitive uses as opposed to only 6 transitive ones: and there are in addition frequent infinitive, participial, or gerundial uses of transitive verbs, in all of which the active nature of the subject-verb-and-object sequence is considerably abated—"on his learning"; "bespeaking a room"; "not absolutely to desire"; "led him thus to postpone."

This relative infrequency of transitive verbal usages in the passage is associated with the even more pronounced tendency towards using abstract nouns as subjects of main or subordinate clauses: "question"; "understanding"; "the same secret principle"; "the principle"; "his business." If one takes only the main clauses, there are four such abstract nouns as subjects, while only three main clauses have concrete and particular subjects ("he," or "they").[3]

I detail these features only to establish that in this passage, at least, there is a clear quantitative basis for the common enough view that James's late prose style is characteristically abstract; more explicitly, that the main grammatical subjects are very often nouns for mental ideas, "question," "principle," etc.; and that the verbs—because they are mainly used either non-transitively, or in infinitive, participial and gerundial forms—tend to express states of being rather than particular finite actions affecting objects.

The main use of abstractions is to deal at the same time with many objects or events rather than single and particular ones: and we use verbs that denote states of being rather than actions for exactly the same reason—their much more general applicability. But in this passage, of course, James isn't in the ordinary sense making abstract or general statements; it's narrative, not expository prose; what need exploring, therefore, are the particular

[3] Sentences one and four are compound or multiple, but in my count I haven't included the second clause in the latter—"there was little fear": though if we can talk of the clause having a subject it's an abstract one—fear.

literary imperatives which impose on his style so many of the verbal and syntactical qualities of abstract and general discourse; of expository rather than narrative prose.

Consider the first sentence. The obvious narrative way of making things particular and concrete would presumably be "when Strether reached the hotel, he first asked 'Has Mr. Waymarsh arrived yet?' " Why does James say it the way he does? One effect is surely that, instead of a sheer stated event, we get a very special view of it; the mere fact that actuality has been digested into reported speech—the question "was about his friend"—involves a narrator to do the job, to interpret the action, and also a presumed audience that he does it for: and by implication, the heat of the action itself must have cooled off somewhat for the translation and analysis of the events into this form of statement to have had time to occur. Lastly, making the subject of the sentence "question" rather than "he," has the effect of subordinating the particular actor, and therefore the particular act, to a much more general perspective: mental rather than physical, and subjective rather than objective; "question" is a word which involves analysis of a physical event into terms of meaning and intention: it involves, in fact, both Strether's mind and the narrator's. The narrator's, because he interprets Strether's act: if James had sought the most concrete method of taking us into Strether's mind—" 'Has Mr. Waymarsh come yet?' I at once asked"—he would have obviated the need for the implied external categoriser of Strether's action. But James disliked the "mere platitude of statement" involved in first-person narrative; partly, presumably, because it would merge Strether's consciousness into the narrative, and not isolate it for the reader's inspection. For such isolation, a more expository method is needed: no confusion of subject and object, as in first-person narration, but a narrator forcing the reader to pay attention to James's primary objective—Strether's mental and subjective state.

The "multidimensional" quality of the narrative, with its continual implication of a community of three minds—Strether's, James's, and the reader's—isn't signalled very obviously until the fourth sentence—"The principle I have just mentioned as operating . . ."; but it's already been established tacitly in every detail of diction and structure, and it remains pervasive. One reason for the special demand James's fictional prose makes on our attention is surely that there are always at least three levels of development —all of them subjective: the characters' awareness of events: the narrator's seeing of them; and our own trailing perception of the relation between these two.

The primary location of the narrative in a mental rather than a physical continuum gives the narrative a great freedom from the restrictions of particular time and place. Materially, we are, of course, in Chester, at the hotel—characteristically "the hotel" because a fully particularised specification—"The Pied Bull Inn" say—would be an irrelevant brute fact which would distract attention from the mental train of thought we are invited to partake in. But actually we don't have any pressing sense of time and place: we feel ourselves to be spectators, rather specifically, of Strether's thought processes, which easily and imperceptibly range forwards and backwards both in time and space. Sentence three, for example, begins in the past, at the Liverpool dock; sentence four looks forward to the reunion later that day, and to its many sequels: such transitions of time and place are much easier to effect when the main subjects of the sentences are abstract: a "principle" exists independently of its context.

The multiplicity of relations—between narrator and object, and between the ideas in Strether's mind—held in even suspension throughout the narrative, is presumably the main explanation for the number of "thats" in the passage, as well as of the several examples of elegant variation. There are 9 "thats"—only two of them demonstrative and the rest relative pronouns (or conjunctions or particles if you prefer those terms); actually there were no less than three more of them in the first edition, which James removed from the somewhat more colloquial and informal New York edition; while there are several other "thats" implied—in "the principle [that] I have just mentioned," for instance.

The number of "thats" follows from two habits already noted in the passage. "That" characteristically introduces relative clauses dealing not with persons but with objects, including abstractions; and it is also used to introduce reported speech— "on his learning that Waymarsh"—not "Mr. Waymarsh isn't here." Both functions are combined in the third sentence where we get a triple definition of a timeless idea based on the report of three chronologically separate events "the same secret principle that had prompted Strether not absolutely to desire Waymarsh's presence at the dock, that had led him thus to postpone for a few hours his enjoyment of it, now operated to make him feel that he could still wait without disappointment."

Reported rather than direct speech also increases the pressure towards elegant variation: the use, for example, in sentence 1 of "his friend," where in direct speech it would be "Mr. Waymarsh" (and the reply—"*He* hasn't come yet"). In the second sentence—"a telegram . . . was produced for the inquirer"—"inquirer" is needed because "him" has already been used for Waymarsh just above; of course, "the inquirer" is logical enough after the subject of the first sentence has been an abstract noun—"question"; and the epithet also gives James an opportunity for underlining the ironic distance and detachment with which we are invited to view his dedicated "inquirer," Strether. Later, when Strether is "the most newly disembarked of the two men," we see how both elegant variation and the grammatical subordination of physical events are related to the general Jamesian tendency to present characters and actions on a plane of abstract categorisation; the mere statement, "Mr. Waymarsh had already been in England for [so many] months," would itself go far to destroy the primarily mental continuum in which the paragraph as a whole exists.

The last general sylistic feature of the passage to be listed above was the use of negative forms. There are 6 "noes" or "nots" in the first 4 sentences; four implied negatives—"postpone"; "without disappointment"; "at the worst"; "there was little fear": and two qualifications that modify positiveness of affirmation—"not wholly" and "to that extent." This abundance of negatives has no doubt several functions: it enacts Strether's tendency to hesitation and qualification; it puts the reader into the right judicial frame of mind; and it has the further effect of subordinating concrete events to their mental reflection; "Waymarsh was not to arrive," for example, is not a concrete statement of a physical event: it is subjective—because it implies an expectation in Strether's mind (which was not fulfilled); and it has an abstract quality—because while Waymarsh's arriving would be particular and physical, his *not* arriving is an idea, a non-action. More generally, James's great use of negatives or near-negatives may also, perhaps, be regarded as part of his subjective and abstractive tendency: there are no negatives in nature but only in the human consciousness.

II

The most obvious grammatical features of what Richard Chase has called Henry James's "infinitely syntactical language" (*The American Novel and its Tradition,* New York, 1957), can, then, be shown to reflect the essential imperatives of his narrative point of view; and they could therefore lead into a discussion of the philosophical qualities of his mind, as they are discussed, for example, by Dorothea Krook in her notable article "The Method of the Later Works of Henry James" (*London Magazine,* I [1954], 55–70); our passage surely exemplifies James's power "to generalise to the limit the particulars of experience," and with it the characteristic way in which both his "perceptions of the world itself, and his perceptions of the logic of the world . . . happen simultaneously, are part of a single comprehensive experience." Another aspect of the connection between James's metaphysic and his method as a novelist has inspired a stimulating stylistic study—Carlo Izzo's "Henry James, Scrittore Sintattico" (*Studi Americani,* II [1956], 127–142). The connection between thought and style finds its historical perspective in John Henry Raleigh's illuminating study "Henry James: The Poetics of Empiricism" (*PMLA,* LXVI [1951], 107–123), which establishes connections between Lockean epistemology and James's extreme, almost anarchic, individualism; while this epistemological preoccupation, which is central to Quentin Anderson's view of how James worked out his father's cosmology in fictional terms (*The American Henry James,* New Brunswick, 1957), also leads towards another large general question, the concern with "point of view," which became a crucial problem in the history and criticism of fiction under the influence of the sceptical relativism of the late nineteenth-century.

In James's case, the problem is fairly complicated. He may be classed as an "Impressionist," concerned, that is, to show not so much the events themselves, but the impressions which they make on the characters. But James's continual need to generalise and place and order, combined with his absolute demand for a point of view that would be plastic enough to allow him freedom for the formal "architectonics" of the novelists' craft, eventually involved him in a very idiosyncratic kind of multiple Impressionism: idiosyncratic because the dual presence of Strether's consciousness and of that of the narrator, who translates what he sees there into more general terms, makes the narrative point of view both intensely individual and yet ultimately social.

Another possible direction of investigation would be to show that the abstractness and indirection of James's style are essentially the result of this characteristic multiplicity of his vision. There is, for example, the story reported by Edith Wharton that after his first stroke James told Lady Prothero that "in the very act of falling . . . he heard in the room a voice which was distinctly, it seemed, not his own, saying: 'So here it is at last, the distinguished thing.'" James, apparently, could not but see even his own most fateful personal experience, except as evoked by some other observer's voice in terms of the long historical and literary tradition of death. Carlo Izzo regards this tendency as typical of the Alexandrian style, where there is a marked disparity between the rich inheritance of the means of literary expression, and the meaner creative world which it is used to express; but the defence of the Jamesian habit of mind must surely be that what the human vision shares with that of animals is presumably the perception of concrete images, not the power to conceive universals: such was Aristotle's notion of man's distinguishing capacity. The universals in the present context are presumably the awareness that behind every petty individual circumstance there ramifies an endless network of general moral, social, and historical relations. Henry James's style can therefore be seen as a supremely civilised effort to relate every event and every moment of life to the full complexity of its circumambient conditions.

Obviously James's multiple awareness can go too far; and in the later novels it often poses the special problem that we do not quite know whether the awareness implied in a given passage is the narrator's or that of his character. Most simply, a pronoun referring to the subject of a preceding clause is always liable to give trouble if one hasn't been very much aware of what the grammatical subject of that preceding clause was; in the last sentence of the paragraph, for example, "the apprehension, already, on Strether's part, that . . . it would, at best, . . . prove the 'note' of Europe," "it" refers to Waymarsh's countenance: but this isn't at first obvious; which is no doubt why, in his revision of the periodical version for the English edition James replaced "it" by "he"—simpler, grammatically, but losing some of the ironic visual precision of the original. More seriously, because the narrator's consciousness and Strether's are both present, we often don't know whose mental operations and evaluative judgments are involved in particular cases. We pass, for instance, from the objective analysis of sentence 3 where the analytic terminology of "the same secret principle" must be the responsibility of the narrator, to what must be a verbatim quotation of Strether's mind in sentence 4: "With all respect to dear old Waymarsh" is obviously Strether's licensed familiarity.

But although the various difficulties of tense, voice, and reference require a vigilance of attention in the reader which some have found too much to give, they are not in themselves very considerable: and what perhaps is much more in need of attention is how the difficulties arising from the multiplicity of points of view don't by any means prevent James from ordering all the elements of his narrative style into an amazingly precise means of expression: and it is this positive, and in the present case, as it seems to me, triumphant, mastery of the difficulties which I want next to consider.

Our passage is not, I think, James either at his most memorable or at his most idiosyncratic: *The Ambassadors* is written with considerable sobriety and has, for example, little of the vivid and direct style of the early part of *The Wings of the Dove,* or of the happy symbolic complexities of *The Golden Bowl.* Still, the passage is fairly typical of the later James; and I think it can be proved that all or at least nearly all the idiosyncrasies of diction or syntax in the present passage are fully justified by the particular emphases they create.

The most flagrant eccentricity of diction is presumably that where James writes "the most newly disembarked of the two men" (lines 16–17). "Most" may very well be a mere slip; and it must certainly seem indefensible to any one who takes it as an absolute rule that the comparative must always be used when only two items are involved.[4] But a defence is at least possible. "Most newly disembarked" means something rather different from "more newly disembarked." James, it may be surmised, did not want to compare the recency of the two men's arrival, but to inform us that Strether's arrival was "very" or as we might say, "most" recent; the use of the superlative also had the advantage of suggesting the long and fateful tradition of transatlantic disembarcations in general.

The reasons for the other main syntactical idiosyncrasies in the passage are much clearer. In the first part of the opening sentence, for example, the separation of subject—"question"—from verb—"was"—by the longish temporal clause "when he reached the hotel," is no doubt a dislocation of normal sentence structure; but, of course, "Strether" must be the first word of the novel: while, even more important, the delayed placing of the temporal clause, forces a pause after "question" and thus gives it a very significant resonance. Similarly with the last sentence; it has several peculiarities, of which the placing of "throughout" seems the most obvious. The sentence has three parts: the first and last are comparatively straightforward, but the middle is a massed block of portentous qualifications: "Mixed with everything was the apprehension—already, on Strether's part, that he would, at best, throughout,—prove the note of Europe in quite a sufficient degree." The echoing doom started by the connotation of "apprehension"—reverberates through "already," ("much more to come later") "on Strether's part" ("even he knows") and "at best" ("the worst has been envisaged, too"); but it is the final collapse of the terse rhythm of the parenthesis that isolates the rather awkwardly placed "throughout," and thus enables James to sound the fine full fatal note; there is no limit to the poignant eloquence of "throughout." It was this effect, of course, which dictated the preceding inversion which places "apprehension" not at the start of the sentence, but in the middle where, largely freed from its syntactical nexus, it may be directly exposed to its salvos of qualification.

The mockingly fateful emphasis on "throughout" tells us, if

[4] Though consider *Rasselas*, ch. xxviii: "Both conditions may be bad, but they cannot both be worst."

nothing had before, that James's tone is in the last analysis ironic, comic, or better, as I shall try to suggest, humorous. The general reasons for this have already been suggested. To use Maynard Mack's distinction (in his Preface to *Joseph Andrews*, Rinehart Editions, New York, 1948), "the comic artist subordinates the presentation of life as experience, where the relationship between ourselves and the characters experiencing it is a primary one, to the presentation of life as a spectacle, where the primary relation is between himself and us as onlookers." In the James passage, the primacy of the relation between the narrator and the reader has already been noted, as has its connection with the abstraction of the diction, which brings home the distance between the narrator and Strether. Of course, the application of abstract diction to particular persons always tends towards irony,[5] because it imposes a dual way of looking at them: few of us can survive being presented as general representatives of humanity.

The paragraph, of course, is based on one of the classic contradictions in psychological comedy—Strether's reluctance to admit to himself that he has very mixed feelings about his friend: and James develops this with the narrative equivalent of *commedia dell'arte* technique: virtuoso feats of ironic balance, coming exaggeration, and deceptive hesitation conduct us on a complicated progress towards the foreordained illumination.

In structure, to begin with, the six sentences form three groups of two: each pair of them gives one aspect of Strether's delay; and they are arranged in an ascending order of complication so that the fifth sentence—72 words—is almost twice as long as any other, and is succeeded by the final sentence, the punch line, which is noticeably the shortest—26 words. The development of the ideas is as controlled as the sentence structure. Strether is obviously a man with an enormous sense of responsibility about personal relationships; so his first question is about his friend. That loyal *empressement*, however, is immediately checked by the balanced twin negatives that follow: "on his learning that Waymarsh *was not* to arrive till evening, he *was not* wholly disconcerted": one of the diagnostic elements of irony, surely, is hyperbole qualified with mock-scrupulousness, such as

[5] As I have argued in "The Ironic Tradition in Augustan Prose from Swift to Johnson," *Restoration and Augustan Prose* (Los Angeles, 1957).

we get in "not wholly disconcerted." Why there are limits to Lambert Strether's consternation is to transpire in the next sentence; Waymarsh's telegram bespeaking a room "only if not noisy" is a laconic suggestion of that inarticulate worthy's habitually gloomy expectations—from his past experiences of the indignities of European hotel noise we adumbrate the notion that the cost of their friendly *rencontre* may be his sleeping in the street. In the second part of the sentence we have another similar, though more muted, hint: "the understanding that they should meet in Chester rather than at Liverpool remained to that extent sound"; "to that extent," no doubt, but to *any other?*—echo seems to answer "No."

In the second group of sentences we are getting into Strether's mind, and we have been prepared to relish the irony of its ambivalences. The negatived hyperbole of "not absolutely to desire," turns out to mean "postpone"; and, of course, a voluntarily postponed "enjoyment" itself denotes a very modified rapture, although Strether's own consciousness of the problem is apparently no further advanced than that "he could still wait without disappointment." Comically loyal to what he would like to feel, therefore, we have him putting in the consoling reflection that "they would dine together at the worst"; and the ambiguity of 'at the worst' is followed by the equally dubious thought: "there was little fear that in the sequel they shouldn't see enough of each other." That they should, in fact, see too much of each other; but social decorum and Strether's own loyalties demand that the outrage of the open statement be veiled in the obscurity of formal negation.

By the time we arrive at the climactic pair of sentences, we have been told enough for more ambitious effects to be possible. The twice-mentioned "secret principle," it appears, is actually wholly "instinctive" (line 17); but in other ways Strether is almost ludicrously self-conscious. The qualified hyperbole of "his business would be a trifle bungled," underlined as it is by the alliteration, prepares us for a half-realised image which amusingly defines Strether's sense of his role: he sees himself, it appears, as the stage-manager of an enterprise in which his solemn obligations as an implicated friend are counterbalanced by his equally ceremonious sense that due decorums must also be attended to when he comes face to face with another friend of long ago—no less a person than Europe. It is, of course, silly of him, as James makes him acknowledge in the characteristic italicising of "the 'note' of Europe";[6] but still, he does have a comically ponderous sense of protocol which leads him to feel that "his business would be a trifle bungled" should he simply arrange for this countenance to present itself to the nearing steamer as the first "note" of Europe. The steamer, one imagines, would not have turned hard astern at the proximity of Waymarsh's sacred rage; but Strether's fitness for ambassadorial functions is defined by his thinking in terms of "arranging" for a certain countenance at the docks to give just the right symbolic greeting.

Strether's notion of what Europe demands also shows us the force of his aesthetic sense. But in the last sentence the metaphor, though it remains equally self-conscious, changes its mode of operation from the dramatic, aesthetic, and diplomatic, to something more scientific: for, although ten years ago I should not have failed to point out, and my readers would not, I suppose, have failed to applaud, the ambiguity of "prove," it now seems to me that we must choose between two possible meanings. James may be using "prove" to mean that Waymarsh's face will "turn out to be" the "note of Europe" for Strether. But "prove" in this sense is intransitive, and "to be" would have to be supplied; it therefore seems more likely that James is using "prove" in the older sense of "to test": Waymarsh is indeed suited to the role of being the sourly acid test of the siren songs of Europe "in quite a sufficient degree," as Strether puts it with solemn but arch understanding.

The basic development structure of the passage, then, is one of progressive and yet artfully delayed clarification; and this pattern is also typical of James's general novelistic method. The reasons for this are suggested in the Preface to *The Princess Casamassima,* where James deals with the problem of maintaining a balance between the intelligence a character must have to be interesting, and the bewilderment which is nevertheless an essen-

[6] See George Knox, "James's Rhetoric Quotes," *College English,* XVII (1956), 293–297.

tial condition of the novel's having surprise, development, and tension: "It seems probable that if we were never bewildered there would never be a story to tell about us."

In the first paragraph of *The Ambassadors* James appraises us both of his hero's supreme qualities and of his associated limitations. Strether's delicate critical intelligence is often blinkered by a highly vulnerable mixture of moral generosity towards others combined with an obsessive sense of personal inadequacy; we see the tension in relation to Waymarsh, as later we are to see it in relation to all his other friends; and we understand, long before Strether, how deeply it bewilders him; most poignantly about the true nature of Chad, Madame de Vionnet—and himself.

This counterpoint of intelligence and bewilderment is, of course, another reason for the split narrative point of view we've already noted: we and the narrator are inside Strether's mind, and yet we are also outside it, knowing more about Strether than he knows about himself. This is the classic posture of irony. Yet I think that to insist too exclusively on the ironic function of James's narrative point of view would be mistaken.

Irony has lately been enshrined as the supreme deity in the critical pantheon: but, I wonder, is there really anything so wonderful about being distant and objective? Who wants to see life only or mainly in intellectual terms? In art as in life we no doubt can have need of intellectual distance as well as of emotional commitment; but the uninvolvement of the artist surely doesn't go very far without the total involvement of the person; or, at least, without a deeper human involvement than irony customarily establishes. One could, I suppose, call the aesthetically perfect balance between distance and involvement, open or positive irony: but I'm not sure that humour isn't a better word, especially when the final balance is tipped in favour of involvement, of ultimate commitment to the characters; and I hope that our next critical movement will be the New Gelastics.

At all events, although the first paragraph alone doesn't allow the point to be established fully here, it seems to me that James's attitude to Strether is better described as humorous than ironical; we must learn like Maria Gostrey, to see him "at last all comically, all tragically." James's later novels in general are most intellectual; but they are also, surely, his most compassionate: and in this particular paragraph Strether's dilemma is developed in such a way that we feel for him even more than we smile at him. This balance of intention, I think, probably explains why James keeps his irony in such a low key: we must be aware of Strether's "secret" ambivalence towards Waymarsh, but not to the point that his unawareness of it would verge on fatuity; and our controlling sympathy for the causes of Strether's ambivalence turns what might have been irony into something closer to what Constance Rourke characterises as James's typical "low-keyed humor of defeat" (*American Humor,* 1931).

That James's final attitude is humorous rather than ironic is further suggested by the likeness of the basic structural technique of the paragraph to that of the funny story—the incremental involvement in an endemic human perplexity which can only be resolved by laughter's final acceptance of contradiction and absurdity. We don't, in the end, see Strether's probing hesitations mainly as an ironic indication by James of mankind's general muddlement; we find it, increasingly, a touching example of how, despite all their inevitable incongruities and shortcomings, human ties remain only, but still, human.

Here it is perhaps James's very slowness and deliberation throughout the narrative which gives us our best supporting evidence: greater love hath no man than hearing his friend out patiently.

III

The function of an introductory paragraph in a novel is presumably to introduce: and this paragraph surely has the distinction of being a supremely complex and inclusive introduction to a novel. It introduces the hero, of course, and one of his companions; also the time; the place; something of what's gone before. But James has carefully avoided giving us the usual retrospective beginning, that pile of details which he scornfully termed a "mere seated mass of information." All the details are scrupulously presented as reflections from the novel's essential centre—the narrator's patterning of the ideas going forwards and backwards in Strether's mind. Of course, this initially makes the novel more difficult, because what we probably think of as primary—event and its setting—is subordinated to what James thinks is—the mental drama of the hero's consciousness, which, of course, is not told but shown: scenically dramatised. At the same time, by selecting thoughts and events which are representative of the book as a whole, and narrating them with an abstractness which suggests their larger import, James introduces the most general themes of the novel.

James, we saw, carefully arranged to make "Strether's first question," the first three words; and, of course, throughout the novel, Strether is to go on asking questions—and getting increasingly dusty answers. This, it may be added, is stressed by the apparent aposiopesis: for a "first" question when no second is mentioned, is surely an intimation that more are—in a way unknown to us or to Strether—yet to come. The later dislocations of normal word-order already noted above emphasise other major themes; the "secret principle" in Strether's mind, and the antithesis Waymarsh-Europe, for instance.

The extent to which these processes were conscious on James's part cannot, of course, be resolved; but it is significant that the meeting with Maria Gostrey was interposed before the meeting with Waymarsh, which James had originally planned as his beginning in the long (20,000) word scenario of the plot which he prepared for *Harper's*. The unexpected meeting had many advantages; not least that James could repeat the first paragraph's pattern of delayed clarification in the structure of the first chapter as a whole. On Strether's mind we get a momentously clear judgment at the end of the second paragraph: "there was detachment in his zeal, and curiosity in his indifference"; but then the meeting with Maria Gostrey, and its gay opportunities for a much fuller presentation of Strether's mind, intervene before Waymarsh himself finally appears at the end of the chapter; only then is the joke behind Strether's uneasy hesitations in the first paragraph brought to its hilariously blunt climax: "It was already upon him even at that distance—Mr. Waymarsh was for *his* part joyless."

One way of evaluating James's achievement in this paragraph, I suppose, would be to compare the opening of James's other novels, and with those of previous writers: but it would take too long to do more than sketch the possibilities of this approach.

James's early openings certainly have some of the banality of the "mere seated mass of information": in *Roderick Hudson* (1876), for example: "Rowland Mallet had made his arrangements to sail for Europe on the 5th of September, and having in the interval a fortnight to spare, he determined to spend it with his cousin Cecilia, the widow of a nephew of his father. . . ." Later, James showed a much more comprehensive notion of what the introductory paragraph should attempt: even in the relatively simple and concrete opening of *The Wings of the Dove* (1902): "She waited, Kate Croy, for her father to come in, but he kept her unconscionably, and there were moments at which she showed herself, in the glass over the mantle, a face positively pale with irritation that had brought her to the point of going away without sight of him. . . ." "She waited, Kate Croy"—an odd parenthetic apposition artfully contrived to prefigure her role throughout the novel —to wait.

One could, I suppose, find this sort of symbolic prefiguring in the work of earlier novelists; but never, I imagine, in association with all the other levels of introductory function that James manages to combine in a single paragraph. Jane Austen has her famous thematic irony in the opening of *Pride and Prejudice* (1813): "It is a truth universally acknowledged, that a single man in possession of a good fortune must be in want of a wife"; but pride and prejudice must come later. Dickens can hurl us overpoweringly into *Bleak House* (1852–3), into its time and place and general theme; but characters and opening action have to wait:

> London. Michaelmas Term lately over, and the Lord Chancellor sitting in Lincoln's Inn Hall. Implacable November weather. As much mud in the streets, as if the waters had but newly retired from the face of the earth, and it would not be wonderful to meet a Megalosaurus, forty feet long or so, waddling like an elephantine lizard up Holborn-Hill. Smoke lowering down from chimney-pots. . . .

In Dickens, characteristically, we get a loud note that sets the tone, rather than a polyphonic series of chords that contain all the later melodic developments, as in James. And either the Dickens method, or the "mere seated mass of information," seem to be commonest kinds of opening in nineteenth-century novels. For openings that suggest something of James's ambitious attempt to achieve a prologue that is a synchronic introduction of all the main aspects of the narrative, I think that Conrad is his closest rival. But Conrad, whether in expository or dramatic vein, tends to an arresting initial vigour that has dangers which James's more muted tones avoid. In *An Outcast of the Islands* (1896), for example:

> When he stepped off the straight and narrow path of his peculiar honesty, it was with an inward assertion of unflinching resolve to fall back again into the monotonous but safe stride of virtue as soon as his little excursion into the wayside quagmires had produced the desired effect. It was going to be a short episode—a sentence in brackets, so to speak, in the flowing tale of his life. . . .

Conrad's sardonic force has enormous immediate impact; but it surely gives too much away: the character, Willems, has been dissected so vigorously that it takes great effort for Conrad—and the reader—to revivify him later. The danger lurks even in the masterly combination of physical notation and symbolic evaluation at the beginning of *Lord Jim* (1900): "He was an inch, perhaps two, under six feet . . .": the heroic proportion is for ever missed, by an inch, perhaps two; which is perhaps too much, to begin with.

It is not for me to assess how far I have succeeded in carrying out the general intentions with which I began, or how far similar methods of analysis would be applicable to other kinds of prose. As regards the explication of the passage itself, the main argument must by now be sufficiently clear, although a full demonstration would require a much wider sampling both of other novels and of other passages in *The Ambassadors*.[7] The most obvious and demonstrable features of James's prose style, its vocabulary and syntax, are direct reflections of his attitude to life

[7] A similar analysis of eight other paragraphs selected at fifty page intervals revealed that, as would be expected, there is much variation: the tendency to use non-transitive verbs, and abstract nouns as subjects, for instance, seems to be strong throughout the novel, though especially so in analytic rather than narrative passages; but the frequent use of "that" and of negative forms of statement does not recur significantly.

and his conception of the novel; and these features, like the relation of the paragraph to the rest of the novel, and to other novels, make clear that the notorious idiosyncrasies of Jamesian prose are directly related to the imperatives which led him to develop a narrative texture as richly complicated and as highly organised as that of poetry.

No wonder James scorned translation and rejoiced, as he so engagingly confessed to his French translator, Auguste Monod, that his later works were "locked fast in the golden cage of the *intraduisible.*" Translation could hardly do justice to a paragraph in which so many levels of meaning and implication are kept in continuous operation; in which the usual introductory exposition of time, place, character, and previous action, are rendered through an immediate immersion in the processes of the hero's mind as he's involved in perplexities which are characteristic of the novel as a whole and which are articulated in a mode of comic development which is essentially that, not only of the following chapter, but of the total structure. To have done all that is to have gone far towards demonstrating the contention which James announced at the end of the Preface to *The Ambassadors,* that "the Novel remains still, under the right persuasion, the most independent, most elastic, most prodigious of literary forms"; and the variety and complexity of the functions carried out in the book's quite short first paragraph also suggest that, contrary to some notions, the demonstration is, as James claimed, made with "a splendid particular economy."

George Bernard Shaw: Prose Against Itself

RICHARD M. OHMANN

[In Chapter III of his book *Shaw: The Style and the Man,* from which this selection is taken, Richard Ohmann does a reprise of some of the themes he had treated in Chapter I, but in the later chapter he comes at these themes from a different angle. "My subject to this point," he says (p. 73), "has been connections between Shaw's basic epistemic mode and its stylistic repercussions. From here on I shall be concerned less with style as a way of knowing and increasingly with the rhetorical and emotional uses to which that way of knowing is put."

Unlike the authors of other critiques in this volume, Professor Ohmann does not concentrate on a single literary work but rather ranges over a wide territory of Shaw's prose for his illustrations and confirmations of Shaw's "stylistics of tension and conflict." Shaw's plays, which because of the nature of the genre lack the authorial voice, create an impression of broadmindedness, of tolerance for a variety of points of view. But in most of his prose works, where the author speaks in his own voice, we see the born scrapper. It is "impossible to see in his prose," Ohmann says, "the cautious, prudent thinker, weighing all possibilities and coming judiciously to rest on one of them with only tentative force." Shaw works mainly by dogmatic assertion and sweeping denial, and because of the very forcefulness of this pattern of affirmation and denial, he carries many readers along with him.

Ohmann examines those strategies of diction and syntax by which Shaw achieves his rhetorical effectiveness, and he tries to show that these devices of style are not only characteristic of Shaw's polemical prose but also symptomatic of Shaw the man. This selection is a good example of the kind of rhetorical criticism that moves back and forth between the work, the author, and the audience—although in this particular selection Ohmann

From *Shaw: The Style and the Man,* by Richard M. Ohmann, 90–101.

focuses mainly on the interrelations between the work and the author.]

Key to Abbreviations in Richard Ohmann's Analysis
(References are to volumes in the Ayot St. Lawrence edition unless otherwise specified)

PPU	*Plays Pleasant and Unpleasant* (2 vols.)
War	*What I Really Wrote About the War*
IWG	*The Intelligent Woman's Guide to Socialism, Capitalism, Sovietism, and Fascism.* Standard Edition (London, 1932)
HH	*Heartbreak House, Great Catherine, Playlets of the War*
Dilemma	*The Doctor's Dilemma, Getting Married, The Shewing-Up of Blanco Posnet*
Delusions	*Doctor's Delusions, Crude Criminology, Sham Education*
Too True	*Too True To Be Good, Village Wooing, On the Rocks. Three Plays by Bernard Shaw* (London, 1934)
EPWW	*Everybody's Political What's What?* (London, 1944)
Back	*Back to Methuselah*
QI	*The Quintessence of Ibsenism, The Perfect Wagnerite, The Sanity of Art*
StJ	*Saint Joan, The Apple Cart*
Essays	*Essays in Fabian Socialism*
JBOI	*John Bull's Other Island, How He Lied to Her Husband, Major Barbara*

UNITY, SAYS SHAW, is fatal to the drama, which must present a conflict. But, he goes on, "the obvious conflicts of unmistakeable good with unmistakeable evil can only supply the crude drama of villain and hero. . . . In such cheap wares I do not deal" (PPU, II, ix). Certainly this self-appraisal is on the whole just. Although many of the plays have one or two hopeless snobs or ignoramuses, out-and-out villains do not abound. Normally, if there *is* a devil, he is so eloquently his own advocate that Shaw himself seems half convinced. To think of the complexity of debate in the better plays is to be reminded of the complexity of judgment they require—the awareness, for instance, that both Joan and her judges have a measure of right on their side, or that Andrew Undershaft is only Prince of Darkness in the sense of having made himself prince in a place where darkness is the natural condition. Shaw habitually forestalls the stock response, says No to the reader's facile verdicts. The dazzling brightness of Shavian dialogue would be impossible if half the burden fell to straw men.

In another context he claims that this dramatic many-sidedness extends to all of his thinking: "My inborn dramatic faculty and professional habit as a playwright prevent me from taking a one-sided view . . ." (War, 23). Now this is a contention that needs to be received with more caution than the other one. Shaw is certainly not one-sided in the sense of being narrow, and he is emphatically not one-sided in the sense of cleaving blindly to an already-formed position in a controversy. But it is nonetheless impossible to see in his prose the cautious, prudent thinker, weighing all possibilities and coming judiciously to rest on one of them with only tentative force. The typical Shavian idea may be idiosyncratic and complex, but once he has adopted it he pushes it on the reader with a quite one-sided tenacity.

The common ground between his dramatic dialogue and his discursive prose is not urbane broadmindedness, but scrappiness. His prose, like his drama, bulges with conflicting voices, full of argument. Since, in the drama, there can hardly be an authorial voice with final jurisdiction over the disputants, the devil always seems to be getting his due. But in the prose his arguments collapse under an avalanche of Shavian scorn; Shaw articulates them in order to drown them out with his own commanding rhetoric. Still, the rejected arguments play an important stylistic part. As the forces of the enemy they elicit the negatives that I have already discussed; but negation is impossible without something to be denied, and it still remains for me to examine the actual stylistics of tension and conflict.

In Chapter II, I argued that directional shifts from speech to speech in the plays have a loose parallel in various forms of syntactical discontinuity that appear in the prose. It is possible to find an even closer analogy for these dramatic shifts in the give and take, mostly give on Shaw's part, between his persona and the opposition. Consider the short sentence of denial, which dismisses arguments that have gone immediately before, thus reversing the direction of the discourse. Such sentences range from the relatively formal and moderate—

> So that will not do. (IWG, 6–7)
> They did not strike me in that way. (HH, 3)
> This was a bad beginning. (Dilemma, 370)

to the relatively curt and disrespectful—

> They are not. (IWG, 1)
> This is impossible. (IWG, 2)
> They won't. (IWG, 44)
> Stuff and nonsense. (IWG, 7)
> That is stupid. (Delusions, 198)
> No. (Too True, 16)

These rejoinders signal conflict rather spectacularly, because of the brevity and abruptness with which they reverse the direction of the argument, and they are a favorite trick of Shaw's. But of course even for him they represent a tiny fraction of all the oscillation between assertion and denial. The transitional words that mark concession and conflict—words such as "although," "but," and "yet"—are responsible for very many changes of direction. Shaw probably does not rely more heavily on these commonplace rhetorical shifts than the average writer, since large units of his prose move in unbroken lines like those of the torrential series (see Chapter I). But a count of such changes of direction as constitute a *denial* of what went before, rather than a mere *qualification,* reveals the extent to which Shaw's prose moves by negation. An unusually large number of the junctions between sentence and sentence involve a collision of opposed forces.

This simple method of giving the opposition its brief say while denying its claims with some kind of negative has an analogue in these slightly less compact forms:

> It is not true that all the atrocities of Capitalism are the expression of human vice and evil will: on the contrary . . . (EPWW, 2)

> It is not that science is free from legends, witchcraft, miracles, biographic boostings of quacks as heroes and saints, and of barren scoundrels as explorers and discoverers. On the contrary . . . (Back, lxxix–lxxx)

Here Shaw allots a sentence or clause to the view he is rejecting, but two things are worth noting: First, although he does not state his refutation until after he has presented the opposite contention, he nullifies that contention before it can gain a toehold by subordinating it grammatically to a main clause that *denies* it—"It is not true that . . ." Second, the position Shaw refutes is put so uncompromisingly that it would claim no credence even if preserved from Shaw's contradiction. He makes no pretense of giving a fair hearing to the accused, whose testimony he exaggerates in order to point up the dichotomy of right and wrong views. The conflict created by such oppositions is the resolved tension of a mind already made up, rather than the balanced tension of indecision and careful weighing.

The same holds true of several shorter forms in the "not———, but———" family:

> Not against the opinions it expresses, but against the facts it records. (QI, 175)
>
> Socialism is not charity nor loving-kindness, nor sympathy with the poor, nor popular philanthropy . . . but the economist's hatred of waste and disorder, the aesthete's hatred of ugliness and dirt, the lawyer's hatred of injustice . . . (EPWW, 78)
>
> picture postcards might have been sold of her as a general: they would not have been sold of her as a sultana. (StJ, 9)
>
> neither sown nor reaped, baked nor brewed, but only collected from the hungry . . . (IWG, 348)

This pattern of denial and affirmation is a rather common one in Shaw's prose. It leads to a species of semantic overlap, since to tell what is not the case in the same breath that one tells what *is* the case is to specify a situation doubly. But the semantic redundancy is not a rhetorical redundancy. In buttressing his assertion with a negation he exposes to scorn either the folly of the other side's views or the venality of its actions. It is important to Shaw not only that truth be broadcast, but that error be pilloried, and the "not———, but———" pattern answers to both aims.

When the opposition has its say within such a short syntactical span, the entire process of refutation can easily be tucked into the pocket of a larger grammatical garment. Take, for example, the by-now-familiar Shavian series, itself an instrument of denial as a whole. Within these catalogues the individual members may embody lesser conflicts. Thus when Shaw disputes the ability of censors to do their job he complains that they cannot distinguish "between art and blackguardism, between morality and virtue, between immorality and vice, between conscientious heresy and mere baseness of mind and foulness of mouth" (Dilemma, 410). Each phrase sets two things against each other that are, to Shaw, quite contradictory. On the four separate conflicts of ideas, the larger conflict between him and the censors depends. Here is a more gross example of tension within the units of a series: the government must assume, he says,

> that everybody is exactly like everybody else, although no two people are alike; that everybody is consistent although everybody is in fact a sackful of contradictions; that all marriages are alike, all love affairs alike, all . . .; although they are all as different as fingerprints. (EPWW, 334)

In each of the three large sections of the series a position gets voiced and then rejected, with the effect of direct contradiction.

The trope of which both these series present special cases is, of course, antithesis, an important framework for stylistic opposition. In it, conflict emerges most dramatically when, as with the second of the two series, Shaw repeats a number of words, allowing their exact correspondence to emphasize the divergence of the others. Thus, in order to suggest the difference between democracy and justice, and dispel the notion that justice is a practical alternative to democracy, Shaw opposes them thus: "The indispensable preliminary to Democracy is the representation of every interest: the indispensable preliminary to justice is the elimination of every interest" (JBOI, xxvii-xxviii). In this respect democracy differs from justice as much as elimination does from representation. Neat opposites of this sort have a peculiar appeal for him:

> Now the tendency of private property is to keep the masses mere beasts of burden. The tendency of Social Democracy is to educate them—to make men of them. (Essays, 59)

> a mystic nexus to replace the cash nexus. (JBOI, 218)

> When the Germans bombed the Cathedral of Rheims, the world rang with the horror of the sacrilege. When they bombed the

> Little Theatre . . . the fact was not even mentioned in the papers. (HH, 36)

They satisfy both the requirements of equivalence and those of conflict, for they compare two events or situations that are precisely alike in some ways and radically different in others.

When Shaw's antitheses build less on repetition of major words, they may build more on the pairing up of grammatical frames. For instance, "The economic change is merely formal: the moral change is enormous" (Essays, 12); or "On decent human terms with one another instead of on competitive capitalistic terms" (IWG, 154). The syntax of one half mirrors that of the other closely enough to show that the two *meanings* are far from alike. But such close repetition either of syntactical frames or of words themselves is more characteristic of neo-classical than of Shavian antithesis, which spreads out into a variety of forms. Its mechanism may be tripped by the repetition of just one word and the metamorphosis of one or two others: "The business of an honest and understanding Government is . . . When Governments are either dishonest or ignorant . . ." (IWG, 292). There is no parallelism at all, nor any word pointing to negation, but the echo of "honest" in "dishonest" and the fainter echo of "understanding" in "ignorant" suffice to put the two sentences in evident conflict. Or the antithesis may emerge only through the total meanings of its parts, as when "soldiers who had done voluntary and heroic service in the field" are set against "persons who had apparently never run a risk or spent a farthing that they could avoid." (HH, 26).

This last is the most common, though not the most noticeable, method of Shavian antithesis. It matches nicely his conviction that society's make-up is badly askew, and his hope that merely exposing contradictions to the light will suffice to turn some readers against them. *The Intelligent Woman's Guide* is particularly full of such contrasts—one woman has a single pair of leaking boots and another has forty pairs of high-heeled shoes (p. 56); a nation is confused if it "spends money on champagne before it has provided milk for its babies" (p. 56); and so on. These contradictions are the nourishment on which socialism thrives, and as such they inevitably play a significant part in

Shaw's political writing, but he favors such modes of contrast whether or not his subject is the sickness of capitalism. They are tightly implicated with typically Shavian debate.

When antithesis works merely by the juxtaposition of disparate meanings it may closely resemble paradox, which also deals in the oddities of reality. All that is needed to push many Shavian antitheses over the line into paradox is closer structuring to insist on the compatibility of seemingly incompatible meanings. Thus, when he says that "our laws make law impossible" (JBOI, 243), he relies on an antithesis between true law and false law to make sense of the apparent contradiction. As Bentley explains, Shaw often uses words in two different senses, "postulates a genuine article—gentleman, science, democracy—and in each case the spurious product which has stolen the market." The paradox of "law" and "laws" is followed by another, "Our liberties destroy all freedom," which, instead of making the same word mean opposite things, makes two supposed synonyms work against each other as opposites. The list of capitalistic injustices moves on to property: "Our property is organized robbery"—another variety of paradox, which operates by equating two words normally taken to be antonyms. Similarly, "Our morality is an impudent hypocrisy." Then the form shifts again with "our wisdom is administered by inexperienced or malexperienced dupes, our power wielded by cowards and weaklings." Here the paradox turns on incongruity rather than overt contradiction. It is not impossible that power should be wielded by weaklings, but such a thing does violate one's sense of rightness. This catalogue of the hypocrisies entailed by a *laissez-faire* system concludes with still another form of paradox-oxymoron: "Our honor false in all its points." In this most compact of antitheses, the adjective undermines the noun. The variegation of this series suggests how numerous are the syntactical means by which Shaw sets up paradox. He falls into it naturally, without rhetorical or stylistic affectation, because it conforms to his vision of the contradictions in human conduct.

I have now run through the most obvious stylistic outcroppings of tension and conflict. A number of more subtle manifestations remain, but subtlety in these matters is really not Shaw's forte. It is possible, for instance, to imply an opposition by stating only one half of it. Thus, in describing medieval economic life,

Shaw says, "If they catch a man buying goods solely in order to sell them a few hours later at a higher price, they treat that man as a rascal," and the man never pleads that it is his "pious duty, to buy in the cheapest market and sell in the dearest" (Essays, 34). The capitalistic counterpart of the medieval attitude lurks outside the sentence, but is not very well concealed; it hangs near the back door in Shaw's statement of what the merchant does *not* plead. The danger of ambiguity prevents him from relying completely on implication.

Or take irony, which I have previously mentioned among the devices of opposition. Of irony in the broad sense—pointing up the disparity between what is and what ought to be—Shaw's prose contains a sufficiency, but it is subsumed under the headings of antithesis and invective. Of irony in the narrower sense—the indirect communication of one's meaning by stating a different one—there is very little in Shaw. He may claim kinship with Swift in sharing that writer's rage over human cruelty and folly, but in satirical method they are scarcely third cousins. When Shaw does fall in ironic step with the reasoning of his opponents, he grows quickly restless, and moves back into his own stride:

> The Webbs' arguments and facts were unanswerable: consequently the problem of how not to do it was solved as usual by simply taking no notice of the proposal. (EPWW, 41)
>
> I dislike cruelty, even cruelty to other people, and should therefore like to see all cruel people exterminated. (Too True, 153)

In the first example "consequently" embodies the logic of the do-nothings: when presented with unanswerable facts, ignore them. But Shaw makes his own stand quite clear, over and above the irony of the connective, by saying that the problem was how *not* to do it, and by inserting the contemptuous "as usual." Nor does the second example play the game of irony more than halfheartedly. "Even" is the key word; it constitutes an admission that Shaw is overfastidious in disliking cruelty, and that his scruples against cruelty to other people are positively unreasonable—it turns the first part of the sentence into a shy confession of peculiarity. But the second clause substitutes the steam roller for the feather duster, leaving no doubt at all of Shaw's real attitude. The full-blooded ironist must be willing to leave himself at least slightly open to misunderstanding, say by very young children and idiots. This risk Shaw is seldom willing to take—nor is the fact surprising when considered against the background of his love for exaggeration and his intolerance of conceptual ambiguity. For such a writer, indirection becomes almost an intellectual impossibility.

The several ways in which Shaw's style points up antithetical features of experience might have been studied in Chapter I as evidence of leveling, for the leveler seeks polarities as well as similarities. The impulse toward antithesis can live peaceably with the habit of equivalence. But on the whole it seemed best to emphasize the extent to which stylistic oppositions of the Shavian sort fit with his chosen mask, that of the attacker of received opinion. A good reason for so classifying his antitheses is that they usually have a strong evaluative slant. In drawing an antithesis the writer need not invoke values at all; he may simply make explicit a distinction for his own sake. But in setting one thing against another Shaw almost invariably exhibits a preference. His "not—— but——" makes a moral distinction in addition to the conceptual one, and the other forms of antithesis develop contrast so as to cry up one term and cry down the other. If the device were not so admirably suited to Shavian scorn I doubt it would have nearly the prominence in his writing that it does.

Grammar and Rhetoric in Criticism: Wallace Stevens' "The Snow Man"

ROBERT M. BROWNE

[WE HAVE SEEN an analysis of John Donne's "The Prohibition," a lyric poem written at the end of the sixteenth century. Now we get a look at an analysis of Wallace Stevens' "The Snow Man," a lyric poem written in the twentieth century. There are some differences, however, both in the kinds of lyric poems examined and in the way they are analyzed. In addition to the rather obvious differences in the tone and mood of the two poems, the Donne poem presents a persuasion-situation in which the "I" in the poem is trying to persuade the "you" of the poem; the Stevens poem, on the other hand, presents no pronounced persuasion-situation, and if it can be classified at all as one of the classical kinds, it is an example of epideictic discourse, the rhetoric of display.

The chief difference in the way the poems are analyzed lies in Browne's preference for remaining *inside* the poem. So, unlike the explicator of Donne's poem, he eschews any analysis of the relation between the poet and the reader and concentrates on the relation between the speaker and the listener in the poem. Browne also assumes a broader purview in his analysis than Mr. Sloan does, touching on the grammatical and poetic elements as well as on the rhetorical. He justifies his method in this way: "I would like to argue here that since every literary work has grammatical, rhetorical, and poetic (aesthetic) structure, a thorough analysis of poetic structure cannot be made without some attention to these other structures." It is interesting to see how he integrates these three approaches in his study of the structure of the poem.]

From *Texas Studies in Literature and Language,* III (Spring 1961), 144–157. Reprinted by permission of the University of Texas Press and Robert M. Browne.

CRITICISM IN OUR TIME has developed great interest in analyzing the poetic symbol and the tropes of irony, paradox, and metaphor. A whole poetic has been built on these devices, and has brought about discoveries of permanent value. Yet is it possible that this poetic has been too restricted in limiting itself to the symbolic and tropical uses of language, and to these particular tropes. In so doing it has notoriously been embarrassed in handling such nonsymbolic and nontropical features as plot and sound-structure. Although it has derived many of its terms and methods from ancient rhetoric, it has not managed or even tried very hard to recover the whole of that tradition, of which tropes are only a part. Nor has it yet made much contact with the flourishing modern discipline of structural linguistics. Instead of being equipped with Greco-Latin rhetoric and modern grammar, critics are likely to have Greco-Latin grammar and *Modern Rhetoric,* a freshman composition text which they will naturally not consult about poetry.

Traditionally, of course, poetic, rhetoric, and grammar (and, less intimately, logic) were closely allied, and the critic was assumed to have fairly high competence in all. I would like to argue here that since every literary work has grammatical, rhetorical, and poetic (aesthetic) structure, a thorough analysis of poetic structure cannot be made without some attention to these other structures. It may be that in a given poem these will turn out to be almost neutral aesthetically, chiefly serving to provide the framework of ordinary speech from which the poetic structure departs, but only rhetorical and grammatical analysis can demonstrate this. Very often these structures will turn out to be highly relevant to poetic structure, not merely an occasion for it but participating in it directly. Then analysis of the poetic structure will require analysis of its grammatical and rhetorical structures as well, and of the relations among all three.

I want here to analyze a poem which seems to me to require this kind of examination, Wallace Stevens' "The Snow Man." I will consider only its structure of meaning, as I intend to take up its sound on another occasion; but within these limits I will aspire to theoretical completeness, to a systematic account of all the relevant aspects of the poem. I am well aware that no system could be complete enough, and no analyst sensitive enough, to discover the full structure of a poem. The system will be good if, without losing its general applicability, it shows itself in practice to be capable of undergoing the modifications, extensions, and refinements necessary to manifest the structure of the individual poem in a reasonably specific manner.

It follows that a particular analysis may fail to illustrate all the possibilities of the system of analysis, and yet may develop certain possible refinements of it which would prove otiose in the analysis of the next poem. Stevens' poem, for instance, displays a relatively simple structure of rational argument, but an unusual complexity of relations between grammatical, rhetorical, and poetic structures. My analysis is therefore not intended as a model for analysis of every poem, but as an example of the methodological usefulness of examining grammatical and rhetorical structure.

"The Snow Man" has been briefly discussed in a number of places but not formally analyzed. Most of the talk about it has concerned its meaning, not its structure, and its meaning as an example of Stevens' characteristic thought rather than as part of the structure of the poem. Two of its most illuminating commentators, C. Roland Wagner (*Accent,* 1952) and Robert Pack (*Wallace Stevens,* 1958), see its key words "winter" and "nothing" as major symbols in Stevens' poetry. Yet both, I think, assume too easily that Stevens has a complete philosophical system. They are about three-quarters in agreement about the meaning of these two terms, yet manage to come to opposed versions of the general meaning of the poem. This is not especially scandalous in itself, since the poem is difficult, but it enforces skepticism about the value of a philosophical rather than philological approach to a poet like Stevens. It may be that some of the meanings of this poem are too uncertain to be specified satisfactorily; but a structurally oriented philological approach ought to be less crippled by such uncertainty, since its concern is with the *structures*—grammatical, rhetorical, and poetic—not with meaning as such.

Like Wagner and Pack, I will offer an analysis of the poem's meaning, an interpretation I think consistent with the facts of the poem and with other poems of Stevens (such as the poem standing before it in *Harmonium,* "Domination of Black"). Structural analysis, not interpretation, is my goal; the analysis should not stand or fall on the value of the interpretation alone. I hope to show that consideration of structure is the only profitable way of approaching meaning, but I am finally only interested in meaning as it enters into structure. If I am partly wrong about specific meanings I need not be wrong about the structure unless the difference in specific meaning radically alters the structure. In any case, the poem is widely admired despite lack of agreement about its meaning. The fact suggests that much of the poem's structure is available to readers even when they disagree about meaning, and that a structural analysis will be most profitable.

I begin with the poem:

The Snow Man

One must have a mind of winter
To regard the frost and the boughs
Of the pine-trees crusted with snow;

And have been cold a long time
To behold the junipers shagged with ice,
The spruces rough in the distant glitter

Of the January sun; and not to think
Of any misery in the sound of the wind,
In the sound of a few leaves,

Which is the sound of the land
Full of the same wind
That is blowing in the same bare place

For the listener, who listens in the snow,
And, nothing himself, beholds
Nothing that is not there and the nothing that is.

Grammatical structure. The poem consists of one long sentence, with a remarkable difference in syntactic character between the first three tercets and the last two. Lines 1–9 have a structure which involves much compounding of syntactic groups both small and large. There is compounding of noun-groups: "the frost and the boughs"; of prepositional groups: "in the sound of the wind, / In the sound of a few leaves"; of noun-plus-modifier groups: "the pine-trees crusted with snow . . . the junipers shagged with ice . . . the spruces rough in the distant glitter"; of main verbs; "have . . . have been"; and, most elaborately, of infinitives and their complements: "To regard . . . snow; . . . To behold . . . sun; . . . to think . . . leaves."

All these elements except the third infinitive make up a seven-line bipartite structure, each part having a verb, complement, and infinitive group, and each matching the other in meaning as well as in grammatical structure. It is obvious that the junipers and spruces are simply more of the same kind of detail as the frost and the pine-trees. What about the rest? Is "must have been cold a long time / To behold" simply an elegant variation on "must have a mind of winter / To regard"? Disregarding the infinitives for a moment, I would argue that the second of these adds only a small increment of new meaning: the notion that one is not born with a mind of winter but acquires it through long exposure. Beyond this, it serves the meaning in the same way that the junipers and spruces do, by further fixing and specifying meanings which are already present in a nebulous way. These functions justify the second verb and complement; one cannot object that Stevens ought either to have repeated the first construction or omitted it the second time. But might he as well have put the second immediately after the first, as follows?

> One must have a mind of winter,
> And have been cold a long time,
> To regard (or behold) the frost and the boughs
> Of the pine-trees crusted with snow,
>
> The junipers shagged with ice,
> The spruces rough in the distant glitter
> Of the January sun . . .

An advocate of stripping poetic language to the bone might prefer this second version, might feel that one infinitive is enough, especially if he shares my belief that "to regard" and "to behold" are almost pure tautology here (the slight difference in dictionary meanings does not seem relevant). In Stevens' version economy of meaning and structure is sacrificed for more compounding and more elaborate symmetry in the syntax. Of course the symmetry could have been achieved without the elegant variation; "to regard" might have appeared twice. The variation, unimportant in itself, provides a clue to a characteristic of the grammatical structure of the first nine lines; in them we find a maximum of grammatical identity (compounding, parallelism) with a maximum of lexical difference (no important word is repeated until "sound" in the very last line of the section).

These nine lines form a unit in that their rhythms, parallelisms, and balance are aesthetically satisfying. Furthermore, the section could easily stand as an independent sentence. It satisfies all the syntactic and semantic norms for a written sentence, one which would have a fairly common pattern: subject, compound predicate, sentence modifier (the third infinitive).

Nevertheless the sentence does not end here. Instead there follows, in 10–13, a series of syntactic units all alike in that each modifies the unit preceding it. There is not one example of the compounding so noticeable before; all is subordination, not coordination, syntaxis rather than parataxis. Thus "sound" in 8 and 9 is modified by "which . . . land"; "land" is modified by "full of the same wind"; "wind" by "that is blowing . . . place"; "is blowing . . . place" by "for the listener"; "listener" by "who . . . snow" and what follows it in 14–15.

The pattern for the entire sentence is thus subject (first word), compound predicate (to "sun"), sentence modifier (7–15). The long sentence modifier falls into three parts, 7–9, 10–13, 14–15. Lines 7–9, we have already seen, fit smoothly into the pattern of 1–7 and seem to round out that pattern. Yet they mark a transition to the characteristic pattern of 10–13; they use function words more freely than do 1–7, and they introduce the device of repeating form-class words (by repeating "sound").

Function words are those words whose syntactical functions within the speech are more important than their reference to realities outside the speech. That function words are more prominent in 7–13 than in 1–7 can be sensed in reading, since words like "of," "in," "which," "that," "the" recur so frequently. Analysis bears this out: almost two-thirds of the words in 7–13 can be classified as function words, but only one-half of the words in the rest of the poem. Form-class words are those words which carry the burden of semantic meaning, the nouns, verbs, adjectives, and adverbs (as these terms are used in contemporary linguistics). There are 17 such words in 7–13, but only 12 different ones; 5 are repeated (counting "listens" as a repetition). By contrast, none of the 23 form-class words in 1–7 are repeated within that section. Thus in 7–13 we have more elaborate syntactical machinery with fewer important words to work on and organize. The syntactical structure is more prominent than the lexical elements it governs. Also, there is a change in the kind of form-class word stressed: descriptive adjectives and participles are very important in the opening part, but they almost disappear after 7.

After the transition of 7–9, and the emergence of syntactic subordination and lexical repetition in 7–13, there is a striking reversion to coordinative structure in 13–15. "Listens" and "beholds" are compound verbs, together governing a compound complement which exhibits the close matching of parts characteristic of the opening of the poem: "Nothing that is not there and the nothing that is." But though the quality of the syntax reverts to that of the beginning, the vocabulary of the last few lines continues to be limited in range, like the middle section. "Beholds" and "snow" are repeated from earlier in the poem, and the only important new word, "nothing," gets repeated twice. There are no adjectives.

Syntactically, then, the sentence's immediate constituents are the subject-predicate sequence of 1–7 and the sentence modifier of 7–15. This bipartite division is emphasized by the change in the quality of diction which takes place in 7. And yet the grammar has a tripartite feel to it because of something about the *quality* of the syntax, heavily paratactic in 1–9, syntactic in 10–13, paratactic again in 13–15. We shall see again, in the rhetorical structure, a similar crossing of bipartite and tripartite patterns.

Rhetorical structure. According to Aristotle's *Rhetoric,* a speech consists of three elements, all of which require consideration here: the speaker, the hearer, and the speech itself. To analyze the rhetorical structure of a poem is to analyze its *internal* rhetoric: not the relation between poet and reader, but that of speaker and hearer. To analyze the external rhetoric of a poem, in the manner of Kenneth Burke, seems to me to treat it as essentially prose.

This poem appears to be soliloquy; no specific imagined addressee seems to be on hand. Lack of a specific hearer also characterizes much scientific or philosophical writing, and

Stevens' critics have felt the temptation to read the poem as a general philosophical statement in picture-language. But though there is no hearer, there is an occasion provided by the title and the opening lines. The winter scenery is not merely exemplary; it is real, and present to the speaker at the moment of speech. Syntactical proof of this is the heavy use of *the,* repeated ten times in the first seven lines. *The* carries the syntactical meaning "identified." When it is used, especially at the beginnings of literary works, of specific objects which have not in fact been identified, *the* suggests a speaker referring to objects physically present before him and needing no formal identification. It is a common way of achieving dramatic immediacy, just as use of the indefinite *a* is a way of establishing distance between speaker and object.

Furthermore, the mere quantity of physical detail in 1–7 establishes that the scene is real and not merely hypothetical or typical, not merely constructed by the speaker to serve the needs of a general statement. There is at least the appearance of general statement in 1 and 4, but it is countered by particularity in the infinitive constructions which follow each line.

If the scenery is real, what about the human agents and acts mentioned? One of them, "the listener," seems certified as real by another set of *the*'s: *the* listener, *the* snow. More difficult is the problem of the "one" of the first line. Is this a real person, a snow man, or a general type? Nothing in the syntax asserts that someone with a mind of winter actually exists; the pronoun is general and impersonal, the actions of the "one" are named in infinitives rather than in finite verbs, and "must have" could be merely hypothetical. Still, if only a general type were meant by "one" it would have been easy to make the scenery general and typical, too, perhaps by suppressing the early use of *the.* It would seem that the acts of regarding, beholding, and not-thinking are in some sense taking place.

If these acts are literally performed, the agent must either be a real person or the snow man of the title, a literal snow man to whom these actions are fancifully ascribed. If the latter, the speaker watches the snow man and is inspired to a series of little pleasantries. He imagines that the snow man, who literally cannot think of misery because he cannot think of anything, has through long exposure acquired a mind of winter to match his body of winter, and *therefore* cannot think of misery. Lines 1–9 would then be a pseudo-logical causal analysis. Note that this interpretation does not rob the poem of all seriousness; if a real unthinking snow man is meant, he is also a symbol of something.

I believe that this interpretation of the first part of the poem is the right one, but on poetic rather than grammatical or rhetorical grounds. It gives the title more meaning, and solidly anchors the poem's more universal meanings in homely fact. Another critic might argue that the title is only metaphoric, not literal-symbolic, and that the "one" refers to a real human being, most likely the speaker himself in a passing mood. Though I feel that such an interpretation impoverishes the poem a little, it seems grammatically and rhetorically tenable, and not in basic disagreement with the one I propose.

More basic disagreements are likely to arise over the identity of "the listener." Is the listener the same person as the viewer of the first line or not? If the viewer is a real snow man he is not likely to be the listener (snow men usually have eyes but less commonly ears). Critics generally tend to equate the viewer and the listener, though none has offered reasons. But it seems to me that even if the viewer is human the grammar and rhetoric of the poem distinguish him from the listener. My arguments do not require the conclusion that the two are numerically distinct; they could each represent successive states of the same mind, most likely the speaker's. But my contention is that in the poem they are treated as different persons.

The word "same" appears in 11 and 12, asserting the identity of the wind with that of 8, and of this bare place with that implied by the whole preceding description. It is true that fallen leaves are mentioned in 9, though none of the trees named earlier is deciduous, but I do not think this means that the scene has changed; if it had changed there would be nothing strange about the viewer's failure to think about the misery of sounds he could not have heard. Actually, the two uses of "same" seem strictly unnecessary; the scene can be assumed to remain unchanged unless a change is strongly indicated. Then why "same"? "Same" is only necessary, it seems to me, if something about the scene is different. If the listener is the viewer, nothing has changed and "same" remains unnecessary. If the listener is not the viewer, then the same scene is having a different impact on a different mind, and this is why the speaker insists that it is the same scene.

The amount of identification the listener gets is another clue. Everything after "listener" modifies that noun. The nonrestrictive relative clause gives added information about the listener; but if he is the viewer, it is superfluous to say that he is "in the snow." Furthermore, why does he so abruptly become a listener? If he is the same, it would have been very easy to make it clear by calling him "this" or "the same" listener.

The rhetorical reasons why viewer and listener seem distinct to me derive from analysis of the speech proper, apart from speaker, hearer, and occasion. The analysis of the occasion has suggested that this speech is in the realm of narrative rather than exposition, that it tells what is happening rather than what is. Yet the narrative is a report of subjective rather than objective events, and it tells of subjective events which might easily form the basis of an exposition. Also, the poem begins with the air of delivering a general proposition or argument such as we associate with exposition. The dynamic and narrative framework thus supports much that is static and expository.

The subjective events referred to in the poem are the perceptions and feelings of the speaker, the viewer, and the listener. The speaker begins by observing the conduct of the viewer, and abruptly (that is, without stating that he is observing a particular person) offers what appears to be a general proposition: "One must have a mind of winter to do so and so." Some critics have assumed that this is to be taken as a general principle supplied from outside the poem, justified by Stevens' general philosophy and characteristic use of symbols, and illustrated in the poem by tropes, symbols, and a concluding general statement. For them the statement is, crudely, that one must have a mind of winter to be able to look at the sights of winter, avoid thinking of misery in its sounds, and see the nothingness of the scene. Consequently, these critics concentrate most attention on the undoubtedly important problem of determining what "winter" and "nothing" mean.

But if I am right about the occasion of the poem, the generalization is a kind of induction from the behavior of the viewer, weighted with overtones of surprise. The generalization is not philosophical. This kind of jumping from a single case to a general conclusion is rhetorical, not logical induction, what Aristotle in the *Rhetoric* called *example.* The speaker does not seem to have arrived at the conclusion through a purposeful search for it; instead he seems to be trying to get some perspective on a surprising situation by universalizing it. There is a subtle interplay between cognitive and affective meaning in these opening lines. The word "must," though in some contexts lacking in affectivity (*One must be intelligent to master physics*) easily takes on affective coloration in the vicinity of such strongly affective phrases as "mind of winter" and "cold a long time." Whatever the exact significance of these phrases, a certain hyperbolic quality is evident from the start. The tone is much more like *One must be a fool to try to keep up with the neighbors these days* than like *One must be intelligent to master physics.*

The cognitive weight of the induction is thus lessened by the presence of affective meanings and by the particularity of the description. Too, the induction is metaphorically rather than literally stated. What is a mind of winter? It is one which is pleased by coldly beautiful winter sights but does not think of any misery in winter sounds which would conventionally be thought of as dreary. Why does it not think of misery? One possible answer is that the mind of winter has achieved a penetration into reality which puts it beyond anthropocentric interpretations of natural phenomena—beyond the pathetic fallacy. This of course requires that the phrase "mind of winter" be glossed primarily by the last line of the poem; the mind of winter beholds the nothingness of the scene. But if I am right, it is the listener who sees nothingness, not the viewer; "mind of winter" can only be glossed by the first nine lines of the poem.

Winter is the season when everything is hard, stiff, frozen; the adjectives "crusted," "shagged," and "rough" bring this out well. According to Robert Pack, winter in Stevens' poetry represents the mind's capacity to contemplate "the material actuality of fact" unaided by the vivifying power of imagination. The mind rests with the hard surfaces of the scene it has come to resemble; it sees no further into the reality of things; hence it is like a snow man.

Mr. Pack feels that "nothing" is like "winter," the mere unimaginative perception of fact. But Mr. Wagner, who has discovered six meanings of "nothingness" in Stevens' poetry, all exemplified in this poem, finds that the chief meaning for "nothing" here is that "human values are seen to be relative and unsubstantial." The listener sees *through* the factual reality to the nothingness beneath. Wagner, like Pack, sees no difference between viewer and listener, yet his gloss on "nothing" fits easily into an interpretation which does distinguish them. The mind of the listener, more flexible and responsive than the viewer's, is aware of the moral or metaphysical emptiness symbolized by the winter bareness. The listener can do this because he is "nothing himself"; it is an old philosophical principle that the mind must have something in common with what it knows, and that the mind in a sense must become what it knows. Paradoxically, the imperceptive viewer and the perceptive listener are much alike; both stand in the snow, both "see nothing": the viewer through lack of insight, the listener precisely because he *has* insight.

The rhetorical "thought" (*dianoia, inventio*) is basically the narration of a process of observation and analysis going on in the mind of the speaker, who is thus not merely an expositor but a dramatic agent. He observes the viewer observing the scene, and accounts to himself for the viewer's insensitivity by means of a generalization; then he observes the sounds unnoticed by the viewer and implicitly contrasts his obtuseness with the acuteness of the listener, who misses none of the significance. It is an evaluatory contrast: knowledge, even of the void, is preferable to ignorance.

But though the basic intellectual act recorded in the poem is a contrast of two types, the contrast does not set up a bipartite structure of thought, as might have been expected. The opening generalization, into which all the details of 1–8 fit, carries the suggestion that this will be a poem whose meanings are ordered by some kind of logic, at least empirical logic. But imagery, subordinate to idea in 1–7, seems to take on a life of its own in 9–13. The focus of the poem seems to be shifting from conceptually-controlled analysis to nonconceptual synthesis of images. Then, in 14–15, images almost disappear and ideas dominate once more; the poem ends as it began, with the analysis of a mind. The pattern of the "thought" is conceptual—nonconceptual—conceptual.

Besides "thought," rhetorical analysis traditionally deals with "style" (*lexis, elocutio*). In analyzing the internal rhetoric of the poem we deal with the style of the speaker on this occasion, not with the poet's style in general. The grammar, previously examined simply as such, must be re-examined for its stylistic effect. The syntactical compounding of the opening part contributes to the rhetorical effects of parallelism and balance; the section exhibits the well-turned grammatical structure which we associate with formal speech or writing. The middle section, on the other hand, would seem out of place in actual formal prose. It beautifully exemplifies the fault condemned in one freshman handbook as "*tandem subordination:* an unhappy series of subordinate clauses each of which depends on an element in the preceding." But its grammar would not be inappropriate to meditative soliloquy, in which one word or idea suggests another. In the final lines the manner of formal prose returns. The compounding is enhanced by adroit antithesis and verbal repetition. There is an ingenious variation on *nothing;* it is twice given its normal indeterminate meaning, then, by the unusual combination with *the,* is made to seem specific and definite; a nothing which is somehow a something.

The style thus has a tripartite structure, like the thought. The beginning and ending are in a style which is balanced, elegant, controlled, a public style associated with serious books, journals, and addresses. The middle section is in a more private style, the style of familiar unpremeditated speech; it is less predictable from part to part, less balanced and neat. The style and thought correspond in their divisions, for organization of thought along conceptual, rational lines is conventionally expected of public speech, and almost as conventionally not expected of private speech.

Poetic structure. If this analysis of thought and style is correct, there would seem to be problems of consistency on the poetic level. If the speech is soliloquy (and a second person in the poem seems unthinkable) why the public manner of the beginning and ending? Is not the speaker's character internally inconsistent?

The answers to these questions must be sought for on really poetic, not rhetorical grounds. If one remains on the rhetorical level, as I think Pack does, one soon begins talking about the external rhetoric of the poem, interpreting the device of soliloquy as a mere sham allowing Stevens to practice his wiles on us the readers. I would argue that Stevens does not violate the persona; the public manner is adopted by the speaker for his own benefit. I suggest that the speaker is dramatizing for himself the contrast between the viewer and the listener by giving each an appropriate style. The viewer, whose conventional mind sees only surfaces, is described by the relatively conventional rhetoric and grammar of the passage in which he appears. It is a mind which imposes a conventional order on things. But there is something about the scene which is not easily reducible to conventional order, something symbolized by the dreary sounds of the scene. These sounds make a sensitive observer think of misery, of disorder, and they are presented in syntactic patterns which are disordered from the point of view of public prose. The sounds are treated at length before mention of the observer, in contrast to the system of the rest of the poem, because the speaker wishes to dramatize for himself the objectively terrible qualities of the scene as a measure of the ultimate victory of the listener over disorder. In the final section this victory is described in a neatly constructed, well-balanced epigram. The manner is once again the public manner of the beginning, but not for the same reason. The listener has not been taken in by the illusory order of the conventional viewer; he has achieved full knowledge of the disorder symbolized by the sound of the wind, and his full knowledge is itself an order: the only satisfactory order, and one which can well be symbolized by a fully ordered syntax. It is a paradox, of course, that none of the misery signified by the sounds is in any way altered; but it is brought under the control of the mind. The very vocabulary of the last part suggests this: it is even plainer than that of the middle part, for the misery is still there; yet out of these neutral, colorless materials the listener makes a more impressive order than does the viewer out of a richer diction.

When I suggest that the middle section is grammatically disordered and symbolizes disorder, I do not mean it is absolutely disordered; I am not committing the fallacy of imitative form.

The section has its own order, characterized by the prominence of function words (somewhat as in the old rhetorical figure of polysyndeton), grammatical subordination (syntaxis) and lexical repetition. The constant expansion of nouns by means of post-nominal modifiers suggests greater and greater precision and refinement of meaning, yet each new modifying structure only adds more syntactical complication without really clarifying things. The effect is reminiscent of Gertrude Stein: grammatical structure temporarily becomes more prominent than the meanings it manifests. The speaker appears to have become intrigued by the aesthetic possibilities of lexical and syntactic structure, and to be essaying a little flight in which linguistic structure interests him as structure and not simply as an instrument.

It might seem that such a deviation on the part of the speaker would destroy the poem by reducing the meaning to gibberish. But the speaker does not eliminate reference to reality in favor of nonsense; enough semantic reference is there to play its essential role in grammatical and rhetorical structure. It simply has a less prominent place than in the other two sections. If this were a poem in which the speaker were a man actively wrestling with a moral or philosophical problem such a deviation would either be a fault of dramatic inconsistency or it would signal a real change of tone on the part of the speaker. But I see no evidence that this is such a dramatic poem; the speaker seems to me as self-possessed in the middle as elsewhere.

Actually, the exploitation of the aesthetic possibilities of language in this section is but an intensification of something characteristic of the speaker throughout the poem. I suggested that there was more syntactical elaborateness in the first part than was necessary; in the last part there is the well-made epigram. The voice heard speaking in this poem is that of a man interested in speech patterns, so much so that he will pay attention to the patterns his speech makes even in soliloquy. I do not see any indication that he is gripped by strong emotion about the nothingness of winter at the moment of speech. He recounts attitudes he may have passed through, but he is on a level superior to them now, and has achieved the detachment his playing with syntax implies. Consequently, the middle section does not violate the integrity of the poem by its subordination of external reference to pattern. It is consistent with the speaker's character, which is that of an epideictic rhetorician, a man interested in verbal display. Such a speaker turns up everywhere in Stevens' poetry. R. P. Blackmur has at various times called him a rhetorician, a dandy; and one of his remarks seems especially applicable to this poem: "The dandy is nothing if not conspicuous, even in the wilderness." [1]

Employment of this kind of speaker in poetry has its defects as well as virtues. The great disadvantage is that the epideictic rhetorician's normal or typical speech is already so far removed from common speech, and epideictic rhetoric so resembles lyric poetry at times, that the intended poem may easily slip into being only a piece of display rhetoric, speech with the pragmatic function of showing a real public that this real poet-rhetorician is a clever fellow with language. I believe that this collapse of poetic into merely rhetorical structure is what Blackmur means when he says in the same essay that Stevens lets one out of three poems run down through "studied carelessness."

But it need not happen, and does not happen in "The Snow Man." The slightest modification of linguistic structure here carries more meaning than it would in the speech of a less word-conscious speaker. The varying of style to suit local subject, normally a requirement of rhetorical structure, is here raised to the poetic level. It is in excess of the rhetorical requirements of the poem, for there is no hearer. Yet it is not primarily aimed at impressing actual readers. If such an intention was present in the poet's mind, it has been transformed. The verbal grammatical and rhetorical virtuosity of the speaker is dramatically consistent and enriches the poetic structure of meaning; verbal display has become a component of the verbal play in which morphological, syntactical, and rhetorical elements consort in the total pattern of the poem.

Not all poems exploit grammatical and rhetorical structure as thoroughly as does this one. But if this analysis is correct, poetic structure may at times arise from a kind of superabundance of grammatical or rhetorical structure or of relations between these. Grammatical structure exists to make meaning available; it uses

[1] R. P. Blackmur, "The Substance That Prevails," *Kenyon Review,* XVII (1955), 107.

parallelism or function words or word order for quite practical reasons. Yet, because these devices are structures, they may be developed beyond the bare needs of intelligibility to become interesting as a set of relations. Rhetorical structure exists to affect a hearer; it may present rational arguments or at least make the speaker seem rational, all in order to persuade. But where there is no need to persuade, as here, the suggestion of intellectual analysis may be developed in the first part, be attenuated in favor of imaginative synthesis in the second, and reappear in the third. The pattern is of no real rhetorical value, but is of interest for its contribution to the poem's tripartite structure.

The poem I have chosen may seem too unusual to demonstrate the importance of grammatical and rhetorical analysis. But though grammatical and rhetorical structures may be more fundamentally a part of poetic structure in this poem than in many, the extreme case may yet be illuminating. If grammatical and rhetorical analysis can shed light on a contemporary poem, it should do no less for poems written earlier, when poets attended more consciously to grammatical and rhetorical doctrine. For such analysis we need the best rhetoric and grammar; not handbooks, but Aristotle and the successors of Bloomfield.

BIBLIOGRAPHY

Bibliography

In Part I, General Background Reading, the items are arranged alphabetically according to authors. In Part II, which lists studies of specific literary works and of specific authors as they relate to rhetoric, I thought that it would be helpful to group the items under *authors as subjects.* Not all of the critiques in Part II are examples of what I have defined as "rhetorical criticism," but even where they are not rhetorical—or consistently rhetorical—they represent some kind of close analysis of a literary text. I make no pretense to completeness in this Bibliography.

KEY TO ABBREVIATIONS

AL	*American Literature*
CCC	*College Composition and Communication*
CE	*College English*
ELH	*Journal of English Literary History*
JEGP	*Journal of English and Germanic Philology*
MP	*Modern Philology*
PMLA	*Publications of the Modern Language Association*
PQ	*Philological Quarterly*
QJS	*Quarterly Journal of Speech*
RES	*Review of English Studies*
SP	*Studies in Philology*
VNL	*Victorian Newsletter*

PART I—GENERAL BACKGROUND READING

Aldrige, John W., ed. *Critiques and Essays on Modern Fiction, 1920–1951* (New York, 1952).

Allen, Don Cameron. "Style and Certitude," *ELH,* XV (1948), 167–75.

Bailey, Dudley, ed. *Essays on Rhetoric* (New York, 1965).

Bailey, Richard W. "Current Trends in the Analysis of Style," *Style,* I (1967), 1–14.

Balliet, Conrad A. "The History and Rhetoric of the Triplet," *PMLA,* LXXX (1965), 528–34.

Bartlett, A. C. *The Larger Rhetorical Patterns in Anglo-Saxon Poetry* (New York, 1935).

Baum, P. F. *The Other Harmony of Prose* (Cambridge, Mass., 1952).

Bennett, A. L. "The Principal Rhetorical Conventions in the Renaissance Personal Elegy," *SP,* LI (1954), 107–26.

Bennett, James R. "An Annotated Bibliography of Selected Writings in English Prose Style," *CCC,* XVI (1965), 248–55.

Bilsky, Manuel. "I. A. Richards's Theory of Metaphor," *MP,* L (1952), 130–37.

Black, Edwin. *Rhetorical Criticism: A Study in Method* (New York, 1965).

———. "Frame of Reference in Rhetoric and Fiction," *Rhetoric and Poetic,* ed. Donald C. Bryant (Iowa City, Ia., 1965), pp. 26–35.

Bland, D. S. "Rhetoric and the Law Student in Sixteenth-Century England," *SP,* LIV (1957), 498–508.

Blankenship, Jane. "A Linguistic Analysis of Oral and Written Style," *QJS,* XLVIII (1962), 419–22.

Bloomfield, Morton W. "A Grammatical Approach to Personification Allegory," *MP,* LX (1963), 161–71.

Booth, Wayne C. *The Rhetoric of Fiction* (Chicago, 1961).

———. "The Revival of Rhetoric," *PMLA,* LXXX (1965), 8–12.

———. "*The Rhetoric of Fiction* and the Poetics of Fictions," *Novel,* I (1968), 105–17.

Boulton, Marjorie. *The Anatomy of Prose* (London, 1954).

Brady, Frank. "Prose Style and the 'Whig' Tradition," *Bulletin of the New York Public Library,* LXVI (1962), 455–63.

Brennan, Joseph X. "Joannes Susenbrotus: A Forgotten Humanist," *PMLA,* LXXV (1960), 485–96.

Bridgman, Richard. *The Colloquial Style in America* (New York, 1966).

Brockett, O. G. "Poetry as Instrument," *Rhetoric and Poetic,* ed. Donald C. Bryant (Iowa City, Ia., 1965), pp. 15–25.

Brockriede, Wayne E. "Bentham's Criticism of Rhetoric and Rhetoricians," *QJS,* XLI (1955), 377–82.

———. "Dimensions of the Concept of Rhetoric," *QJS,* LIV (1968), 1–12.

Brooks, Cleanth, and Robert Penn Warren. *Understanding Poetry* (New York, 1938; 1950; 3rd ed. 1960).

Brown, Huntington. *Prose Styles: Five Primary Types* (Minneapolis, Minn., 1966).

Brown, James. "Eight Types of Puns," *PMLA,* LXXI (1956), 14–26.

Bryant, Donald C. "Aspects of the Rhetorical Tradition: The Intellectual Foundation," *QJS*, XXXVI (April 1950), 169–76; (October 1950), 326–332.

———. "Rhetoric: Its Function and Its Scope," *QJS*, XXXIX (1953), 401–24.

———. "'A Peece of a Logician': The Critical Essayist as Rhetorician," *The Rhetorical Idiom*, ed. Donald C. Bryant (Ithaca, N.Y., 1958), pp. 293–303.

———. "The Uses of Rhetoric in Criticism," *Rhetoric and Poetic*, ed. Donald C. Bryant (Iowa City, Ia., 1965), pp. 1–14.

Burke, Kenneth. *A Rhetoric of Motives* (New York, 1950).

———. "A Dramatistic View of the Origins of Language: Part One," *QJS*, XXXVIII (October 1952), 251–64; "Part Two," (December 1952), 446–60; "Part Three," XXXIX (February 1953), 79–92; "Postscripts on the Negative," (April 1953), 209–16.

Burklund, Carl E. "The Presentation of Figurative Language," *QJS*, XLI (1955), 383–90.

Burwick, Frederick, "Associationist Rhetoric and Scottish Prose Style," *Speech Monographs*, XXXIV (1967), 21–34.

Campbell, Jackson J. "Knowledge of Rhetorical Figures in Anglo-Saxon England," *JEGP*, LXVI (1967), 1–20.

Candelaria, Frederick, ed. *Perspectives on Style* (Boston, 1968).

Chayes, Irene H. "Rhetoric as Drama: An Approach to the Romantic Ode," *PMLA*, LXXIX (1964), 67–79.

Christensen, Francis. "John Wilkins and the Royal Society's Reform of Prose Style," *Modern Language Quarterly*, VII (1946), 279–90.

Clark, Donald Lemen. *Rhetoric and Poetry in the Renaissance: A Study of Rhetorical Terms in English Renaissance Literary Criticism* (New York, 1922).

———. *Rhetoric in Greco-Roman Education* (New York, 1957).

———. "The Place of Rhetoric in a Liberal Education," *QJS*, XXXVI (1950), 291–95.

———. "Rhetoric and the Literature of the English Middle Ages," *QJS*, XLV (1959), 19–28.

Clark, Robert D. "Biography and Rhetorical Criticism," *QJS*, XLIV (1958), 182–86.

Cohen, Herman. "Hugh Blair's Theory of Taste," *QJS*, XLIV (1958), 265–74.

Colie, R. L. "The Rhetoric of Transcendence," *PQ*, XLIII (1964), 145–70.

Cope, Jackson I. "Joseph Glanvill, Anglican Apologist: Old Ideas and New Style in the Restoration," *PMLA,* LXIX (1954), 223–50.

———. "Seventeenth-Century Quaker Style," *PMLA,* LXXI (1956), 725–54.

Corbett, Edward P. J. *Classical Rhetoric for the Modern Student* (New York, 1965).

———. "Rhetoric and Teachers of English," *QJS,* LI (1965), 375–81.

———. "What Is Being Revived?" *CCC,* XVIII (1967), 166–72.

Crane, William G. *Wit and Rhetoric in the Renaissance: The Formal Basis of Elizabethan Prose Style* (New York, 1937).

Croft, Albert J. "The Functions of Rhetorical Criticism," *QJS,* XLII (1956), 283–91.

Croll, Morris W. *Style, Rhetoric, and Rhythm,* ed. J. Max Patrick and Robert O. Evans, with John M. Wallace and R. J. Schoeck (Princeton, N.J., 1966).

Culler, A. Dwight. "Method in the Study of Victorian Prose," *VNL,* No. 9 (1957), 1–4. See answers to this article: R. C. Schweik. "Method in the Study of Victorian Prose: A Criticism," *VNL,* No. 10 (1957), 15–16; Martin J. Svaglic. "Method in the Study of Victorian Prose: Another View," *VNL,* No. 11 (1957), 1–5.

Dahl, Torsten. "Alliteration in English Prose," *English Studies,* XL (1959), 449–54.

Davidson, Donald. "Grammar and Rhetoric: The Teacher's Problem," *QJS,* XXXIX (1953), 425–36.

Dobrée, Bonamy. "Some Remarks on Prose in England Today," *Sewanee Review,* LXIII (1955), 631–46.

Doherty, Paul C. "Stylistics—A Bibliographical Survey," *The CEA Critic,* XXVIII (1966), 1, 3–4.

Duhamel, P. Albert. "The Function of Rhetoric as Effective Expression," *Journal of the History of Ideas,* X (1949), 344–56.

———. "The Logic and Rhetoric of Peter Ramus," *MP,* XLVI (1949), 163–71.

———. "The Ciceronianism of Gabriel Harvey," *SP,* XLIX (1952), 155–70.

Ehrenpreis, Irvin. "Personae," *Restoration and Eighteenth-Century Literary Essays in Honor of Alan Dugald McKillop* (Chicago, 1963), pp. 25–37.

Elledge, Scott. "The Background and Development in English Criticism of the Theories of Generality and Particularity," *PMLA,* LXII (1947), 147–82.

Embler, Weller. "Style Is as Style Does," *ETC.: A Review of General Semantics,* XXIV (1967), 447–53.

Engelhardt, George J. "The Relation of Sherry's *Treatise of Schemes and Tropes* to Wilson's *Arte of Rhetorique*," *PMLA*, LXII (1947), 76–82.

Fisch, Harold. "The Puritans and the Reform of Prose Style," *ELH*, XIX (1952), 229–48.

Fogarty, Daniel. *Roots for a New Rhetoric* (New York, 1959).

Foster, F. M. K. "Cadence in English Prose," *JEGP*, XVI (1917), 456–62.

Frazer, Ray. "The Origin of the Term 'Image,'" *ELH*, XXVII (1960), 149–61.

Frye, Northrop. "Rhetorical Criticism: Theory of Genre," *Anatomy of Criticism* (Princeton, N.J., 1957), pp. 243–337.

Fussell, Paul. *The Rhetorical World of Augustan Humanism: Ethics and Imagery from Swift to Burke* (Oxford, 1965).

Geraldine, Sister Mary. "Erasmus and the Tradition of Paradox," *SP*, LXI (1964), 41–63.

Gibson, Walker. *Tough, Sweet, and Stuffy: An Essay on Modern American Prose Styles* (Bloomington, Ind., 1966).

———. "Authors, Speakers, Readers, and Mock Readers," *CE*, XI (1950), 265–69.

Gilbert, Allan H. "Logic in the Elizabethan Drama," *SP*, XXXII (1935), 527–45.

Golden, James L., and Edward P. J. Corbett, eds. *The Rhetoric of Blair, Campbell, and Whately* (New York, 1968).

Golden, James L. "The Rhetorical Theory of Adam Smith," *Southern Speech Journal*, XXXIII (1968), 200–215.

Gorrell, Robert M., ed. *Rhetoric: Theories for Application* (Champaign, Ill., 1967).

———. "Structure in Thought," *CE*, XXIV (1963), 591–98.

Graves, Robert, and Alan Hodge. *Reader Over Your Shoulder: A Handbook for Writers of English Prose* (New York, 1961).

Greene, Donald J. "Is There a 'Tory' Prose Style?" *Bulletin of the New York Public Library*, LXVI (1962), 449–54.

Griffin, Leland M. "The Rhetoric of Historical Movements," *QJS*, XXXVIII (1952), 184–88.

Grube, G. M. A. "Rhetoric and Literary Criticism," *QJS*, XLII (1956), 339–44.

Gruner, Charles R. "Is Wit to Humor What Rhetoric is to Poetic?" *Central States Speech Journal*, XVI (1965), 17–22.

———. "An Experimental Study of Satire as Persuasion," *Speech Monographs*, XXXII (1965), 149–153.

Gruner, Charles R. "A Further Experimental Study of Satire as Persuasion," *Speech Monographs,* XXXIII (1966), 184–85.

Hamm, Victor M. "Meter and Meaning," *PMLA,* LXIX (1954), 695–710.

Hardison, O. B. *The Enduring Moment: A Study of the Idea of Praise in Renaissance Literary Theory and Practice* (Chapel Hill, N.C., 1962).

Harris, Victor. "The Arts of Discourse in England, 1500–1700," *PQ,* XXXVII (1958), 484–94.

Harris, Wendell V. "Style and the Twentieth-Century Novel," *Western Humanities Review,* XVIII (1964), 127–40.

Hatzfeld, Helmut. "The Language of the Poet," *SP,* XLIII (1946), 93–120.

Herrick, Marvin T. "The Early History of Aristotle's *Rhetoric* in England," *PQ,* V (1926), 242–57.

———. "The Place of Rhetoric in Poetic Theory," *QJS,* XXXIV (1948), 1–22.

———. "The Theory of the Laughable in the Sixteenth Century," *QJS,* XXXV (1949), 1–16.

Hirsch, E. D., Jr. "Objective Interpretation," *PMLA,* LXXV (1960), 463–79.

Hochmuth, Marie. "I. A. Richards and the 'New Rhetoric,'" *QJS,* XLIV (1958), 1–16.

———. "Kenneth Burke and the 'New Rhetoric,'" *QJS,* XXXVIII (1952), 133–44.

Hoffman, Frederick J. "Violence and Rhetoric in the '30's," *Modern Novel in America, 1900–1950* (Chicago, 1951), pp. 160–68.

Holland, Virginia. "Rhetorical Criticism: A Burkeian Method," *QJS,* XXXIX (1953), 444–50.

———. "Kenneth Burke's Dramatistic Approach in Speech Criticism," *QJS,* XLI (1955), 352–8.

Howell, A. C. "*Res et Verba:* Words and Things," *ELH,* XIII (1946), 131–42.

Howell, Wilbur Samuel. *Logic and Rhetoric in England, 1500–1700* (Princeton, 1956).

———. "Ramus and English Rhetoric: 1574–1681," *QJS,* XXXVII (1951), 299–310.

Hudson, Hoyt H. "Rhetoric and Poetry," *Historical Studies of Rhetoric and Rhetoricians,* ed. Raymond F. Howes (Ithaca, N.Y., 1961), pp. 369–79.

Hume, Robert D. "Intention and the Intrinsic in Literature," *CE,* XXIX (1968), 355–65.

Hunt, Everett L. "Rhetoric and General Education," *QJS*, XXXV (1949), 275–79.

———. "Rhetoric as a Humane Study," *QJS*, XLI (1955), 114–17.

Jones, Richard F. "The Rhetoric of Science in England of the Mid-Seventeenth Century," *Restoration and Eighteenth-Century Literary Essays in Honor of Alan Dugald McKillop* (Chicago, 1963), pp. 5–24.

———. "Science and English Prose Style in the Third Quarter of the Seventeenth Century," *PMLA*, XLV (1930), 977–1009.

Jones, William Powell. *The Rhetoric of Science: A Study of Scientific Ideas and Imagery in Eighteenth-Century English Poetry* (Berkeley, 1966).

Joos, Martin. *The Five Clocks* (Bloomington, Indiana, 1962).

Kennedy, George. *The Art of Persuasion in Greece* (Princeton, N.J., 1963).

Kernan, Alvin. *The Cankered Muse: Satire of the English Renaissance* (New Haven, Connecticut, 1959).

Kroeber, A. L. "Parts of Speech in Periods of Poetry," *PMLA*, LXXIII (1958), 309–14.

La Drière, Craig. "Rhetoric as 'Merely Verbal' Art," *English Institute Essays, 1948*, ed. D. A. Robertson, Jr. (New York, 1949), pp. 123–52.

Langworthy, Charles A. "Verse-Sentence Patterns in English Poetry," *PQ*, VII (1928), 283–98.

Larson, Richard L., ed. *Rhetoric* (Indianapolis, Ind., 1968).

———. "Sentences in Action: A Technique for Analyzing Paragraphs," *CCC*, XVIII (1967), 16–22.

Lechner, Sister Joan Marie. *Renaissance Concepts of the Commonplaces* (New York, 1962).

Leed, Jacob, ed. *The Computer and Literary Style: Introductory Essays and Studies* (Kent, Ohio, 1967).

Lemon, Lee T. *The Partial Critics* (New York, 1965).

Levine, George. "Nonfiction as Art," *VNL*, No. 30 (1966), 1–6.

———, and William A. Madden, eds. *The Art of Victorian Prose* (New York, 1968).

Lodge, David. *Language of Fiction: Essays in Criticism and Verbal Analysis of the English Novel* (New York, 1966).

Lotspeich, C. M. "Poetry, Prose, and Rhythm," *PMLA*, XXXVII (1922), 293–310.

Lutwack, Leonard. "Mixed and Uniform Prose Styles in the Novel," *Journal of Aesthetics and Art Criticism*, XVIII (1960), 350–57.

McCartney, Eugene S. "Zeugma in Vergil's *Aeneid* and in English," *PQ,* VIII (1929), 79–94.

McCullen, Joseph T. "Renaissance Rhetoric: Use and Abuse," *Discourse,* V (1962), 252–64.

McDonald, Charles Osborne. *The Rhetoric of Tragedy: Form in Stuart Drama* (Amherst, Mass., 1966).

———. "Restoration Comedy as Drama of Satire: An Investigation into Seventeenth-Century Aesthetics," *SP,* LXI (1964), 522–44.

Maclean, Norman. "From Action to Image: Theories of the Lyric in the Eighteenth Century," *Critics and Criticism,* ed. R. S. Crane (Chicago, 1952), pp. 408–60.

McLuhan, H. M. "Poetic vs. Rhetorical Exegesis," *Sewanee Review,* LII (1944), 266–76.

Malloch, A. E. "The Technique and Function of the Renaissance Paradox," *SP,* LIII (1956), 191–203.

Martin, Harold C. "The Development of Style in Nineteenth-Century American Fiction," *English Institute Essays, 1958,* ed. Harold C. Martin (New York, 1959), pp. 114–41.

———, and Richard M. Ohmann. "A Selective Bibliography on Style," *English Institute Essays, 1958* (New York, 1959), pp. 192–200.

Martin, Howard H. "Puritan Preachers on Preaching: Notes on American Colonial Rhetoric," *QJS,* L (1964), 285–92.

———. " 'Style' in the Golden Age," *QJS,* XLIII (1957), 374–82.

Miles, Josephine. *Style and Proportion: The Language of Prose and Poetry* (Boston, 1967).

———. "Eras in English Poetry," *PMLA,* LXX (1955), 853–75.

———. "Toward a Theory of Style and Change," *Journal of Aesthetics and Art Criticism,* XXII (1963), 63–67.

Milic, Louis T. *Style and Stylistics: An Analytical Bibliography* (New York, 1967).

———. "Theories of Style and Their Implications for the Teaching of Composition," *CCC,* XVI (1965), 66–69.

Miller, Henry Knight. "The Paradoxical Encomium, with Special Reference to Its Vogue in England, 1600–1800," *MP,* LIII (1956), 145–178.

Mitchell, W. Fraser. *English Pulpit Oratory from Andrewes to Tillotson* (London, 1932).

Moore, Arthur K. "Lyric Voices and Ethical Proofs," *Journal of Aesthetics and Art Criticism,* XXIII (1965), 429–39.

Murphy, James J. "Saint Augustine and the Christianization of Rhetoric," *Western Speech,* XXII (1958), 24–29.

———. "Saint Augustine and the Debate about a Christian Rhetoric," *QJS,* XLVI (1960), 400–10.

Murphy, James J. "The Earliest Teaching of Rhetoric at Oxford," *Speech Monographs,* XXVII (1960), 345–47.

———. "The Arts of Discourse, 1050–1400," *Medieval Studies,* XXIII (1961), 194–205.

———. "The Medieval Arts of Discourse: An Introductory Bibliography," *Speech Monographs,* XXIX (1962), 71–78.

———. "Rhetoric in Fourteenth-Century Oxford," *Medium Aevum,* XXXIV (1965), 1–20.

———. "Aristotle's *Rhetoric* in the Middle Ages," *QJS,* LII (1966), 109–15.

Myers, Henry Alonzo. "The Usefulness of Figurative Language," *QJS,* XXVI (1940), 236–43.

Nadeau, Ray. "Thomas Farnaby: Schoolmaster and Rhetorician of the English Renaissance," *QJS,* XXXVI (1950), 340–44.

Natanson, Maurice. "The Limits of Rhetoric," *QJS,* XLI (1955), 133–39.

Nelson, William. "The Teaching of English in Tudor Grammar Schools," *SP,* XLIX (1952), 119–143.

Nichols, Marie Hochmuth. "Kenneth Burke: Rhetorical and Critical Theory," *Rhetoric and Criticism* (Baton Rouge, La., 1963), pp. 79–92.

Nist, John. "Sound and Sense: Some Structures of Poetry," *CE,* XXIII (1962), 291–95.

Nitchie, Elizabeth. "Longinus and the Theory of Poetic Imitation in Seventeenth and Eighteenth Century England," *SP,* XXXII (1935), 580–97.

Ohmann, Richard. "Prolegomena in the Analysis of Prose Style," *English Institute Essays, 1958,* ed. Harold C. Martin (New York, 1959), pp. 1–24.

———. "Methods in the Study of Victorian Style," *VNL,* XXVII (1965), 1–4.

———. "Literature as Sentences," *CE,* XXVII (1966), 261–67.

Olson, Elder., ed. *Aristotle's Poetics and English Literature* (Chicago, 1965).

———. "An Outline of Poetic Theory," *Critics and Criticism,* ed. R. S. Crane (Chicago, 1952), pp. 546–66.

Ong, Walter J. "Voice as Summons for Belief," *English Institute Essays, 1957* (New York, 1958), pp. 80–105.

———. "Oral Residue in Tudor Prose Style," *PMLA,* LXXX (1965), 145–54.

———. "Fouquelin's French Rhetoric and the Ramist Vernacular Tradition," *SP,* LI (1954), 127–42.

Osborn, Michael M. "The Evolution of the Theory of Metaphor," *Western Speech,* XXXI (1967), 121–30.

Ostroff, Anthony. "Notes Toward a Theory of Diction," *QJS,* XLIV (1958), 166–74.

Parrish, Wayland Maxfield. "Whately and His Rhetoric," *QJS,* XV (1929), 58–79.

Perrine, Laurence. "The Importance of Tone in the Interpretation of Literature," *CE,* XXIV (1963), 389–95.

Poirier, Richard. *A World Elsewhere: The Place of Style in American Literature* (New York, 1966).

Posner, Rebecca. "The Use and Abuse of Stylistic Statistics," *Archivum Linguisticum,* XV (1963), 111–39.

Ragsdale, J. Donald. "Invention in English 'Stylistic' Rhetorics: 1600–1800," *QJS,* LI (1965), 164–67.

Randolph, Mary Claire. "The Structural Design of the Formal Verse Satire," *PQ,* XXI (1942), 368–84.

Reid, Loren D. "The Perils of Rhetorical Criticism," *QJS,* XXX (1944), 416–28.

Reynolds, George F. "Literature for An Audience," *SP,* XXVIII (1931), 810–19.

Richards, I. A. *The Philosophy of Rhetoric* (New York, 1936).

———. "The Places and the Figures," *Speculative Instruments* (London and Chicago, 1955), pp. 155–69.

Rickert, Edith. *New Methods for the Study of Literature* (Chicago, 1927).

Riffaterre, Michael. "Criteria for Style Analysis," *Word,* XV (1959), 154–74.

———. "Stylistic Context," *Word,* XVI (1960), 207–18.

Rix, Herbert David. "The Editions of Erasmus's *De Copia,*" *SP,* XLIII (1946), 595–618.

Rodgers, Paul C., Jr. "Alexander Bain and the Rise of the Organic Paragraph," *QJS,* LI (1965), 399–408.

Rosenfield, Lawrence W. "Rhetorical Criticism and An Aristotelian Notion of Process," *Speech Monographs,* XXXIII (1966), 1–16.

Rosenheim, Edward, Jr. "Anger as a Fine Art," *CCC,* XVI (1965), 80–84.

Rosenthal, Paul I. "The Concept of Ethos and the Structure of Persuasion," *Speech Monographs,* XXXIII (1966), 114–26.

Routh, James. "Prose Rhythms," *PMLA,* XXXVIII (1923), 685–97.

Sack, Sheldon. *Fiction and the Shape of Belief* (Berkeley, 1964).

Saintsbury, George. *A History of English Prose Rhythm* (Bloomington, Ind., reissue 1965).

Salper, Donald. "The Imaginative Component of Rhetoric," *QJS,* LI (1965), 307–10.

Scanlan, Ross. "Rhetoric and the Drama," *QJS,* XXII (1936), 635–42.

Schwartz, Elias. "*Mimesis* and the Theory of Signs," *CE,* XXIX (1968), 343–54.

Schwartz, Joseph. "Kenneth Burke, Aristotle, and the Future of Rhetoric," *CCC,* XVII (1966), 210–16.

———, and John Rycenga, eds. *The Province of Rhetoric* (New York, 1965).

Sharp, Robert Lathrop. "Some Light on Metaphysical Obscurity and Roughness," *SP,* XXXI (1934), 497–518.

Shurr, William. "Cicero and English Prose Style," *Classical Bulletin,* XXXIII (1961), 49–50.

Sloan, Thomas O. "Restoration of Rhetoric to Literary Study," *The Speech Teacher,* XVI (1967), 91–97.

Sowards, J. K. "Erasmus and the Apologetic Textbook: A Study of the *De Duplici Copia Verborum ac Rerum,*" *SP,* LV (1958), 122–35.

Sowton, Ian. "Hidden Persuaders as a Means of Literary Grace: Sixteenth-Century Poetics and Rhetoric in England," *University of Toronto Quarterly,* XXXII (1962), 55–69.

Spacks, Patricia Meyer. "Horror-Personification in Late Eighteenth-Century Poetry," *SP,* LIX (1962), 560–78.

Spencer, John, and Michael Gregory. "An Approach to the Study of Style," *Linguistics and Style,* ed. John Spencer (London, 1964), pp. 57–105.

Spilka, Mark. "The Necessary Stylist: A New Critical Revision," *Modern Fiction Studies,* VI (1960–61), 283–97.

Sprott, S. E. "Cicero's Theory of Prose Style," *PQ,* XXXIV (1955), 1–17.

Staton, Walter F., Jr. "The Characters of Style in Elizabethan Prose," *JEGP,* LVII (1958), 197–207.

Steinmann, Martin, Jr., ed. *New Rhetorics* (New York, 1967).

———. "Rhetorical Research," *CE,* XXVII (1966), 278–85.

Sutherland, James. "Some Aspects of Eighteenth-Century Prose," *Essays on the Eighteenth Century Presented to David Nichol Smith* (Oxford, 1945), pp. 94–110.

Tanenhaus, Gussie Hecht. "Bede's *De Schematibus et Tropis*—A Translation," *QJS,* XLVIII (1962), 237–53.

Taylor, Warren. *A Dictionary of the Tudor Figures of Rhetoric* (Chicago, 1937).

Thale, Jerome. "Style and Anti-Style: History and Anti-History," *CE,* XXIX (1968), 286–92, 301–2.

Thonssen, Lester, and A. Craig Baird. *Speech Criticism: The Development of Standards for Rhetorical Appraisal* (New York, 1948).

Tillotson, Geoffrey. "The Methods of Description in Eighteenth- and Nineteenth-Century Poetry," *Restoration and Eighteenth-Century Literary Essays in Honor of Alan Dugald McKillop* (Chicago, 1963), pp. 235–38.

Torrence, Donald L. "A Philosophy for Rhetoric from Bertrand Russell," *QJS*, XLV (1959), 153–65.

Tuve, Rosemond. *Elizabethan and Metaphysical Imagery* (Chicago, 1947).

———. "Imagery and Logic: Ramus and Metaphysical Poetics," *Journal of the History of Ideas*, III (1942), 365–400.

Ullman, B. L. "Renaissance—The Word and the Underlying Concept," *SP*, XLIX (1952), 105–18.

Ullmann, Stephen. "Style and Personality," *RES*, VI (1965), 21–31.

Wallerstein, Ruth C. "The Development of the Rhetoric and Metre of the Heroic Couplet, especially in 1625–1645," *PMLA*, L (1935), 166–209.

Warburg, Jeremy. "Idiosyncratic Style," *RES*, VI (1965), 56–65.

Watkins, Lloyd I. "Lord Brougham's Authorship of Rhetorical Articles in *The Edinburgh Review*," *QJS*, XLII (1956), 55–63.

Weaver, Richard M. "Some Rhetorical Aspects of Grammatical Categories," *The Ethics of Rhetoric* (Chicago, 1953), pp. 115–142.

———. "Language Is Sermonic," *Dimensions of Rhetorical Scholarship*, ed. Roger E. Nebergall (Norman, Okla., 1963), pp. 49–63.

Weinberg, Bernard. "Formal Analysis in Poetry and Rhetoric," *Rhetoric and Poetic*, ed. Donald C. Bryant (Iowa City, Ia., 1965), pp. 36–45.

Weinbrot, Howard D. "The Pattern of Formal Verse Satire in the Restoration and the Eighteenth Century," *PMLA*, LXXX (1965), 394–401.

Weitzmann, Francis White. "Notes on the Elizabethan *Elegie*," *PMLA*, L (1935), 435–43.

Welker, John J. "The Position of the Quarterlies on Some Classical Dogmas," *SP*, XXXVII (1940), 542–62.

Wellek, René, and Austin Warren. *Theory of Literature* (New York, 1949).

Whittemore, Reed. "Literature as Persuasion," *The Fascination of the Abomination* (New York, 1963).

Wichelns, Herbert A. "Some Differences between Literary Criticism and Rhetorical Criticism," *Historical Studies of Rhetoric and Rhetoricians*, ed. Raymond F. Howes (Ithaca, N.Y., 1961), pp. 217–25.

Wichelns, Herbert A. "The Literary Criticism of Oratory," *The Rhetorical Idiom,* ed. Donald C. Bryant (Ithaca, N.Y., 1958), pp. 5–42.

Williamson, George. *The Senecan Amble: A Study of Prose from Bacon to Collier* (Chicago, 1951).

———. "The Rhetorical Pattern of Neo-Classical Wit," *MP,* XXXIII (1935), 55–81.

———. "Senecan Style in the Seventeenth Century," *PQ,* XV (1936), 321–51.

Wilson, Harold S. "George of Trebizond and Early Humanist Rhetoric," *SP,* XL (1943), 367–79.

———. "Gabriel Harvey's Orations on Rhetoric," *ELH,* XII (1945), 167–82.

Wimsatt, W. K., Jr., ed. *Explication as Criticism: Selected Papers from English Institutes, 1941–1952* (New York, 1963).

———, and Cleanth Brooks. "Rhetoric and Neo-Classic Wit," *Literary Criticism: A Short History* (New York, 1957), pp. 221–51.

Winterowd, W. Ross. *Rhetoric: A Synthesis* (New York, 1968).

PART II—STUDIES OF SPECIFIC WORKS AND AUTHORS

Henry Adams

Folsom, James K. "Mutation as Metaphor in *The Education of Henry Adams,*" *ELH,* XXX (1963), 162–74.

Joseph Addison

Lannering, Jan. *Studies in the Prose Style of Joseph Addison* (Cambridge, Mass., 1951).

Mays, Morley J. "Johnson and Blair on Addison's Prose Style," *SP,* XXXIX (1942), 638–49.

Stevick, Philip. "Familiarity in the Addisonian Familiar Essay," *CCC,* XVI (1965), 169–73.

Maxwell Anderson

Roby, Robert C. "Two Worlds: Maxwell Anderson's *Winterset,*" *CE,* XVIII (1957), 195–202.

Sherwood Anderson

Love, Glen A. "*Winesburg, Ohio* and the Rhetoric of Silence," *AL,* XL (1968), 38–57.

Lancelot Andrewes

Webber, Joan. "Celebration of Word and World in Lancelot Andrewes's Style," *JEGP,* LXIV (1965), 255–69.

Matthew Arnold

Gollin, Richard M. "'Dover Beach': The Background of its Imagery," *English Studies,* XLVIII (1967), 493–511.

Holloway, John. "Matthew Arnold," *The Victorian Sage.* Norton Library ed. (New York, 1965), pp. 202–43.

Hunt, Everett Lee. "Matthew Arnold: The Critic as Rhetorician," *Historical Studies of Rhetoric and Rhetoricians,* ed. Raymond F. Howes (Ithaca, N.Y., 1961), pp. 322–44.

Major, John Campbell, "Matthew Arnold and Attic Prose Style," *PMLA,* LIX (1944), 1086–1103.

W. H. Auden

Bennett, Daphne Nicholson. "Auden's 'September 1, 1939': An Interpreter's Analysis," *QJS,* XLII (1956), 1–13.

Bloom, Robert. "The Humanization of Auden's Early Style," *PMLA,* LXXXIII (1968), 443–54.

Jarrell, Randall. "Changes of Attitude and Rhetoric in Auden's Poetry," *Southern Review,* VII (1941), 326–49.

Jane Austen

Crane, R. S. "Jane Austen: *Persuasion,*" *The Idea of the Humanities and Other Essays Critical and Historical,* 2 vols. (Chicago, 1967), II, 283–302.

Harvey, W. J. "The Plot of *Emma,*" *Essays in Criticism,* XVII (1967), 48–63.

Kearful, Frank J. "Satire and the Form of the Novel: The Problem of Aesthetic Unity in *Northanger Abbey,*" *ELH,* XXXII (1965), 511–27.

Francis Bacon

Wallace, Karl R. *Francis Bacon on Communication and Rhetoric* (Chapel Hill, N.C., 1943).

———. "Aspects of Modern Rhetoric in Francis Bacon," *QJS,* XLII (1956), 398–406.

———. "Discussion in Parliament and Francis Bacon," *QJS,* XLIII (1957), 12–21.

Saul Bellow

Shulman, Robert. "The Style of Bellow's Comedy," *PMLA,* LXXXIII (1968), 109–17.

Beowulf

Engelhardt, George J. "*Beowulf:* A Study in Dilatation," *PMLA,* LXX (1955), 825–52.

Leyerle, John. "The Interlace Structure of *Beowulf*," *University of Toronto Quarterly*, XXXVII (1967), 1–17.

Whallon, William. "The Diction of *Beowulf*," *PMLA*, LXXVI (1961), 309–19.

Whitelock, Dorothy. *The Audience of Beowulf* (Oxford, 1951).

William Blake

Bloom, Harold. "Dialectic in *The Marriage of Heaven and Hell*," *PMLA*, LXXIII (1958), 501–4.

Tillyard, E. M. W. "The Two Village Greens," *Poetry: Direct and Oblique* (London, 1934), pp. 7–16. Goldsmith's *Deserted Village* and Blake's *Echoing Green*.

James Boswell

Golden, James L. "James Boswell on Rhetoric and Belles-Lettres," *QJS*, L (1964), 266–76.

Emily Brontë

Pearsall, Robert. "The Presiding Tropes of Emily Brontë," *CE*, XXVII (1966), 267–73.

Sir Thomas Browne

Moloney, Michael F. "Metre and *Cursus* in Sir Thomas Browne's Prose," *JEGP*, LVIII (1959), 60–67.

Parker, E. L. "The Cursus in Sir Thomas Browne," *PMLA*, LIII (1938), 1037–53.

Tempest, Norton R. "Rhythm in the Prose of Sir Thomas Browne," *RES*, III (1927), 308–18.

Warren, Austin. "The Style of Browne," *Kenyon Review*, XIII (1951), 674–87.

Whallon, William. "Hebraic Synonymy in Sir Thomas Browne," *ELH*, XXVIII (1961), 335–53.

Robert Browning

Altick, Richard D. "'A Grammarian's Funeral': Browning's Praise of Folly?" *Studies in English Literature, 1500–1900*, III (1963), 446–60.

Preyer, Robert. "Two Styles in the Verse of Robert Browning," *ELH*, XXXII (1965), 62–84.

Schweik, Robert C. "The Structure of 'A Grammarian's Funeral,'" *CE*, XXII (1961), 411–12.

Weaver, Bennett. "A Primer Study in Browning's Satire," *CE*, XIV (1952), 76–81.

Edmund Burke

Boulton, J. T. "Exposition and Proof: The Apostrophe in Burke's *Reflections*," *Renaissance and Modern Studies*, II (1958), 38–69.

Bryant, Donald C. "Edmund Burke: New Evidence, Broader View," *QJS*, XXXVIII (1952), 435–45.

———. "Burke's *Present Discontents:* The Rhetorical Genesis of a Party Testament," *QJS*, XLII (1956), 115–26.

Johnson, S. F. "Hardy and Burke's 'Sublime,'" *English Institute Essays, 1958*, ed. Harold C. Martin (New York, 1959), pp. 55–86.

Joy, Neill R. "Burke's *Speech on Conciliation with the Colonies:* Epic Prophecy and Satire," *Studies in Burke* (formerly *The Burke Newsletter*), IX (1967), 753–62.

Snow, Vernon F. "Robert C. Johnson's Appraisal of Edmund Burke's Eloquence," *QJS*, XLII (1956), 243–49.

Weaver, Richard M. "Edmund Burke and the Argument from Circumstance," *The Ethics of Rhetoric* (Chicago, 1953), pp. 55–84.

Robert Burns

Buchan, A. N. "Word and Word-Tune in Burns," *SP*, XLVIII (1951), 40–48.

George Gordon, Lord Byron

Lovell, Ernest J., Jr. "Irony and Image in *Don Juan*," *The Major English Romantic Poets*, ed. Clarence D. Thorpe, Carlos Baker, and Bennett Weaver (Carbondale, Ill., 1957), pp. 129–48.

Thomas Carlyle

Roellinger, Francis X., Jr. "The Early Development of Carlyle's Style," *PMLA*, LXXII (1957), 936–51.

Holloway, John. "Carlyle" and "Carlyle as Prophet-Historian," *The Victorian Sage*. Norton Library ed. (New York, 1965), pp. 21–57 and 58–85.

Geoffrey Chaucer

Baldwin, Charles Sears. "Cicero on Parnassus," *PMLA*, XLII (1927), 106–12. Chaucer on the "colours of rethoryk."

Baum, Paull F. "Chaucer's Puns," *PMLA*, LXXI (1956), 225–46.

———. "Chaucer's Puns: A Supplementary List," *PMLA*, LXXIII (1958), 167–70.

Hamilton, Marie Padgett. "Notes on Chaucer and the Rhetoricians," *PMLA*, XLVII (1932), 403–9.

Harrison, Benjamin S. "Medieval Rhetoric in *The Book of the Duchess*," *PMLA*, XLIX (1934), 428–42.

———. "The Rhetorical Inconsistency of Chaucer's Franklin," *SP,* XXXII (1935), 55–61.

Hill, Mary A. "Rhetorical Balance in Chaucer's Poetry," *PMLA,* XLII (1927), 845–61.

Kökeritz, Helge. "Rhetorical Word-Play in Chaucer," *PMLA,* LXIX (1954), 937–52.

Manly, John Matthews. "Chaucer and the Rhetoricians," *The Proceedings of the British Academy,* XII (1926), 95–113.

Murphy, James J. "A New Look at Chaucer and the Rhetoricians," *RES,* XV (1964), 1–20.

Silverstein, Theodore. "Wife of Bath and the Rhetoric of Enchantment: Or, How to Make a Hero See in the Dark," *MP,* LVIII (1961), 153–73.

Teager, Florence E. "Chaucer's Eagle and the Rhetorical Colors," *PMLA,* XLVII (1932), 410–18.

Wilson, William S. "The Eagle's Speech in Chaucer's *Hous of Fame,*" *QJS,* L (1964), 153–58.

Samuel Taylor Coleridge

Gose, Elliott B., Jr. "Coleridge and the Luminous Gloom: An Analysis of the 'Symbolical Language' in 'The Rime of the Ancient Mariner,'" *PMLA,* LXXV (1960), 238–44.

Fogle, Stephen F. "The Design of Coleridge's 'Dejection,'" *SP,* XLVIII (1951), 49–55.

House, Humphry. "The Ancient Mariner," *Coleridge: The Clark Lectures, 1951–52* (London, 1953), pp. 84–113.

Howes, Raymond F. "Coleridge and Rhetoric," *Quarterly Journal of Speech Education,* XII (1926), 145–56.

———. "Samuel Taylor Coleridge in Lecture-Box and Pulpit," *Historical Studies of Rhetoric and Rhetoricians,* ed. Raymond F. Howes (Ithaca, N.Y., 1961), pp. 309–21.

Neumann, Joshua H. "Coleridge on the English Language," *PMLA,* LXIII (1948), 642–61.

Owen, Charles A., Jr. "Structure in *The Ancient Mariner,*" *CE,* XXIII (1962), 261–67.

Warren, Robert Penn. "A Poem of Pure Imagination," *Kenyon Review,* VIII (1946), 402–18. "The Rime of the Ancient Mariner."

William Collins

Quintana, Ricardo. "The Schemes of Collins's *Odes on Several . . . Subjects,*" *Restoration and Eighteenth-Century Literary Essays in Honor of Alan Dugald McKillop* (Chicago, 1963), pp. 371–80.

Spacks, Patricia Meyer. "Collins' Imagery," *SP,* LXII (1965), 719–36.

Wasserman, Earl R. "Collins' 'Ode on the Poetical Character,'" *ELH,* XXXIV (1967), 92–115.

E. E. Cummings

Friedman, Norman. "Diction, Voice, and Tone: The Poetic Language of E. E. Cummings," *PMLA,* LXXII (1957), 1036–59.

Joseph Conrad

Eschbacher, Robert L. "*Lord Jim,* Classical Rhetoric, and the Freshman Dilemma," *CE,* XXV (1963), 22–25.

Stephen Crane

Albrecht, Robert C. "Content and Style in *The Red Badge of Courage,*" *CE,* XXVII (1966), 487–92.

William Davenant

Cope, Jackson I. "Rhetorical Genres in Davenant's *First Day's Entertainment at Rutland House,*" *QJS,* XLV (1959), 191–94.

Charles Dickens

Kincaid, James R. "Laughter in *Oliver Twist,*" *PMLA,* LXXXIII (1968), 63–70.

Quirk, Randolph. "Some Observations on the Language of Dickens," *Review of English Literature,* II (1961), 19–28.

Wentersdorf, Karl. "Mirror-Images in *Great Expectations,*" *Nineteenth-Century Fiction,* XXI (1966), 203–24.

Daniel Defoe

Girdler, Lew. "Defoe's Education at Newington Green Academy," *SP,* L (1953), 573–91.

Koonce, Howard L. "Moll's Muddle: Defoe's Use of Irony in *Moll Flanders,*" *ELH,* XXX (1964), 377–94.

John Denham

Wasserman, Earl R. "Denham: *Cooper's Hill,*" *The Subtler Language: Critical Readings of Neoclassic and Romantic Poems* (Baltimore, 1959), pp. 35–88.

John Donne

Andreasen, N. J. C. "Theme and Structure in Donne's *Satyres,*" *Studies in English Literature,* III (1963), 59–75.

Brooks, Cleanth. "The Language of Paradox," *The Well Wrought Urn* (New York, 1947), pp. 3–21. Donne's "Canonization."

Clair, John A. "Donne's 'The Canonization,'" *PMLA,* LXXX (1965), 300–2.

Empson, William. "Donne and the Rhetorical Tradition," *Kenyon Review*, XI (1949), 571–87.

Freccero, John. "Donne's 'Valediction Forbidding Mourning,'" *ELH*, XXX (1963), 335–76.

Hickey, Robert L. "Donne's Art of Memory," *Tennessee Studies in Literature*, III (1958), 29–36.

Quinn, Dennis. "Donne's Christian Eloquence," *ELH*, XXVII (1960), 276–97.

Sloan, Thomas O. "The Rhetoric in the Poetry of John Donne," *Studies in English Literature, 1500–1900*, III (1963), 31–44.

———. "The Persona as Rhetor: An Interpretation of Donne's *Satyre III*," *QJS*, LI (1965), 14–27.

Stein, Arnold. "Donne's Harshness and the Elizabethan Tradition," *SP*, XLI (1944), 390–409.

Umbach, Herbert H. "The Merit of Metaphysical Style in Donne's Easter Sermons," *ELH*, XII (1945), 108–25.

———. "The Rhetoric of Donne's Sermons," *PMLA*, LII (1947), 354–58.

Wallerstein, Ruth C. "Rhetoric in the English Renaissance: Two Elegies," *English Institute Essays, 1948*, ed. D. A. Robertson, Jr. (New York, 1949), pp. 153–78. Donne's elegy on Prince Henry and Milton's "Lycidas."

Warren, Austin. "Donne's 'Extasie,'" *SP*, LV (1958), 472–80.

Webber, Joan. *Contrary Music: The Prose Style of John Donne* (Madison, Wis., 1963).

———. "The Prose Styles of John Donne's *Devotions upon Emergent Occasions*," *Anglia*, LXXIX (1962), 138–52.

Wiggins, Elizabeth Lewis. "Logic in the Poetry of John Donne," *SP*, XLII (1945), 41–60.

The Dream of the Rood

Schlauch, Margaret. "'The Dream of the Rood' as Prosopopoeia," *Essays and Studies in Honor of Carleton Brown* (New York, 1940), pp. 23–34.

John Dryden

Ellis, Amanda M. "Horace's Influence on Dryden," *PQ*, IV (1925), 39–60.

Feder, Lillian. "John Dryden's Use of Classical Rhetoric," *PMLA*, LXIX (1954), 1258–78.

Fujimura, Thomas H. "Dryden's *Religio Laici:* An Anglican Poem," *PMLA*, LXXVI (1961), 205–17.

Hamm, Victor M. "Dryden's *Religio Laici* and Roman Catholic Apologetics," *PMLA,* LXXX (1965), 190–98.

Jack, Ian. "Mock-Heroic: *MacFlecknoe,*" *Augustan Satire: Intention and Idiom in English Poetry, 1660–1750* (Oxford, 1952; 1957), pp. 43–52.

Levine, Jay Arnold. "Dryden's *Song for St. Cecilia's Day, 1687,*" *PQ,* XLIV (1965), 38–50.

Maurer, A. E. Wallace. "The Structure of Dryden's *Astraea Redux,*" *Papers on Language and Literature,* II (1966), 13–20.

Vieth, David M. "Irony in Dryden's 'Ode to Anne Killigrew,'" *SP,* LXII (1965), 91–100.

Wallerstein, Ruth C. "On the Death of Mrs. Killigrew: The Perfection of a Genre," *SP,* XLIV (1947), 519–28.

Wassermann, Earl R. "Dryden: Epistle to Charleton," *The Subtler Language: Critical Readings of Neoclassic and Romantic Poems* (Baltimore, 1959), pp. 15–33.

Jonathan Edwards

Baumgartner, Paul R. "Jonathan Edwards: The Theory Behind His Use of Figurative Language," *PMLA,* LXXVIII (1963), 321–25.

George Eliot

Holloway, John. "George Eliot," *The Victorian Sage.* Norton Library ed. (New York, 1965), pp. 111–57.

T. S. Eliot

Bates, Ronald. "A Topic in *The Wasteland:* Traditional Rhetoric and Eliot's Individual Talent," *Wisconsin Studies in Contemporary Literature,* V (1964), 85–104.

Wright, Keith. "Rhetorical Repetition in T. S. Eliot's Early Verse," *RES,* VI (1965), 93–100.

———. "Word-Repetition in T. S. Eliot's Early Verse," *Essays in Criticism,* XVI (1966), 201–6.

Ralph Waldo Emerson

Adams, Richard P. "Emerson and the Organic Metaphor," *PMLA,* LXIX (1954), 117–30.

Finnigan, David F. "The Man Himself: Emerson's Prose Style," *Emerson Society Quarterly,* No. 39 (1965), pp. 13–15.

Lauter, Paul. "Emerson's Revisions of *Essays* (First Series)," *AL,* XXXIII (1961), 143–58.

Lee, Roland F. "Emerson Through Kierkegaard: Toward a Definition of Emerson's Theory of Communication," *ELH,* XXIV (1957), 229–48.

Meyer, Sam. "Teaching the Rhetorical Approach to the Poem," *Rhetoric: Theories for Application,* ed. Robert M. Gorrell (Champaign, Ill., 1967), pp. 82–9. Analysis of Emerson's "Concord Hymn, Sung at the Completion of the Battle Monument, July 4, 1837."

Moss, Sidney P. "Analogy: The Heart of Emerson's Style," *Emerson Society Quarterly,* No. 39 (1965), pp. 21–24.

Everyman

Van Laan, Thomas F. "*Everyman:* A Structural Analysis," *PMLA,* LXXVIII (1963), 465–75.

William Faulkner

Antrim, Harry. "Faulkner's Suspended Style," *University of Kansas City Review,* XXXII (1965), 122–28.

Baldanza, Frank. "The Structure of *Light in August,*" *Modern Fiction Studies,* XIII (1967), 67–78.

Beck, William. "William Faulkner's Style," *William Faulkner: Two Decades of Criticism,* ed. Frederick J. Hoffman and Olga W. Vickery (East Lansing, Mich., 1951), pp. 142–56.

Larsen, Eric. "The Barrier of Language: The Irony of Language in Faulkner," *Modern Fiction Studies,* XIII (1967), 19–32.

Lind, Ilse Dusoir. "The Design and Meaning of *Absalom! Absalom!*" *PMLA,* LXX (1955), 887–912.

McElderry, B. R., Jr. "The Narrative of *Light in August,*" *CE,* XIX (1958), 200–207.

Slatoff, Walter J. "The Edge of Order: The Pattern of Faulkner's Rhetoric," *Twentieth-Century Literature,* III (1957), 107–27.

Vickery, Olga W. "Gavin Stevens: from Rhetoric to Dialectic," *Faulkner Studies,* II (1953), 1–4. On *Requiem for a Nun.*

———. "*The Sound and the Fury: A Study in Perspective,*" *PMLA,* LXIX (1954), 1017–37.

Zink, Karl E. "Flux and the Frozen Moment: The Imagery of Stasis in Faulkner's Prose," *PMLA,* LXXI (1956), 285–301.

Zoellner, Robert H. "Faulkner's Prose Style in *Absalom! Absalom!*" *AL,* XXX (1959), 486–502.

Henry Fielding

Crane, R. S. "The Concept of Plot and the Plot of *Tom Jones,*" *Critics and Criticism* (Chicago, 1952), pp. 616–47.

Farrell, William J. "Fielding's Familiar Style," *ELH,* XXXIV (1967), 65–77.

———. "The Mock-Heroic Form of *Jonathan Wild,*" *MP,* LXIII (1966), 216–26.

John Galsworthy

Simrell, V. E. "John Galsworthy: The Artist as Propagandist," *QJS*, XIII (1927), 225–36.

Sir Gawain

Borroff, Marie. *Sir Gawain and the Green Knight: A Stylistic and Metrical Study* (New Haven, 1962).

Edward Gibbon

Hayes, Curtis W. "A Study in Prose Styles: Edward Gibbon and Ernest Hemingway," *Texas Studies in Literature and Language*, VII (1966), 371–86.

Frost, William. "The Irony of Swift and Gibbon: A Reply to F. R. Leavis," *Essays in Criticism*, XVII (1967), 41–47.

Oliver Goldsmith

Tillyard, E. M. W. "The Two Village Greens," *Poetry: Direct and Oblique* (London, 1934), pp. 7–16. Goldsmith's *Deserted Village* and Blake's *Echoing Green*.

Miner, Earl. "The Making of *The Deserted Village*," *Huntington Library Quarterly*, XXII (1959), 125–41.

Quintana, Ricardo. "*The Deserted Village:* Its Logical and Rhetorical Elements," *CE*, XXVI (1964), 204–14.

Stephen Gosson

Kinney, Arthur F. "Stephen Gosson's Art of Argumentation in *The School of Abuse*," *Studies in English Literature, 1500–1900*, VII (1967), 41–54.

John Gower

Daniels, R. Balfour. "Rhetoric in Gower's *To King Henry the Fourth, In Praise of Peace*," *SP*, XXXII (1935), 62–73.

Murphy, James J. "John Gower's *Confessio Amantis* and the First Discussion of Rhetoric in the English Language," *PQ*, XLI (1962), 401–11.

Thomas Gray

Bateson, F. W. "Gray's *Elegy* Reconsidered," *English Poetry: A Critical Introduction* (London, 1950), pp. 181–93.

Brooks, Cleanth. "Gray's Storied Urn," *The Well Wrought Urn* (New York, 1947), pp. 105–123. Gray's *Elegy*.

Dyson, A. E. "The Ambivalence of Gray's Elegy," *Essays in Criticism*, VII (1957), 257–61.

Ellis, Frank H. "Gray's *Elegy:* the Biographical Problem in Literary Criticism," *PMLA,* LXVI (1951), 971–1008.

Peckham, Morse. "Gray's Epitaph Revisited," *Modern Language Notes,* LXXI (1956), 409–11.

Starr, H. W. "'A Youth to Fortune and to Fame Unknown': a Re-Evaluation," *JEGP,* XLVIII (1949), 97–107.

Sutherland, John. "The Stonecutter in Gray's Elegy," *MP,* LV (1957), 11–13.

Thomas Hardy

Holloway, John. "Hardy," *The Victorian Sage.* Norton Library ed. (New York, 1965), pp. 244–89.

Johnson, S. F. "Hardy and Burke's 'Sublime,'" *English Institute Essays, 1958,* ed. Harold C. Martin (New York, 1959), pp. 55–86.

Nathaniel Hawthorne

Battaglia, Francis Joseph. "*The House of the Seven Gables:* New Light on Old Problems," *PMLA,* LXXXII (1967), 579–90.

Gross, Robert Eugene. "Hawthorne's First Novel: The Future of a Style," *PMLA,* LXXVIII (1963), 60–68.

Prosser, Michael H. "A Rhetoric of Alienation as Reflected in the Works of Nathaniel Hawthorne," *QJS,* LIV (1968), 22–28.

Ernest Hemingway

Carpenter, Frederick I. "Hemingway Achieves the Fifth Dimension," *PMLA,* LXIX (1954), 711–18.

Christensen, Francis. "Notes Toward a New Rhetoric: I. Sentence Openers; II. A Lesson from Hemingway," *CE,* XXV (1963), 7–18.

Crane, R. S. "Ernest Hemingway: 'The Killers,'" *The Idea of the Humanities and Other Essays Critical and Historical,* 2 vols. (Chicago, 1967), II, 303–14.

Crane, R. S. "Ernest Hemingway: 'The Short Happy Life of Francis Macomber,'" *The Idea of the Humanities and Other Essays Critical and Historical,* 2 vols. (Chicago, 1967), II, 315–26.

Hayes, Curtis W. "A Study in Prose Styles: Edward Gibbon and Ernest Hemingway," *Texas Studies in Literature and Language,* VII (1966), 371–86.

George Herbert

Bowers, Fredson. "Herbert's Sequential Imagery," *MP,* LIX (1962), 202–13.

Walker, John David. "The Architectonics of George Herbert's *The Temple,*" *ELH,* XXIX (1962), 289–305.

Robert Herrick

Brooks, Cleanth. "What Does Poetry Communicate?" *The Well Wrought Urn* (New York, 1947), pp. 67–79. Herrick's "Corinna's Going a-Maying."

Spitzer, Leo. "Herrick's 'Delight in Disorder,'" *Essays on English and American Literature* (Princeton, N.J., 1962), pp. 132–38.

John Heywood

McCain, John W., Jr. "Oratory, Rhetoric, and Logic in the Writing of John Heywood," *QJS*, XXVI (1940), 44–47.

Richard Hooker

Stueber, Sister M. Stephanie. "The Balanced Diction of Hooker's *Polity*," *PMLA*, LXXI (1956), 808–26.

Yoder, Samuel A. "*Dispositio* in Richard Hooker's 'Laws of Ecclesiastical Polity,'" *QJS*, XXVII (1941), 90–97.

Gerard Manley Hopkins

Hill, Archibald A. "An Analysis of *The Windhover:* An Experiment in Structural Method," *PMLA*, LXX (1955), 968–78.

Nist, John. "Gerard Manley Hopkins and Textural Intensity," *CE*, XXII (1961), 497–500.

Payne, Michael. "Syntactical Analysis and 'The Windhover,'" *Renascence*, XIX (1967), 88–92.

Thomas Henry Huxley

Blinderman, Charles S. "Semantic Aspects of T. H. Huxley's Literary Style," *Journal of Communication*, XXII (1962), 171–78.

Houghton, Walter E. "The Rhetoric of T. H. Huxley," *University of Toronto Quarterly*, XVIII (1949), 159–75.

Jensen, J. Vernon. "The Rhetorical Influence of Thomas Henry Huxley on the United States," *Western Speech*, XXXI (1967), 29–36.

Henry James

Crow, Charles R. "The Style of Henry James: *The Wings of the Dove*," *English Institute Essays, 1958*, ed. Harold C. Martin (New York, 1959), pp. 172–89.

Durkin, Sister Mary Brian. "Henry James's Revisions of the Style of *The Reverberator*," *AL*, XXXIII (1961), 330–49.

Gibson, Priscilla. "The Uses of James's Imagery: Drama Through Metaphor," *PMLA*, LXIX (1954), 1076–84.

Knox, George. "James's Rhetoric of 'Quotes,'" *CE*, XVII (1956), 293–97.

Short, R. W. "The Sentence-Structure of Henry James," *AL*, XVIII (1946), 71–88.

Ward, J. A. "James's Idea of Structure," *PMLA*, LXXX (1965), 419–26.

Samuel Johnson

Elder, A. T. "Thematic Patterning and Development in Johnson's Essays," *SP*, LXII (1965), 610–32.

Emden, Cecil S. "Rhythmical Features of Dr. Johnson's Prose," *RES*, XXV (1949), 38–54.

Moore, Wilbur E. "Samuel Johnson on Rhetoric," *QJS*, XXX (1944), 165–8.

O'Flaherty, Patrick. "Johnson as Satirist: A New Look at *The Vanity of Human Wishes*," *ELH*, XXXIV (1967), 78–91.

Wimsatt, W. K., Jr. *The Prose Style of Samuel Johnson* (New Haven, Conn., 1941; paperback 1963).

———. *Philosophical Words: A Study of Style and Meaning in the "Rambler" and "Dictionary" of Samuel Johnson* (New Haven, Conn., 1948).

Ben Jonson

Barish, Jonas A. "Baroque Prose in the Theater: Ben Jonson," *PMLA*, LXXIII (1958), 184–95.

Caldiero, Frank. "Ben Jonson's Course in Freshman English," *CE*, XIX (1957), 7–11.

Howell, A. C. "A Note on Ben Jonson's Literary Methods," *SP*, XXVIII (1931), 710–19.

Jones, Robert C. "The Satirist's Retirement in Jonson's 'Apologetical Dialogue,'" *ELH*, XXXIV (1967), 447–67.

Knoll, Robert E. "How to Read *The Alchemist*," *CE*, XXI (1960), 456–60.

Neumann, Joshua H. "Notes on Ben Jonson's English," *PMLA*, LIV (1939), 736–63.

Sackton, Alexander H. *Rhetoric as a Dramatic Language in Ben Jonson* (New York, 1948).

Schelling, Felix E. "Ben Jonson and the Classical School," *PMLA*, XIII (1898), 221–49.

Stein, Arnold. "Plain Style, Plain Criticism, Plain Dealing, and Ben Jonson," *ELH*, XXX (1963), 306–16.

Thayer, C. G. "Theme and Structure in *The Alchemist*," *ELH*, XXVI (1959), 23–35.

Trimpi, Wesley. *Ben Jonson's Poems: A Study of the Plain Style* (Stanford, 1962).

Trimpi, Wesley. "Jonson and the Neo-Latin Authorities for the Plain Style," *PMLA*, LXXVII (1962), 21–26.

James Joyce

Anderson, Chester G. "James Joyce's 'Tilly,'" *PMLA*, LXXIII (1958), 285–98.

Cope, Jackson I. "James Joyce: Test Case for a Theory of Style," *ELH*, XXI (1954), 221–36.

Doherty, James. "Joyce and *Hell Opened to Christians:* The Edition He Used for His 'Hell Sermons,'" *MP*, LXI (1963), 110–19.

Hayman, David. "From *Finnegans Wake:* A Sentence in Progress," *PMLA*, LXXIII (1958), 136–54.

Manso, Peter. "The Metaphoric of Joyce's *Portrait*," *Modern Fiction Studies*, XIII (1967), 221–36.

Poss, Stanley. "*Ulysses* and the Comedy of the Immobilized Act," *ELH*, XXIV (1957), 65–83.

Prescott, Joseph. "James Joyce: A Study in Words," *PMLA*, LIV (1939), 304–15.

Russell, John. "From Style to Meaning in 'Araby,'" *CE*, XXVIII (1966), 170–71; Richard Ohmann, "Reply," *ibid.*, pp. 171–73.

Tompkins, Phillip K. "The Rhetoric of James Joyce," *QJS*, LIV (1968), 107–21.

Thrane, James R. "Joyce's Sermon on Hell: Its Source and Its Background," *MP*, LVII (1960), 172–98.

John Keats

Bland, D. S. "'Logical Structure' in the *Ode to Autumn*," *PQ*, XXXIII (1954), 219–22.

Brooks, Cleanth. "Keats's Sylvan Historian: History without Footnotes," *The Well Wrought Urn* (New York, 1947), pp. 151–66. "Ode on a Grecian Urn."

Burke, Kenneth. "Symbolic Action in a Poem by Keats," *A Grammar of Motives* (New York, 1945), pp. 447–63. "Ode on a Grecian Urn."

Spitzer, Leo. "The 'Ode on a Grecian Urn,' or Content vs. Metagrammar," *Essays on English and American Literature* (Princeton, N. J., 1962), pp. 67–97.

Wasserman, Earl R. *The Finer Tone: Keats' Major Poems* (Baltimore, 1953). Analyses of "Ode on a Grecian Urn," "La Belle Dame Sans Merci," "The Eve of St. Agnes," "Lamia," and "Ode to a Nightingale."

D. H. Lawrence

Nichols, Ann Eljenholm. "Syntax and Style: Ambiguities in Lawrence's 'Twilight in Italy,'" *CCC*, XVI (1965), 261–66.

Abraham Lincoln

Brice, Marshall M. "Lincoln and Rhetoric," *CCC*, XVII (1966), 12–14.

Weaver, Richard M. "Abraham Lincoln and the Argument from Definition," *The Ethics of Rhetoric* (Chicago, 1953), pp. 85–114.

John Lyly

Barish, Jonas A. "The Prose Style of John Lyly," *ELH*, XXIII (1956), 14–35.

King, Walter J. "John Lyly and Elizabethan Rhetoric," *SP*, LII (1955), 149–61.

Thomas Babington Macaulay

Fraser, G. S. "Macaulay's Style as an Essayist," *Review of English Literature*, I (1960), 9–19.

Svaglic, Martin J. "Classical Rhetoric and Victorian Prose," *The Art of Victorian Prose*, ed. George Levine and William A. Madden (New York, 1968), pp. 268–88. Analysis of Macaulay's essay on Milton.

Wood, Margaret. "Lord Macaulay, Parliamentary Speaker: His Leading Ideas," *QJS*, XLIV (1958), 375–84.

James Madison

Ashin, Mark. "The Argument of Madison's 'Federalist, No. 10,'" *CE*, XV (1953), 37–45.

Bernard Mandeville

Edwards, Thomas R., Jr. "Mandeville's Moral Prose," *ELH*, XXXI (1964), 195–212.

Christopher Marlowe

Peet, Donald. "The Rhetoric of *Tamburlaine*," *ELH*, XXVI (1959), 137–55.

Wyler, Siegfried. "Marlowe's Technique of Communicating with an Audience, as seen in his *Tamburlaine*, Part I," *English Studies*, XLVIII (1967), 306–16.

Andrew Marvell

Brooks, Cleanth. "Marvell's 'Horatian Ode,'" *English Institute Essays, 1946* (New York, 1947), pp. 127–58.

Cunningham, J. V. "Logic and Lyric," *MP*, LI (1953), 33–41. Analysis of syllogistic logic of Marvell's *The Garden*.

Empson, William. "Marvell's Garden," *Some Versions of Pastoral* (London, 1935), pp. 119–45.

Hogan, Patrick G. "Marvell's 'Vegetable Love,'" *SP*, LX (1963), 1–11.

Hyman, Lawrence W. "Marvell's *Garden*," *ELH*, XXV (1958), 13–22.

Kermode, Frank. "The Argument of Marvell's 'Garden,'" *Essays in Criticism*, II (1952), 225–41.

Spitzer, Leo. "Marvell's 'Nymph Complaining for the Death of Her Fawn': Sources versus Meaning," *Essays on English and American Literature* (Princeton, N. J., 1962), pp. 98–115.

Wallace, John M. "Marvell's Horatian Ode," *PMLA*, LXXVII (1962), 33–45.

Philip Massinger

Hoy, Cyrus. "Verbal Formulae in the Plays of Philip Massinger," *SP*, LVI (1959), 600–18.

H. L. Mencken

Simrell, V. E. "H. L. Mencken the Rhetorician," *QJS*, XIII (1927), 399–412.

Stenerson, Douglas C. "Mencken's Early Newspaper Experience: The Genesis of a Style," *AL*, XXXVII (1965), 153–66.

John Milton

Barker, Arthur. "The Pattern of Milton's *Nativity Odes*," *University of Toronto Quarterly*, X (1940), 167–81.

———. "Structural Pattern in *Paradise Lost*," *PQ*, XXVIII (1949), 17–30.

Battestin, Martin C. "John Crowe Ransom and *Lycidas*: A Reappraisal," *CE*, XVII (1956), 223–28.

Broadbent, J. B. "Milton's Rhetoric," *MP*, LVI (1959), 224–42.

Brooks, Cleanth. "The Light Symbolism in 'L'Allegro-Il Penseroso,'" *The Well Wrought Urn* (New York, 1947), pp. 50–66.

Cheek, Macon. "Of Two Sonnets of Milton," *Renaissance Papers* (Columbia, S. C., 1956), pp. 82–91. "On Having Arrived at the Age of Twenty-Three" and "On His Blindness."

Clark, Donald Lemen. *John Milton at St. Paul's School: A Study of Ancient Rhetoric in Renaissance Education* (New York, 1948).

———. "Milton's Rhetorical Exercises," *QJS*, XLVI (1960), 297–301.

Clark, Evert Mordecai. "Milton's English Poetical Vocabulary," *SP*, LIII (1956), 220–38.

Condee, Ralph W. "The Structure of Milton's 'Epitaphium Damonis,'" *SP*, LXII (1965), 577–94.

Cope, Jackson I. *The Metaphoric Structure of Paradise Lost* (Baltimore, 1962).

Ekfelt, Fred Emil. "The Graphic Diction of Milton's English Prose," *PQ*, XXV (1946), 46–69.

———. "Latinate Diction in Milton's English Prose," *PQ*, XXVIII (1949), 53–71.

Frye, Northrop. "Literature as Context: Milton's *Lycidas*," *University of North Carolina Studies in Comparative Literature*, XXIII (1959), 44–55.

———. "The Typology of *Paradise Regained*," *MP*, LIII (1956), 227–38.

Gilman, Wilbur E. "Milton's Rhetoric on the Tyranny of Kings," *Historical Studies of Rhetoric and Rhetoricians*, ed. Raymond F. Howes (Ithaca, N.Y., 1961), pp. 239–52.

Hunter, G. K. "The Structure of Milton's *Areopagitica*," *English Studies*, XXXIX (1958), 117–19.

Kranidas, Thomas. "'Decorum' and the Style of Milton's Antiprelatical Tracts," *SP*, LXII (1965), 176–87.

Lawry, Jon S. "'Eager Thought': Dialectic in *Lycidas*," *PMLA*, LXXVII (1962), 27–32.

Madsen, William G. "Earth the Shadow: Typological Symbolism in *Paradise Lost*," *PMLA*, LXXV (1960), 519–26.

More, Paul Elmer, "How to Read 'Lycidas,'" *On Being Human* (Princeton, N. J., 1936), pp. 184–202.

Neumann, Joshua H. "Milton's Prose Vocabulary," *PMLA*, LX (1945), 102–20.

Pearce, Donald R. "The Style of Milton's Epic," *The Yale Review*, LII (1963), 427–44.

Price, Alan F. "Incidental Imagery in *Areopagitica*," *MP*, XLIX (1952), 217–22.

Ransom, John Crowe. "A Poem Nearly Anonymous," *The World's Body* (New York, 1938), pp. 1–28. Milton's *Lycidas*.

Shawcross, John T. "The Balanced Structure of *Paradise Lost*," *SP*, LXII (1965), 696–718.

Shumaker, Wayne. "Flowerets and Sounding Seas: A Study of the Affective Structure of *Lycidas*," *PMLA*, LXVI (1951), 485–94.

Slakey, Roger L. "Milton's Sonnet 'On His Blindness,'" *ELH*, XXVII (1960), 122–30.

Stein, Arnold. "Milton's War in Heaven—An Extended Metaphor," *ELH*, XVIII (1951), 201–20.

Svendsen, Kester. "Adam's Soliloquy in Book X of *Paradise Lost,*" *CE,* X (1949), 366–70.

Thompson, E. N. S. "Milton's Prose Style," *PQ,* XIV (1935), 1–15.

Tuve, Rosemond. *Images and Themes in Five Poems by Milton* (Cambridge, Mass., 1957). "The Structural Figures of *L'Allegro* and *Il Penseroso,*" pp. 15–36; "*The Hymn* on the Morning of Christ's Nativity," pp. 37–72; "Theme, Pattern, and Imagery in *Lycidas,*" pp. 73–111; "Image, Form, and Theme in *A Mask,*" pp. 112–161.

Wallerstein, Ruth C. "Rhetoric in the English Renaissance: Two Elegies," *English Institute Essays, 1948,* ed. D. A. Robertson, Jr. (New York, 1949), pp. 153–178. Donne's elegy on Prince Henry and Milton's *Lycidas.*

Weaver, Richard M. "Milton's Heroic Prose," *The Ethics of Rhetoric* (Chicago, 1953), pp. 143–63.

Whaler, James. "Compounding and Distribution of Similes in *Paradise Lost,*" *MP,* XXVIII (1931), 313–27.

Widmer, Kingsley. "The Iconography of Renunciation: the Miltonic Simile," *ELH,* XXV (1958), 258–69.

Woodhouse, A. S. P. "Tragic Effect in *Samson Agonistes,*" *University of Toronto Quarterly,* XXVIII (1958), 205–22.

Wright, Nathalia. "Milton's Use of Latin Formularies," *SP,* XL (1943), 390–98.

Sir Thomas More

Pineas, Rainer. "Thomas More's Use of Humor as a Weapon of Religious Controversy," *SP,* LVIII (1961), 97–114.

Bevington, David M. "The Dialogue in *Utopia:* Two Sides to the Question," *SP,* LVIII (1961), 496–509.

Elliott, Robert C. "The Shape of *Utopia,*" *ELH,* XXX (1963), 317–34.

Heiserman, A. R. "Satire in the *Utopia,*" *PMLA,* LXXVIII (1963), 163–74.

Morte Arthure

Finlayson, John. "Rhetorical 'Descriptio' of Place in the Alliterative *Morte Arthure,*" *MP,* LXI (1963), 1–11.

Thomas Nashe

Summersgill, Travis L. "The Influence of the Marprelate Controversy Upon the Style of Thomas Nashe," *SP,* XLVIII (1951), 145–60.

John Henry Newman

Clancey, Richard W. "Dublin Discourses: Rhetorical Method in Textual Revisions," *Renascence,* XX (1968), 59–74.

Gill, John M. "Newman's Dialectic in *The Idea of a University*," *QJS*, XLV (1959), 415–18.

Holloway, John. "Newman," *The Victorian Sage*. Norton Library ed. (New York, 1965), pp. 158–201.

Houghton, Walter. *The Art of Newman's "Apologia"* (New Haven, Conn., 1945).

Levine, George. "The Prose of the *Apologia Pro Vita Sua*," *VNL*, XXVII (1965), 5–8.

Svaglic, Martin J. "The Structure of Newman's *Apologia*," *PMLA*, LXVI (1951), 138–48.

Townsend, F. G. "Newman and the Problem of Critical Prose," *VNL*, No. 11 (1957), 22–25.

John Oldham

Macken, Cooper R. "The Satiric Technique of John Oldham's *Satyrs Upon the Jesuits*," *SP*, LXII (1965), 78–90.

The Pearl

Johnson, Wendell Stacy. "The Imagery and Diction of *The Pearl*: Toward an Interpretation," *ELH*, XX (1953), 161–80.

Piers Plowman

Kaske, R. E. "The Use of Simple Figures of Speech in *Piers Plowman B*: A Study in the Figurative Expression of Ideas and Opinions," *SP*, XLVIII (1951), 571–600.

Edgar Allan Poe

Spitzer, Leo. "A Reinterpretation of 'The Fall of the House of Usher,'" *Essays on English and American Literature* (Princeton, N. J., 1962), pp. 51–66.

Stauffer, Donald Barlow. "The Two Styles of Poe's 'Ms. Found in a Bottle,'" *Style*, I (1967), 107–20.

Alexander Pope

Beaumont, Charles A. "The Rising and Falling Metaphor in Pope's 'Essay on Man,'" *Style*, I (1967), 121–30.

Brooks, Cleanth. "The Case of Miss Arabella Fermor," *The Well Wrought Urn* (New York, 1947), pp. 80–104. Analysis of the *Rape of the Lock*.

Empson, William. "Wit in the *Essay on Criticism*," *Hudson Review*, II (1950), 559–77.

Fogle, Richard Harter. "Metaphors of Organic Unity in Pope's *Essay on Criticism*," *Tulane Studies in English*, XIII (1963), 51–58.

Hughes, R. E. "Pope's *Essay on Man:* The Rhetorical Structure of Epistle I," *Modern Language Notes,* LXX (1955), 177–81.

Kallich, Martin. *Heav'n's First Law: Rhetoric and Order in Pope's Essay on Man* (DeKalb, Illinois, 1967).

———. "Unity and Dialectic: The Structural Role of Antithesis in Pope's *Essay on Man," Papers on English Language and Literature,* I (1965), 109–24.

———. "The Conversation and the Frame of Love: Images of Unity in Pope's *Essay on Man," Papers on Language and Literature,* II (1966), 21–37.

Krieger, Murray. "Contextualism and the Relegation of Rhetoric," *Rhetoric and Poetic,* ed. Donald C. Bryant (Iowa City, Ia., 1965), pp. 46–58. On the *Epistle to Dr. Arbuthnot.*

Mack, Maynard, ed. *Essential Articles for the Study of Alexander Pope* (Hamden, Conn., 1964).

———. " 'Wit and Poetry and Pope': Some Observations on His Imagery," *Pope and His Contemporaries: Essays Presented to George Sherburn* (Oxford, 1949), pp. 20–40.

Maresca, Thomas E. *Pope's Horatian Poems* (Columbus, Ohio, 1966). Analyses of "The First Satire of the Second Book of Horace, Imitated"; "An Epistle to Dr. Arbuthnot"; "The Second Epistle of the Second Book of Horace, Imitated"; "The First Epistle of the First Book of Horace, Imitated."

Mengel, Elias F., Jr. "Patterns of Imagery in Pope's *Arbuthnot," PMLA,* LXIX (1954), 189–97.

Quintana, Ricardo. " 'The Rape of the Lock' as a Comedy of Continuity," *Review of English Literature,* VII (1966), 9–19.

Surtz, Edward L. "Epithets in Pope's *Messiah," PQ,* XXVII (1948), 209–18.

Wasserman, Earl R. "Pope: *Windsor Forest," The Subtler Language: Critical Readings in Neoclassic and Romantic Poems* (Baltimore, 1959), pp. 89–168.

———. "Pope's *Ode for Musick," ELH,* XXVIII (1961), 163–86.

Wimsatt, W. K., Jr. "Rhetoric and Poems: The Example of Pope," *English Institute Essays, 1948,* ed. D. A. Robertson, Jr. (New York, 1949), pp. 153–178.

Zoellner, Robert E. "Poetic Cosmology in Pope's *An Essay on Man." CE,* XIX (1958), 157–62.

Rochester, Earl of (John Wilmot)

Fujimura, Thomas H. "Rochester's 'Satyr Against Mankind': An Analysis," *SP,* LV (1958), 576–90.

William Shakespeare

Baldwin, T. W. *William Shakespere's Small Latine & Lesse Greeke*, 2 vols. (Urbana, Ill., 1944).

Brooks, Cleanth. "The Naked Babe and the Cloak of Manliness," *The Well Wrought Urn* (New York, 1947), pp. 22–49. Shakespeare's *Macbeth.*

Burke, Kenneth. "Trial Translation (from *Twelfth Night*)," *Philosophy of Literary Form* (Baton Rouge, La., 1941), pp. 344–49.

Calderwood, James L. "Shakespeare's Evolving Imagery: 2 *Henry VI*," *English Studies,* XLVIII (1967), 481–93.

Charney, Maurice. "Shakespeare's Antony: A Study of Image Themes," *SP,* LIV (1957), 149–61.

———. "Shakespeare's Style in *Julius Caesar* and *Antony and Cleopatra*," *ELH,* XXVI (1959), 355–67.

Frye, Roland Mushat. "Rhetoric and Poetry in *Julius Caesar*," *QJS,* XXXVII (1951), 41–48.

Heilman, Robert B. *Magic in the Web: Action and Language in Othello* (Lexington, Ky., 1956).

Joseph, Sister Miriam. *Shakespeare's Use of the Arts of Language* (New York, 1947).

Kennedy, George. "Antony's Speech at Caesar's Funeral," *QJS,* LIV (1968), 99–106.

Maclean, Norman. "Episode, Scene, Speech, and Word: The Madness of Lear," *Critics and Criticism,* ed. R. S. Crane (Chicago, 1952), pp. 595–615.

Robinson, James E. "The Ritual and Rhetoric of *A Midsummer Night's Dream*," *PMLA,* LXXXIII (1968), 380–91.

Spencer, Benjamin T. "*Antony and Cleopatra* and the Paradoxical Metaphor," *Shakespeare Quarterly,* IX (1958), 373–78.

Thaler, Alwin. "Shakespeare on Style, Imagination, and Poetry," *PMLA,* LIII (1938), 1019–36.

Willcock, Gladys D. "Shakespeare and Rhetoric," *Essays and Studies,* XXIX (1943), 50–61.

(It would be an endless task to list here all the close explications of Shakespeare's works. For a handy guide to critiques of individual works, see the Bibliography in Paul N. Siegel, *His Infinite Variety: Major Shakespearean Criticism Since Johnson* (Philadelphia and New York, 1964), pp. 413–24.)

George Bernard Shaw

Berst, Charles A. "The Devil and *Major Barbara*," LXXXIII (1968), 71–79.

Crompton, Louis. "*Major Barbara:* Shaw's Challenge to Liberalism," *Prairie Schooner*, XXXVII (1963), 229–44.

———. "Shaw's *Heartbreak House*," *Prairie Schooner*, XXXIX (1965), 17–32.

Grossman, Manuel L. "Propaganda Techniques in Selected Essays of George Bernard Shaw," *Southern Speech Journal*, XXXII (1967), 225–36.

Mills, John A. "Language and Laughter in Shavian Comedy," *QJS*, LI (1965), 433–41.

Nichols, Marie Hochmuth. "George Bernard Shaw: Rhetorician and Public Speaker," *Rhetoric and Criticism* (Baton Rouge, La., 1963), pp. 109–29.

Regan, Arthur E. "The Fantastic Reality of Bernard Shaw: A Look at *Augustus* and *Too True*," *The Shaw Review*, XI (1968), 2–10.

West, E. J. "*Saint Joan:* A Modern Classic Reconsidered," *QJS*, XL (1954), 249–59.

Percy Bysshe Shelley

Fogle, Richard Harter. "The Imaginal Design of Shelley's 'Ode to the West Wind,'" *ELH*, XV (1948), 219–26.

Ford, Newell F. "Paradox and Irony in Shelley's Poetry," *SP*, LVII (1960), 648–62.

Reiman, Donald H. "Structure, Symbol, and Theme in 'Lines Written Among the Euganean Hills,'" *PMLA*, LXVII (1962), 404–13.

Wasserman, Earl R. *The Subtler Language: Critical Readings of Neoclassic and Romantic Poems* (Baltimore, 1959). "Shelley: *Mont Blanc*," pp. 189–240; "Shelley: *The Sensitive Plant*," pp. 241–84; "Shelley: *Adonais*," pp. 285–361.

———. "*Adonais:* Progressive Revelation As a Poetic Mode," *ELH*, XXI (1954), 274–326.

Wilcox, Stewart C. "The Sources, Symbolism, and Unity of Shelley's *Skylark*," *SP*, XLVI (1949), 560–76.

———. "Imagery, Ideas, and Design in Shelley's *Ode to the West Wind*," *SP*, XLVII (1950), 634–49.

Richard Brinsley Sheridan

Schiller, Andrew. "*The School for Scandal:* The Restoration Unrestored," *PMLA*, LXXI (1956), 694–704.

Sir Philip Sidney

Browne, Robert M. "Rhetorical Analysis and Poetic Structure," *Rhetoric: Theories for Application*, ed. Robert M. Gorrell (Champaign, Ill., 1967), pp. 90–98. Analyses of Sidney's two sonnets "With How Sad Steps, O Moon" and "Leave Me, O Love."

Challis, Lorna. "The Use of Oratory in Sidney's *Arcadia*," *SP*, LXII (1965), 561–76.

Duhamel, P. Albert. "Sidney's *Arcadia* and Elizabethan Rhetoric," *SP*, XLV (1948), 134–50.

Howe, Ann Romayne. "*Astrophel and Stella:* 'Why and How,'" *SP*, LXI (1964), 150–69.

Malloch, A. E. "'Architectonic' Knowledge and Sidney's *Apologie*," *ELH*, XX (1953), 181–85.

Myrick, Kenneth. "The *Defence of Poesie* as a Classical Oration," *Sir Philip Sidney as a Literary Craftsman* (Cambridge, Mass., 1935; 2nd ed., Lincoln, Nebraska, 1965), pp. 51–83.

Thorne, J. P. "A Ramistical Commentary on Sidney's *An Apologie for Poetrie*," *MP*, LIV (1957), 158–64.

John Skelton

Fish, Stanley. "Aspects of Rhetorical Analysis: Skelton's *Philip Sparrow*," *Studia Neophilologica*, XXXIV (1962), 216–38.

Tobias Smollett

Strauss, Albrecht B. "On Smollett's Language: A Paragraph in *Ferdinand Count Fathom*," *English Institute Essays, 1958*, ed. Harold C. Martin (New York, 1959), pp. 25–54.

Edmund Spenser

Alpers, Paul J. "Narrative and Rhetoric in the *Faerie Queene*," *Elizabethan Poetry: Modern Essays in Criticism*, ed. Paul J. Alpers (New York, 1967), pp. 380–400.

Carscallen, James. "The Goodly Frame of Temperance: The Metaphor of Cosmos in the *Faerie Queene*, Book II," *University of Toronto Quarterly*, XXXVII (1968), 136–55.

Craig, Martha. "The Secret Wit of Spenser's Language," *Elizabethan Poetry: Modern Essays in Criticism*, ed. Paul J. Alpers (New York, 1967), pp. 447–72.

Dundas, Judith. "The Rhetorical Basis of Spenser's Imagery," *Studies in English Literature, 1500–1900*, VIII (1968), 59–76.

Fletcher, James V. "Some Observations on the Changing Style of the *Faerie Queene*," *SP*, XXXI (1934), 152–59.

Kaller, Kathrine. "Art, Rhetoric, and Holy Dying in the *Faerie Queene* with Special Reference to the Despair Canto," *SP*, LXI (1964), 128–39.

Nicholson, Margaret Erskine. "Realistic Elements in Spenser's Style," *SP*, XII (1924), 382–98.

Padelford, Frederick M., and William C. Maxwell. "The Compound Words in Spenser's Poetry," *JEGP*, XXV (1926), 489–516.

Pope, Emma Field. "Renaissance Criticism and the Diction of the *Faerie Queene*," *PMLA*, XLI (1926), 575–619.

Rix, Herbert David. *Rhetoric in Spenser's Poetry* (State College, Pa., 1940).

Sirluck, Ernest. "A Note on the Rhetoric of Spenser's 'Despair,'" *MP*, XLVII (1949), 8–11.

Sonn, Carl Robinson. "Spenser's Imagery," *ELH*, XXVI (1959), 156–70.

John Steinbeck

Tuttelton, James W. "Steinbeck in Russia: The Rhetoric of Praise and Blame," *Modern Fiction Studies*, XI (1965), 79–89.

Laurence Sterne

Booth, Wayne C. "The Self-Conscious Narrator in Comic Fiction before *Tristram Shandy*," *PMLA*, LXVII (1951), 163–85.

Stedmond, J. M. "Style and *Tristram Shandy*," *Modern Language Quarterly*, XX (1959), 243–51.

Jonathan Swift

Beaumont, Charles Allen. *Swift's Classical Rhetoric* (Athens, Ga., 1961). Analyses of "A Modest Proposal," pp. 15–43; "An Argument Abolishing Christianity," pp. 44–86; "A Vindication of Lord Carteret," pp. 87–118; "The Answer to the *Craftsman*," pp. 119–37.

Cook, Richard. "Swift as a Tory Rhetorician," *Texas Studies in Language and Literature*, IV (1963), 72–78.

———. "The Uses of *Saeva Indignatio:* Swift's Political Tracts (1710–1714) and His Sense of Audience," *Studies in English Literature*, II (1963), 287–307.

Corbett, Edward P. J. "A Method of Analyzing Prose Style, with a Demonstration Analysis of Swift's *A Modest Proposal*," *Reflections on High School English*, ed. Gary Tate (Tulsa, Okla., 1966), pp. 106–24. Reprinted in *Teaching Freshman Composition* (New York, 1967), pp. 294–312.

Elliott, Robert C. "Swift's *Tale of a Tub:* An Essay in Problems of Structure," *PMLA*, LXVI (1951), 441–55.

Frost, William. "The Irony of Swift and Gibbon: A Reply to F. R. Leavis," *Essays in Criticism*, XVII (1967), 41–47.

Kelling, Harold D. "Reason in Madness: *A Tale of a Tub*," *PMLA*, LXIX (1954), 198–222.

Milic, Louis T. *A Quantitative Approach to the Style of Jonathan Swift* (The Hague, 1967).

———. "Unconscious Ordering in the Prose of Swift," *The Computer and Literary Style,* ed. Jacob Leed (Kent, Ohio, 1966), pp. 79–106.

Quinlan, Maurice J. "Swift's Use of Literalization as a Rhetorical Device," *PMLA,* LXXXII (1967), 516–21.

Rosenheim, Edward W., Jr. *Swift and the Satirist's Art* (Chicago, 1963).

Sams, Henry W. "Swift's Satire of the Second Person," *ELH,* XXVI (1959), 36–44.

Stephens, Lamarr. "'A Digression in Praise of Digressions' as a Classical Oration: Rhetorical Satire in Section VII of Swift's *A Tale of a Tub,*" *Tulane Studies in English,* XIII (1963), 41–49.

Edward Taylor

Griffith, Clark. "Edward Taylor and the Momentum of Metaphor," *ELH,* XXXIII (1966), 448–60.

Mignon, Charles W. "Diction in Edward Taylor's *Preparatory Meditations,*" *American Speech,* XLI (1966), 254–60.

Alfred, Lord Tennyson

Brooks, Cleanth. "The Motivation of Tennyson's Weeper," *The Well Wrought Urn* (New York, 1947), pp. 167–77. Analysis of "Tears, Idle Tears."

Reed, John R. "The Design of Tennyson's 'The Two Voices,'" *University of Toronto Quarterly,* XXXVII (1968), 186–96.

Spitzer, Leo. "'Tears, Idle Tears' Again," *Essays on English and American Literature* (Princeton, N.J., 1962), pp. 37–50.

William Thackeray

Blodgett, Harriet. "Necessary Presence: The Rhetoric of the Narrator in *Vanity Fair,*" *Nineteenth-Century Fiction,* XXII (1967), 211–23.

Craig, G. Armour. "On the Style of *Vanity Fair,*" *English Institute Essays, 1958,* ed. Harold C. Martin (New York, 1959), pp. 87–113.

Taube, Myron. "Contrast as a Principle of Structure in *Vanity Fair,*" *Nineteenth-Century Fiction,* XVIII (1963), 119–35.

Dylan Thomas

Beardsley, Monroe C., and Sam Hynes. "Misunderstanding Poetry: Notes on Some Readings of Dylan Thomas," *CE,* XXI (1960), 315–22.

Montague, Gene. "Rhetoric in Literary Criticism," *CCC,* XIV (1963), 168–75. Analysis of Thomas's "Today This Insect."

Henry David Thoreau

Broderick, John C. "The Movement of Thoreau's Prose," *AL*, XXXIII (1961), 133–142.

Lane, Lauriat, Jr. "On the Organic Structure of *Walden*," *CE*, XXI (1960), 195–202.

Moldenhauer, Joseph J. "The Extra-vagant Maneuver: Paradox in *Walden*," *The Graduate Journal*, VI (1964), 132–46.

———. "The Rhetorical Function of Proverbs in *Walden*," *Journal of American Folklore*, LXXX (1967), 151–59.

Ross, Francis D. "Rhetorical Procedure in Thoreau's 'Battle of the Ants,'" *CCC*, XVI (1965), 14–18.

Cyril Tourneur

Lisca, Peter. "*The Revenger's Tragedy:* A Study in Irony," *PQ*, XXXVIII (1959), 242–51.

Thomas Traherne

Clements, A. L. "On the Mode and Meaning of Traherne's Mystical Poetry: 'The Preparative,'" *SP*, LXI (1964), 500–21.

Webber, Joan. "'I and Thou' in the Prose of Thomas Traherne," *Papers on Language and Literature*, II (1966), 258–64.

Mark Twain

Fussell, E. S. "The Structural Problem of the *Mysterious Stranger*," *SP*, XLIX (1952), 95–104.

Gerber, John C. "The Relation between Point of View and Style in the Works of Mark Twain," *English Institute Essays, 1958*, ed. Harold C. Martin (New York, 1959), pp. 142–71.

Henry Vaughan

Farnham, Fern. "The Imagery of Henry Vaughan's 'The Night,'" *PQ*, XXXVIII (1959), 425–35.

Izaak Walton

Oliver, H. J. "Izaak Walton's Prose Style," *RES*, XXI (1945), 280–88.

Robert Penn Warren

Douglas, Wallace W. "Drug Store Gothic: The Style of Robert Penn Warren," *CE*, XV (1954), 265–72.

John Webster

Price, Hereward T. "The Function of Imagery in Webster," *PMLA*, LXX (1955), 717–39.

Edith Wharton

Hopkins, Viola. "The Ordering Style of *The Age of Innocence*," *AL*, XXX (1958), 345–57.

Walt Whitman

Azarnoff, Roy S. "Walt Whitman's Concept of the Oratorical Ideal," *QJS*, XLVII (1961), 169–72.

Chatman, Vernon V. "Figures of Repetition in Whitman's 'Songs of Parting,'" *Bulletin of the New York Public Library*, LXIX (1965), 77–82.

Coffman, Stanley K., Jr. "Form and Meaning in Whitman's 'Passage to India,'" *PMLA*, LXX (1955), 337–49.

Hollis, C. Carroll. "Whitman and the American Idiom," *QJS*, XLIII (1957), 408–20.

Miller, James E., Jr. "'Song of Myself' as Inverted Mystical Experience," *PMLA*, LXX (1955), 636–61.

———. "Whitman's 'Calamus': The Leaf and the Root," *PMLA*, LXXII (1956), 249–71.

Spitzer, Leo. "*Explication de Texte* Applied to Walt Whitman's Poem 'Out of the Cradle Endlessly Rocking,'" *Essays on English and American Literature* (Princeton, N.J., 1962), pp. 14–36.

John Greenleaf Whittier

Pickard, John B. "Imagistic and Structural Unity in 'Snowbound,'" *CE*, XXI (1960), 338–43.

Oscar Wilde

Foster, Richard. "Wilde as Parodist: A Second Look at *The Importance of Being Earnest*," *CE*, XVIII (1956), 18–23.

Reinert, Otto. "Satiric Strategy in *The Importance of Being Earnest*," *CE*, XVIII (1956), 14–18.

Thomas Wolfe

Natanson, Maurice. "The Privileged Moment: A Study in the Rhetoric of Thomas Wolfe," *QJS*, XLIII (1957), 143–50.

William Wordsworth

Brooks, Cleanth. "Wordsworth and the Paradox of Imagination," *The Well Wrought Urn* (New York, 1947), pp. 124–50. Analysis of "Ode on Intimations of Immortality."

Murray, Roger N. "Synecdoche in Wordsworth's 'Michael,'" *ELH*, XXXII (1965), 502–10.

Parrish, Stephen Maxfield. "'The Thorn': Wordsworth's Dramatic Monologue," *ELH*, XXIV (1957), 153–63.

Sonn, Carl Robinson. "An Approach to Wordsworth's Earlier Imagery," *ELH*, XXVII (1960), 208–222.

Trilling, Lionel. "The Immortality Ode," *The Liberal Imagination* (New York, 1950), pp. 129–53.

William Butler Yeats

Brooks, Cleanth. "Yeats's Great Rooted Blossomer," *The Well Wrought Urn* (New York, 1947), pp. 178–91. Analysis of "Among School Children."

Hahn, Sister M. Norma. "Yeats's 'The Wild Swans at Coole': Meaning and Structure," *CE*, XXII (1961), 419–21.

Masson, David I. "Word and Sound in Yeats's 'Byzantium,'" *ELH*, XX (1953), 136–60.

Spitzer, Leo. "On Yeats's Poem 'Leda and the Swan,'" *Essays on English and American Literature* (Princeton, N.J., 1962), pp. 3–13.